MW01405488

72 STORIES

From the Baseball Collection of

GEDDY LEE

With

DANIEL RICHLER

Photographs by

RICHARD SIBBALD

HARPER
An Imprint of HarperCollinsPublishers

*In memory of my good friend and
baseball guru J.W. Jones.
Thank you for all those years guiding me
down the rabbit hole.*

TABLE OF CONTENTS

INTRODUCTION 4

The 3,000-HIT CLUB 13
1993 ALL-STAR GAME 14
HANK AARON 16
JIM ABBOTT 18
NEIL ARMSTRONG, FRANK SINATRA and OTHER STARS IN THE SKY 20
THE BEATLES 22
MOE BERG 24
BARRY BONDS 26
BOB CAIN vs. EDDIE GAEDEL 28
ROD CAREW 30
JOE CARTER 32
FIDEL CASTRO 34
ROBERTO CLEMENTE 36
TY COBB 38
EDDIE COLLINS 40
SAM E. CRAWFORD 42
MARTÍN DIHIGO 44
JOE DIMAGGIO 46
DWIGHT EISENHOWER 48
JOHNNY EVERS 50
THE EXPOS 52
WHITEY FORD 54
JIMMIE FOXX 56
LOU GEHRIG 58
BOB GIBSON 60
JOSH GIBSON 62
HANK GREENBERG 64
LEFTY GROVE 66
ROY HALLADAY 68
GABBY HARTNETT 70
ROGERS HORNSBY 72
JOE JACKSON 74
JAPAN 1931 and 1934 TOURS 76
ICHIRO SUZUKI, SHOHEI OHTANI and SADAHARU OH 78
RANDY JOHNSON 80
WALTER JOHNSON 82

JOHN F. KENNEDY 84
SANDY KOUFAX 86
NAP LAJOIE 88
KENESAW MOUNTAIN LANDIS 90
DON LARSEN 92
BILL LEE 94
CONNIE MACK 96
MICKEY MANTLE 98
ROGER MARIS 100
CHRISTY MATHEWSON 102
WILLIE MAYS 104
JOHN MCGRAW 106
STAN MUSIAL 108
ODDBALLS 110
MEL OTT 112
SATCHEL PAIGE 114
ROBIN ROBERTS 116
JACKIE ROBINSON 118
BABE RUTH 120
NOLAN RYAN 122
TOM SEAVER 124
BERT SHEPARD 126
SMITTY and THE CRO 128
GEORGE SOSNAK 130
WARREN SPAHN 134
TRIS SPEAKER 136
DAVE STIEB 138
JOHNNY VANDER MEER 140
RUBE WADDELL 142
HONUS WAGNER 144
TED WILLIAMS 146
1906 WORLD SERIES (ED WALSH and MORDECAI BROWN) 148
1992 WORLD SERIES 150
1927 NEW YORK YANKEES 152
MISCELLANEOUS MEMORABILIA 154
RUSH 158

ACKNOWLEDGEMENTS 160

INTRODUCTION

BASEBALL WAS IN my bones long before music started to seriously divert my attention. As a kid in the Sixties, I collected bubble gum cards with my school buddies, watched the New York Yankees beamed across the border from Buffalo TV stations, and took the streetcar downtown to watch the Maple Leafs, Toronto's Triple-A International League team—my first excursions independent of my parents. Then, after a decade-long sojourn during which I put everything I had into a fledgling band called Rush, I rediscovered my childhood passion while on the road, at the dawn of cable television when the only things on during the day were soaps, quiz shows, infomercials and—courtesy of the two superstations, WGN Chicago and TBS Atlanta—baseball! And by the end of the Seventies I had the fever again. Two years after the Blue Jays were founded, I had my own season tickets, and if I was abroad on tour during the season, I'd do just about anything to keep on top of the game.

I remember being on tour in the U.K. in 1981, playing at the Bingley Hall in Birmingham and staying nearby in some crappy hotel. It was the night before our first show and I was hurtin' something bad to be missing Game 6 of the World Series. Jetlagged and in desperation, I twiddled and twiddled the radio that was built into the wall, and finally heard, crackling through the air, Vin Scully's voice. Huzzah! I had found the Armed Forces Network broadcasting live from Los Angeles. I lay in bed in the dark, transported through the wee hours, listening in vivid detail to the event happening thousands of miles away: Pedro Guerrero stepping up to the plate and hitting a three-run shot to win it for the Dodgers—a one-man show that capped a 9-2 victory and gave them their first championship title in six years. Scully was the greatest baseball broadcaster of all time, don't you think? His eloquence, he having cut his teeth in the radio era, is a lost art. He had a poetic, even philosophical way of describing every nuance of the action, even without the back and forth of a colour commentator beside him sometimes. Man, could he orate! He put you right there, like you had your own seat behind home plate.

Through the Eighties, then, I was absolutely mad for the game, devoting much of my spare time to learning the nuances of the gameplay and who the current players were, devouring reference books, biographies and novels about the sport, especially after broadcasters had made references to historical moments, players and plays that went over my head. But in 1988 or thereabouts, with a day off before our show at Kemper Arena in Kansas City, I was taking a walk around the Crowne Plaza adjacent to our hotel, when I came upon a shop called The Legacy. In the window and festooning the walls within were framed photographs, mostly Americana, of famous Presidents and the like, every frame mounted with an engraved plate and a cutout of the featured individual's autograph. I went inside and rummaged through the raft of ephemera for sale.

"Hobby" is an odd word to use when you consider just how seriously we take autograph hunting, but that is what it's called. I was definitely always a hobbyist in the obsessional sense; once I'd get started, there'd be no finish. I had a friend who worked for the Blue Jays, who at the end of each season used to present my brother and me with a gift of baseballs signed by current American League and All-Star teams (a cool and thoughtful thing for him to do), but that was the totality of my collection then, and the idea of expanding it had never occurred to me, but in The Legacy that day, I suddenly found myself captivated by the older photos of stars from the game's long and colourful past. It was like a door on another world, another time, had been left ajar, and I couldn't resist sticking my head inside. I felt compelled to buy something, but most of the prices were daunting.

Since I had no experience in this area, I cautiously settled on a couple of inexpensive signed photographs, each of which had stories that drew me in....

The first commemorated Bobby Thomson's "Shot Heard 'Round the World" of 1951, the legendary ninth inning home run that won the pennant for the New York Giants and broke the hearts of long-suffering Dodger fans. It was a story I knew well, having read Roger Kahn's *The Boys of Summer*, the marvellous memoir of his youth and love-letter to "dem bums."[1] The photo was signed by Thomson himself, an image I'd see many times in subsequent years, but sometimes also signed by that game's losing pitcher, Ralph Branca. Ouch, you had to feel for the guy! Holding the photo in my hands, I recalled an interview recorded right after his crushing defeat in which he spoke of inwardly pleading with the ball to fall into his left fielder's glove—but alas, it was not to be. Years after that game it was revealed that the Giants had set up a telescope and buzzer system signaling to Thomson what pitch was coming.[2] Apparently, Branca knew about this for years, but while he stopped speaking to Thomson, he never said a word in public—a show of fine character that he was able to swallow such a bitter pill so graciously.

The other photo I purchased that day was of Satchel Paige, the charismatic and dominant pitching star of the Negro Leagues who finally made the Majors in 1948, at the ripe old age of forty-two (joining the Cleveland Indians), making him not just the American League's first-ever Black pitcher but also the oldest rookie to debut in the majors—a milestone that still stands. On top of his sheer talent, what always impressed me was his supercool personality in America's terrible era of segregation. As much as stories of Jackie Robinson's courage told of one man breaking the colour barrier in 1947, Paige's illuminated how Black players actually lived, at times even thrived, in the barnstorming years before Robinson's momentous accomplishment.

I'm embarrassed to say that as a naive, white, Jewish, Canadian nebbish, I'd been woefully ignorant of the Negro Leagues. Having spent an inordinate amount of time in front of a TV set in the Fifties and Sixties, my awareness of racial strife in America was mostly framed by what I saw on the Big Three American television networks, NBC, CBS and ABC. I watched newscasts covering conflicts in the Deep South, the Selma to Montgomery March, the oratory of Martin Luther King, the race riots in Harlem, Philadelphia and Detroit, and I'd seen the Hollywood version of being Black in America acted out in *Gone with the Wind*, *To Kill a Mockingbird* and *Guess Who's Coming to Dinner*, but while to my young brain that world puzzled and saddened me, it all seemed to be happening far from the melting pot of my more humdrum Toronto suburb. The antisemitism I would experience first-hand, and what little I knew of the way Canada treated First Nations People and its many waves of immigrants, seemed (in its deceptively nice, polite way) less noisy and violent.

The more I came to learn about baseball's history and the more I understood how forbidding the colour barrier had been, the more I

---

[1] Both a term of endearment and derision for fans of the Dodgers then.

[2] Using technology to steal the catcher's signs? Isn't that cheating?! Yeah, I'm talkin' to *you*, 2017 and 2018 Astros.

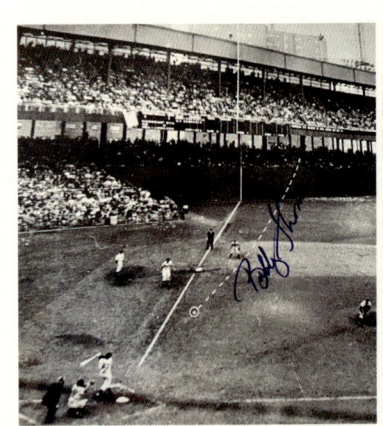

The first two baseball acquisitions that sent me tumbling down the rabbit hole: photos signed by Bobby Thomson and Satchell Paige.

learned about the institutional depth of racism in all of North America. So, like Jackie Robinson, Satchel Paige represented a whole lot of things to me, but mostly he was the consummate survivor (a word that reverberated powerfully in my household), a man who pitched in two very different worlds and kept pitching until he was an astounding fifty-nine years of age! He was longevity itself, so much my kind of hero that for years I kept his Six Rules for a Happy Life taped to my dressing room case on the road with Rush, and which is featured in full later in this book. (I have to admit that in the course of my own life I've not adhered to any one of his nuggets of wisdom—for example, "Avoid fried meats, which angry up the blood" and "Go very light on vices such as carrying on in society"; quite the opposite, in fact, but I still recommend them to you without hesitation!)

So, I left the store that day with not just a humble bag of swag, but something more profound: a lightning bolt had struck me, galvanizing me to delve even deeper into the game that I already loved but was still only into knee-deep. I began to understand that through these signed artifacts which had passed through the actual hands of some great and talented people, I could see more clearly into the game's vaunted past; each item was a window onto history and a piece of time itself. I was discovering how American history and its National Pastime, from the late 1800s to the present, were inextricably intertwined. I then got it into my head to acquire, if I could, a few significant baseballs signed by legends of the game—Babe Ruth, Lou Gehrig, Cobb, Cy Young, Paige et al.—but I didn't have a clue how to begin. So I phoned The Legacy's owner, J.W. Jones, as kind a gentleman as you'd want to meet. A longtime hobbyist and collector of signatures himself, he'd been the head of Human Resources for a large corporation for many years, but decided in 1989 to leave that lucrative position and follow his passion (and have more fun) and purchased the store from its founders.

I didn't know it, but the first question that popped out of my mouth was one that every rookie baseball collector asks: "How much would a ball signed by Babe Ruth cost?" The Babe's stature as the Home Run King made him the game's most timeless icon and the ideal starting point for any collection. J.W. chuckled and embarked on a lesson in what determines the value of any given single-signed baseball: the condition of the ball, the clarity and authenticity of the autograph, and most importantly, its provenance. There's also, of course, the matter of rarity. The Bambino was a gregarious chap who loved to hit home runs, eat hot dogs and sign autographs for fans—in direct contrast with his teammate, Lou Gehrig, a relatively aloof character who did his talking on the field and did not like to sign. Hence, while Ruth might arguably be the more universally famous of the two, a Gehrig signature is more expensive because it's harder to find. Nonetheless, J.W. said he could probably find me a good "Ruth" for around eight to ten thousand dollars, and I bit. (Eventually, of course, I had to have a Gehrig too.)

To steal a phrase from *Casablanca*, this was the beginning of a beautiful friendship—a decades-long trawl of the history of baseball, propelled by the whims and unevenness of my knowledge of the game—and J.W. would remain my mentor for thirty years. He was a fount of invaluable information, guiding me around the world of auction houses and collectors and drawing my attention to the more obscure but colourful players of the game whose objects would become part of my collection. Those game-used baseballs brought me closer to the athletes, transporting me right onto the field during their moments of triumph and failure. I fell in love with the idea that baseballs could tell a story,[3] not of the players alone but the actual moments in the games that distinguished them. Evocative stuff!

THE SPORTS MEMORABILIA craze that swept the U.S. in the 1980s boosted the value of many baseball artefacts. A lot of players, particularly those retired, would go to conventions and sign things for cash, just like Star Trek illuminati attending the Comicons. Mickey Mantle, who had become penurious in his later

---

3   See also a certain *Big Beautiful Book of Bass*.

years, was able to restore his former lifestyle by selling off many items that had suddenly become extra valuable; George Sosnak, whose folk art baseballs are featured in this book, would set up a booth and paint you a ball for fifty or a hundred bucks, a helluva bargain, given that they now go for five, six, seven, eight thousand; but the craze also muddied matters. Pete Rose, for instance, will set up a booth and put just about anything on a baseball, like "I'm sorry for the economic downturn of 2008"; I have one that says, "I'm sorry I bet on baseball" and another, "I'm sorry I shot JFK." That's pretty funny, and for a while I collected them, but then I stopped because I realized that what he's doing in taking the blame for all these catastrophic events in world history is trying to make light of his own crime—as if to say, "I did everything. And I did nothing."

I was having a blast, speaking to J.W. once a week as I travelled all over the world with the band. Because I'd get too excited and would overbid like mad, it was good to rely on someone with some sense and a bit of a remove, but me being me, if I were in the middle of the night in England, say, or after a show in Italy, I'd still call or send panicked emails saying, "Where are we at? Am I the high bidder? Bid more!" And if a bidding war was going on all night and the time zone I was in favoured me, I'd say, "Just give me your login info and go to sleep." Dangerous! Being able to bid online, and being able to afford to do it myself, raised the temperature—and, I dare say, the price. It wasn't unlike gambling, especially in the days when authentication was not as rigorous as it is today, and I fell victim more than a couple of times. (Sellers, of course, count on that. I've seen the same with wristwatch auctions at Phillips in Geneva, with insane bids rising just because two gazillionaires have decided they both need to have the same thing; it happened recently with a record price on an Omega Speedmaster . . . that turned out to be a fake.)

But no collector worth his salt has ever built a collection without buying at least one fake (and if they tell you any different, they're lying). Back in the day there were very few authentication houses; it was mainly a field of self-styled experts who'd verify a specific type of signature for you. Determining, say, whether that Babe Ruth ball you just bought had been signed by the man himself or was a "secretarial" signature, required an experienced eye for the nuances of his autograph—while if you wanted a ball signed by The Beatles you'd go to the "Beatles guy." These days, every item you find at an auction house comes with full certification from an accepted authenticator, so it's doubly authenticated, but mistakes can still be made. As a wise collector once said, "Who's authenticating the authenticator?"

I've been on both sides of the baseball, so to speak—the collector as well as the signer of autographs that people collect—which has given me some interesting insights: my scrawl has evolved over the years, sometimes going through changes in the course of a couple of hours. On tour to promote my *Big Beautiful Book of Bass*, I'd do signings and by the five-hundredth find my hand cramping; as a result, there were sure to be small but noticeable differences from the first to the last, starting out as "Geddy Lee" but ending up more like "Jerry Lewis." Thus, while they're all me and perfectly authentic, the proof of provenance becomes as important as the autograph itself.

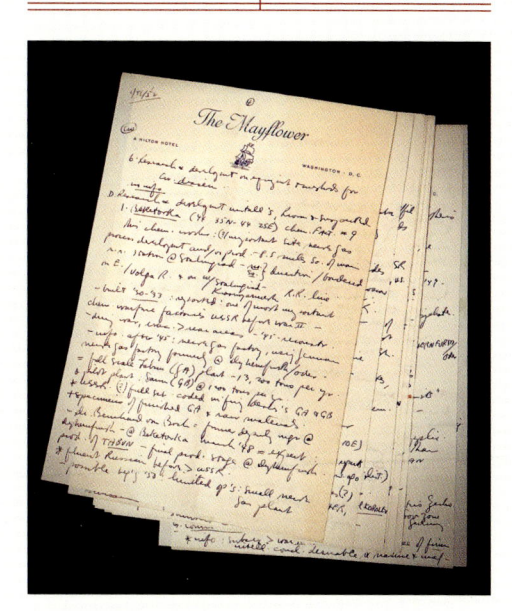

Told you I was nuts! Among the various Moe Berg artefacts I've collected are these pages of scientific notes Moe Berg scribbled out while at the Mayflower Hotel in D.C. during the Cold War.

ANYHOW, SO BEGAN a steady, regular scouring of catalogues from auction houses both big and small, opening dialogues with private sellers, as my collection grew and grew. Collectormania is such that at first you're almost too excited, snapping up things all over the map: single-signed baseballs, team baseballs, photographs, books, pins, pennants, uniforms, trophies, watches, toys, games . . . Watch out! There's a fine line between collecting and hoarding. Eventually you learn that the very best collections are more focused, so I tried to streamline, concentrating on single-signed baseballs of Hall of Fame players, and er . . . a few other things I fell in love with that I felt would surely enhance the overall collection because, quite frankly . . . getting carried away is too much fun! For example, after I read

The Catcher was a Spy, the fascinating story of Moe Berg's work with the Office of Strategic Services (the forerunner to the CIA), I not only acquired several balls but also notepaper on which he'd scribbled scientific equations during the war, and tried to buy the film rights to his life story—only to find that George Clooney's company had beat me to it. (That movie was eventually made with Paul Rudd starring as Berg and pulling off a pretty good likeness, but in my view didn't do justice to the man's eccentric life.)

Still awake? Okay, good, because if you know me, I can and *will* go on for hours about this stuff. (Hmm... maybe I should write a book?) But I'm sharing all of this partly to illustrate how difficult it actually was for me to build a disciplined collection. I'm too easily distracted—or too *interested*, depending on your point of view—and enjoy being pulled in different directions by a great story or a fascinating individual. By the early Nineties I was most definitely in heat, as J.W. and I continued to beat the bushes for the coolest items, concentrating on single-signed baseballs from Hall of Famers—although I couldn't resist certain others along the way; game-used balls were of great interest to me, but as you will see in this book, I also bought balls signed by Frank Sinatra, The Beatles, The Rolling Stones, Neil Armstrong and Fidel Castro, as well as Muhammad Ali, Wayne Gretzky, Leroy Neiman (who drew those black-stockinged Femlins in *Playboy*), the Dalai Lama, Tony Blair and one signed "Jesus Christ" but whose provenance requires a, uh, leap of faith. Then baseballs signed by U.S. Presidents became a collection unto themselves, which I suppose is weird because I'm a Canadian and (as of yet) there's not a single Canadian Prime Minister amongst them. For me, the *crème de la crème* of Presidential baseballs, some featured in this book, are ones thrown out as the first pitch on Opening Day, a tradition started by William Howard Taft in 1910. (I don't have a Taft baseball, but I do have a signed photo of him tossing the horsehide sphere!)

Such is my weakness for game-used items that a nice part of my collection consists of balls from no-hitters, rare home run balls or game balls marking significant milestones that players have achieved (reaching 1,000 or 2,000 hits, winning 30 games, etc.). For the most part, these are the actual balls that were in play and, as such, were part of an historic moment. I don't generally collect bats, meanwhile, mainly because they're a bit unwieldy and awkward to display, but I do have some that also played a part in baseball history—as I tell in the Mickey Mantle chapter.

Whatever you choose to collect, it has to come from a place of passion. For me, at least, it cannot only be a financial investment. Moreover, while it's true that collectibles rarely go down in value, you can never be sure that you'll make money on a piece. Which is why I say *buy what you love*, not what you think you should own. That being said, there is a particular conceit to collecting—the foolish and in some ways greedy belief that you really can own a piece of the past by squirreling it away in your own private treasure trove. The desire to want it all to yourself is something that any honest collector must fess up to—to themselves, at least. I'll admit that over the years it's crossed my mind more than once, yet I carry on regardless, powerless to rein in my obsessive nature. But in the end what makes me happiest is the love of the chase combined with the filling in of gaps in my knowledge; in some ways, that means more to me than the things themselves.

I used to wonder why some longtime collectors were willing to ever sell off or trade good pieces, but I learned that building a proper collection is a full-time endeavor that requires constant feeding. If you're not prepared to keep adding, the collection risks feeling stale, at which point it may be time to think about letting it go to someone more passionate (and, if possible, turn a profit for all your trouble). Let's face it, you never truly own these things anyway; you're merely paying for the privilege of minding them for as long as you can before handing them on to the next caretaker.

IN LATE AUGUST of 2007, on the Snakes and Arrows tour, I flew to Kansas City a day before our concert to visit the Negro Leagues Baseball Museum with J.W. The museum, located in the historic 18th & Vine Jazz District, is a magical place designed with a Field of Legends baseball diamond at its heart, featuring life-size bronze statues of some of the league's greatest players in their customary positions around the field: catcher Josh Gibson, pitcher Satchel Paige, shortstop Judy Johnson, and standing at home plate, bat in hand, Martín Dihigo.

In the halls surrounding the field are displays that walk you through a detailed history of the league. I was embarrassed to learn how little I knew; not least how successful the league had actually been, which was the main factor that led Branch Rickey and few of the more open-minded Major League GMs to look seriously at

MY (SORT OF) CAREER IN BASEBALL

My BFF Alex and I at Anaheim Stadium in 1992, and Alex tackling me after I threw a first pitch in Arlington, Texas in 2004. (The crowd was unamused but I was laughing hysterically.)

Here I am in Dunedin, Florida in 1992, eagerly awaiting my first fly ball (which of course I missed). This baseball stuff ain't so easy....

In Toronto there was a local pickup team that Rush sponsored, named and bought uniforms for: Those Darn Fish. We didn't end up playing with them very often because we were on the road so much, but when we were home they had to let us play because we were the token owners.

*Opening Day 2013, Rogers Centre, Toronto.
LEFT: I wasn't going to fuck this one up, so I went early to warm up. Veteran pitcher Duane Ward told me to throw from up on the mound instead of in front of it as most people do. "That way, you'll be throwing downhill," he said, and he was right: I threw a curveball for an effin' strike!
RIGHT: Talking to one of my fave baseball peeps, the Blue Jays' manager John Gibbons.*

*Batting practice with the Angels in 1992.
(I was not offered a contract afterwards.)*

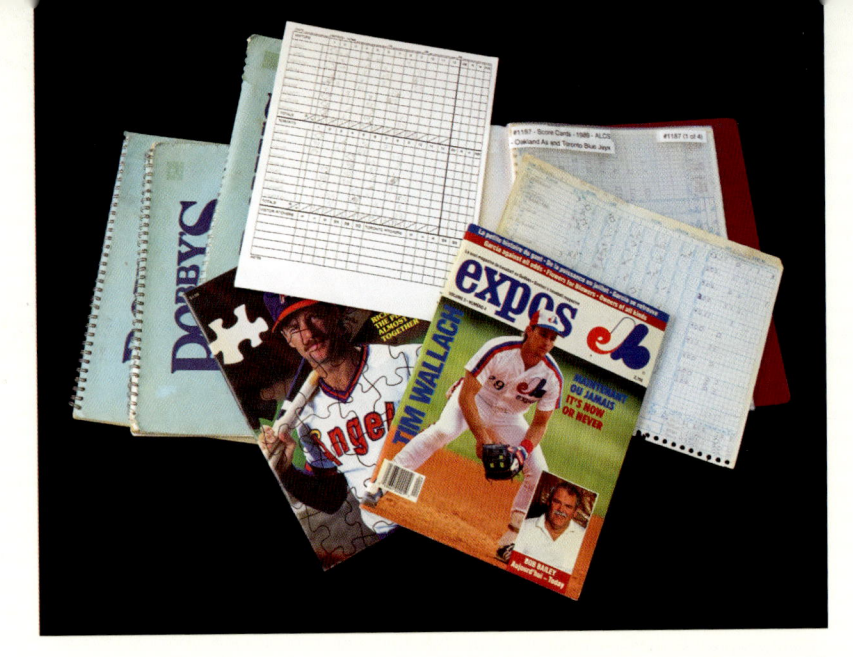

Just a few of the dozens of scorecards I've filled out over the years. And of course I kept them all!

---

bringing black players into the Majors. (No, they weren't especially motivated by a sense of racial injustice, but rather to help turn their flagging post-war ticket sales around; tapping into an abundant source of impressive baseball talent, expanding their audience and, as it happened, integrating the sport, simply made good business sense.) It was a moving and immensely informative visit for me, but I was dismayed that J.W. and I were pretty much the only visitors there, and as we left that gem of a place, I feared for its future.

That concern lingered with me for months, so I suppose it was meant to be that later the same year J.W. came across an auction lot containing a quantity of signed baseballs from a range of Negro League players. Individually, the signatures were exceedingly rare, but almost impossible to find in such a large grouping. J.W. suggested that acquiring the lot would be an opportunity to show support for the museum in the form of a donation, which immediately resonated with me. Looking more closely at the auction catalogue, we found that the collection had been divided into three lots of approximately two hundred signed baseballs each. On the day of the sale, I was en route from Milan to Oslo near the end of the European leg of our tour, and what with the time change, couldn't get in front of a computer or phone, so I asked J.W. to bid on all three lots.

As I described earlier, we were usually in constant contact during bids, especially when prices were rising stratospherically, but since I was unavailable this time and he didn't feel comfortable spending my money too freely, he set himself some limits. When I got off the plane, I learned that even within those limits, he'd suc-

TOP: *The collection at the Negro Leagues Museum in Kansas City, which sits off the third baseline and behind a statue of Ray Dandridge.*
BOTTOM LEFT: *With Todd, J.W. and Anna Jones.* BOTTOM RIGHT: *Bob Kendrick, the museum's Director, making the dedication speech.*

72 Stories **10** *Geddy Lee*

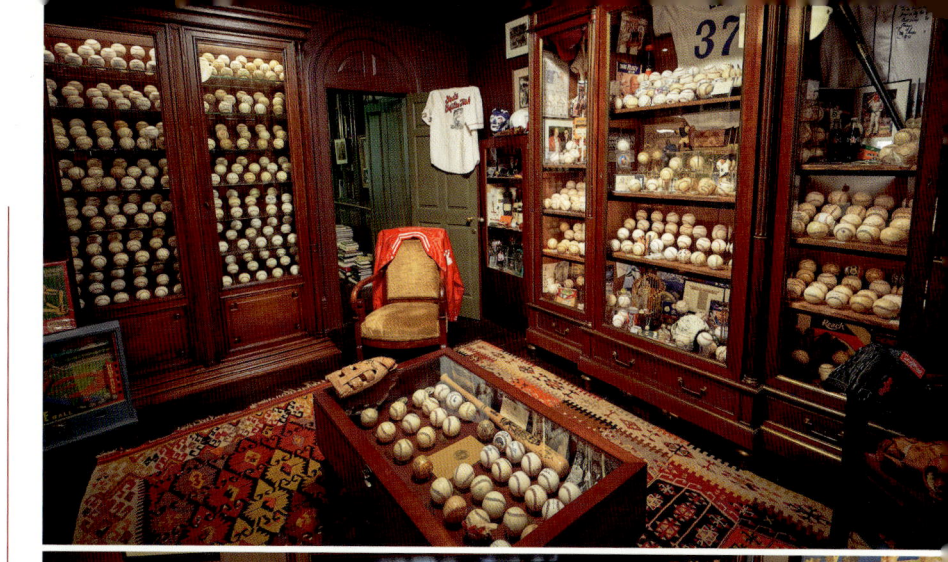

Where I began . . . and where it ended up. What can I say? It was an effin' blast!

ceeded in purchasing one of the three lots—two hundred and thirteen single-signed baseballs. Pretty darn good, but compared to what I'd have had to pay for that many Major Leaguers, it struck me as shockingly undervalued and I immediately regretted not giving him free rein to buy all three lots. When we received the baseballs and saw what good condition they were in, I asked him and the auction house to see if the other winners might sell their purchases to me. We reached a deal with one, a fellow representing the William "Judy" Johnson Memorial Foundation, for two hundred more baseballs, so the donation would now total just over four hundred.

In the meantime, J.W. had contacted Raymond Doswell, the curator of the Negro Leagues Museum, who said he'd be delighted to accept such a gift. On June 6th, 2008, I was invited to a small but heartfelt unveiling ceremony and was very surprised to see my name in the middle of the display, now billed as the Geddy Lee Collection. I had not intended for the donation to draw any attention to myself, but I reckoned that if it ultimately drew baseball fans from the world of rock and roll and helped keep the museum's doors open, that would be very nice indeed. In the end, I'm proud to have played a part—with full acknowledgment of J.W.'s role—in memorializing the history of the game I love.

I SPENT CLOSE to three decades collecting baseball ephemera with the help of J.W. Jones, so it was a terrible blow to me when in 2018 he passed away, and it took the heart out of the hobby for me. In fact, I have not bought a single baseball item since. I'm now passing some of my treasures on to younger, more enthusiastic collectors, but until then I'll remain extremely proud of the vast collection I built with the help of my buddy from the Midwest, and I don't regret a penny or second I spent getting to the heart of what the great game of baseball means to me.

To come clean, I should tell you that the day after a truck carrying all those precious memories pulled away from my home, my wife Nancy ventured into my office and said, "Wait. I don't get it . . . It doesn't look like they took anything away!"

Busted! I guess she never knew just how much I really had.

THE P. GOLDSMITH SONS CO. CINCINNATI, O. U.S.A.
GOLDSMITH TRADE MARK
NO. 97
HORSE HIDE COVER
9 INCH 5 OZ
1 OZ RUBBER
OFFICIAL LEAGUE BALL
GUARANTEED 18 INNINGS

THE 3,000-HIT CLUB

THIS IS SURELY one of the most unique 3,000-hit balls extant, a time traveller handed down from caretaker to caretaker for over a hundred years. From its first signature inked in 1920, it goes all the way up to the present day: the most recent members of the elite club signed at my personal request after I acquired it in 2013.

As its letter of certification avers, "Of the twenty-eight men ever to summit the storied plateau, twenty-two appear on this ancient Official League ball. In chronological order we also find Ty Cobb, Eddie Collins, Tris Speaker, Stan Musial, Hank Aaron, Willie Mays, Al Kaline, Pete Rose, Lou Brock, Carl Yastrzemski, Rod Carew, Robin Yount, George Brett, Dave Winfield, Eddie Murray, Paul Molitor, Tony Gwynn, Wade Boggs, Cal Ripken, Rickey Henderson, Rafael Palmeiro and Craig Biggio." But the number continues to rise, because I myself have added Ichiro Suzuki, Albert Pujols, and most recently Miguel Cabrera, bringing the current total to 25. Note how hard it is to see Ichiro Suzuki's signature because the ball is getting so full, and how he had to write over the word GUARANTEED, while alas, poor Ty Cobb, is fading away.

I have fantastic memories of meeting and asking those few players for their signatures—a fair turnabout of roles, with me now as an eager fan boy. One such memory is of Albert Pujols, who I've met a few times through my friendships with the Cardinals: he's always been incredibly kind to me, and this story speaks to his personality: at one point I also had a 500-home run ball, for which I similarly gathered a few signatures, but was missing Ken Griffey Jr., who was known to be reluctant to sign for strangers. A pal of mine who worked for the Cards offered to help me out, and when Griffey came to town for a series, he asked him on my behalf. Griffey refused, saying, "Sorry, I'm under exclusive contract for signings." Ok, fair enough . . . Now, Albert Pujols happened to overhear their conversation, and during batting practice strode across the outfield to chat with Griffey. My pal doesn't know what Pujols said to him out there, but afterwards, the centre fielder returned to the clubhouse and said, "Okay, give me that ball. I'll sign it." And he did! Not only did Albert, who barely knew me, literally go out of his way to convince him, but in 2018, when he himself crossed the 3,000 hit line, he signed it too. What a wonderful guy.

And what about the difficulty achieving those 3,000 hits? Well, first, you have to be a damn fine hitter, and second, you have to have a long, healthy career. While modern athletes are in much better condition, like finely tuned cars, they also seem more injury prone, rarely seeming to enjoy the longevity of the legends of old. We baseball nuts often ask, "Are milestones like 500 homers, 3,000 hits and 300 wins a thing of the past?" I sure hope not, because to me these feats are testaments to greatness that fuel our enduring fascination with this beautiful and timeless game.

I like this shot because Ichiro and I are so relaxed. You can see how thrilled I am talking to him!

72 Stories   **13**   Geddy Lee

1993 ALL-STAR GAME

IN 1993 I RECEIVED a letter inviting me to sing the national anthem before an All-Star game in Baltimore's Oriole Park at Camden Yards. I was really in baseball heat in those days, watching every game I could, so I gladly accepted.

I recall going out to do a soundcheck in the middle of the afternoon. There were no monitors, but I could hear my voice rambling around the empty cavernous building with an unbelievable delay that drastically affected the pace I was singing at. Still, because I was very much a fly-by-the-seat-of-my-pants dude, I thought, *It'll be fine, whatever.* Meanwhile, James Earl Jones, who was singing for the U.S. side, came up to me and said something to the effect of, "I really like the Canadian anthem. It's a simple melody but a nicely written song." I said, "Oh, it doesn't really compare to the glory of the 'Star-Spangled Banner,'" and he replied in his Darth Vader voice, "It *does* have a certain *martial* glory," which I thought was an interesting descriptor.

I had a couple of pals there on the team, Randy Johnson and Mark Langston, and all day I found myself meeting players I knew or others I admired who introduced themselves to me, which was a thrill: Jeff Montgomery (a Rush fan I'd met at shows) was one, and Bryan Harvey the Marlins' relief pitcher showed me unexpected kindness, coming up to me out of the blue to give me a baseball for my son Jules, which I thought was one of the sweetest gestures.

But as I was waiting to do my thing, seconds before I went on, a woman from the TV network said to me, "You'll be happy to know that tonight we have eighty million viewers." And I'm thinking to myself, I *really* don't need to know that! What? Does she want me to shit my pants on the way to the mound?

So, yes, I was nervous. I mean, you're standing there, and every great ballplayer of that year is looking at you, and I had family in the audience, and there's the echo and the delay. I sang it *a cappella*—just me, myself and me. Like an idiot, I didn't even bring a pitch pipe; I mean, you can get yourself in a pickle if you start too high, you know? Maybe I thought it would look unprofessional, I dunno. I figured I'd just wing it, and in the end, according to Alex, I sang the slowest rendition of the Canadian national anthem ever to be performed in public. I sheepishly said to him, "I was trying to get the most out of my screen time, dude."

Since then, I've been asked numerous times to sing the anthem for Blue Jays games or other games around the States. There are some people who can't say no and keep doing it, but I'm not one of them. To me it's a thing you do just once, or else it becomes a career, not the honour that it truly was.

Me and Darth Vader before the game.

72 Stories   **14**   Geddy Lee

★ OFFICIAL BALL ★
1993 ALL-STAR GAME
BALTIMORE ★ ORIOLES
1993 ALL ★ STAR GAME

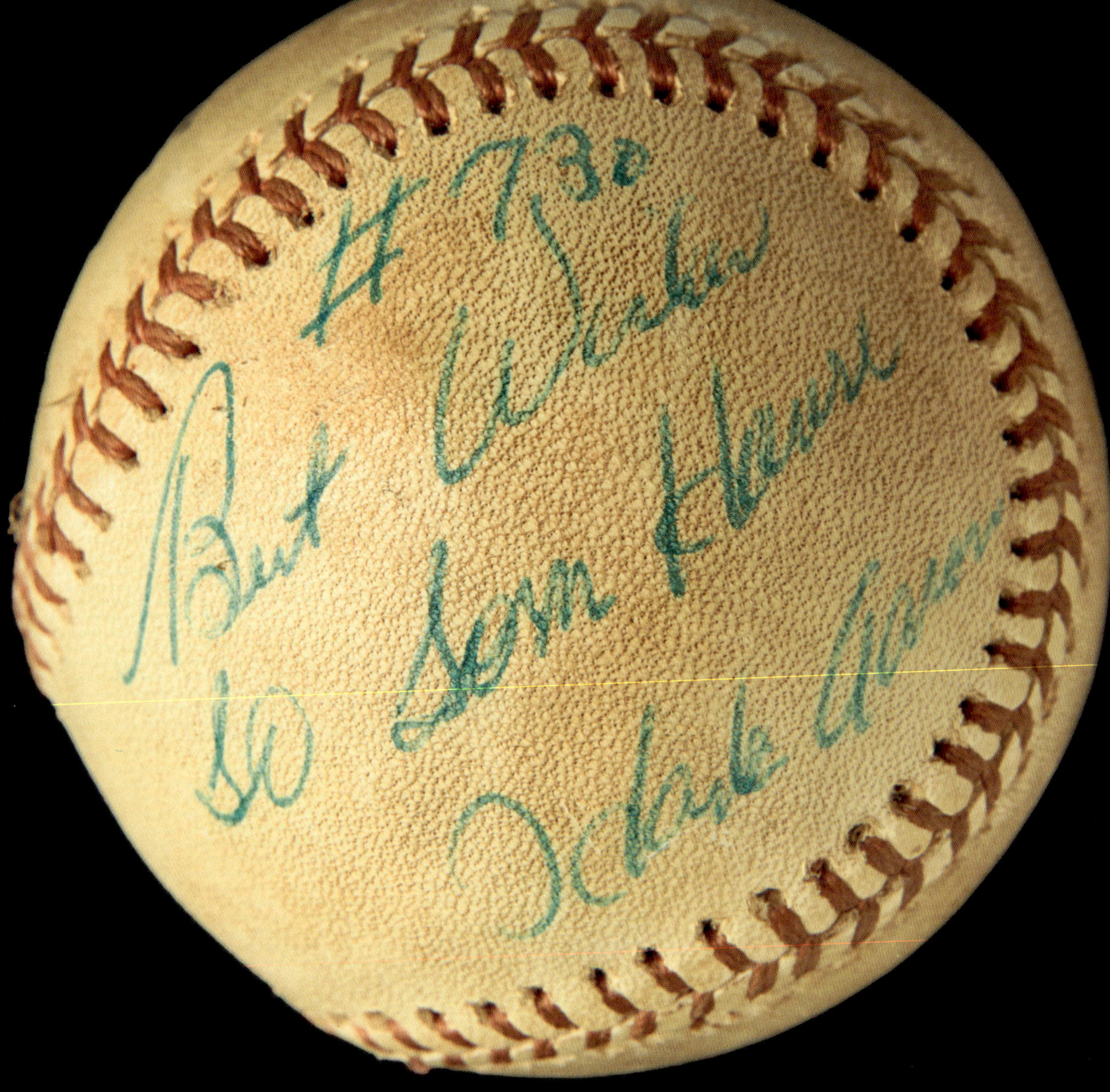
#730
Best Wishes
To Sam
Hank Aaron

HANK AARON

APRIL 8TH, 1974, Fulton County Stadium in Atlanta. Second inning, Bad Henry at bat.

Live on TV, the Braves' announcer Milo Hamilton: "He's sittin' on 714. Here's the pitch by Downing. Swinging. There's a drive into left center field. That ball is gonna be . . . *outta* here! It's gone! It's 715! There's a new home run champion of all time, and it's Henry Aaron!"

And the Dodgers' announcer Vin Scully: "What a marvellous moment for baseball! What a marvellous moment for Atlanta and the state of Georgia. What a marvellous moment for the country and the *world*. A black man is getting a standing ovation in the Deep South for breaking a record of an all-time baseball idol. . . . "

What bigger moment could there be? "I just thank God it's all over," Aaron said while still on the field, expressing the mixed emotions of a man who like Roger Maris had been bombarded by the media and received hate mail and death threats from the general public, except that he was a Black man in what was forever a white man's game, and in the American South, surpassing Babe Ruth's all-time home run leadership.

So many of my favourite moments recounted in this book have to do with milestones that aren't simply about baseball; they're *human* stories, stories of human struggle, of players overcoming their nerves and adversity and achieving greatness. A collection of this kind celebrates greatness in all its forms, and no one is more deserving of that accolade than Hank Aaron. It's sometimes easy to forget that African Americans were banned from playing in the Major and Minor Leagues until 1947. I don't know what the game would be like today without players of all different creeds and colours, and thank goodness for it—especially at a time when, dishearteningly, those hatreds are being reignited. Aaron not only surpassed Babe Ruth's all-time home run record, but moved the game *and* the nation forward on a journey begun by Jackie Robinson.

For years after playing, Aaron worked with Major League baseball in a front office role, and I had the very good fortune of meeting him when he was seated near me at a game in Toronto. I shook his hand, and we exchanged just a couple of words. He was gentle and very polite. I was in awe of this giant of a human. So then, when I had the opportunity to purchase a home run ball of his, his 730th (he finished his career with 755), you can imagine how I felt.

According to its certification, "On August 19th, 1974, the Braves hosted the St. Louis Cardinals. That game proved to be a veritable clinic in slugging as Atlanta sparked to an 11-6 victory. Atlanta's first scoring came in the bottom of the third when megastar Hank Aaron stepped into the box with two out and a runner on first. The Cardinals hurler Claude Osteen delivered a fat one and Hammerin' Hank got all of it for his 730th home run. That ball has survived these past years and now become available thanks in no small part to the guy who caught the ball as a bullpen spectator, Atlanta relief pitcher Tom House [who went on to be a very respected pitching coach]. Beautifully, House surrendered the ball to Hank, who in turn documented the event on a side panel and returned it to his teammate as a keepsake."

Here's a guy who's hit another historic home run, and the teammate retrieves it and offers it to him, but he says no, *you* keep it. I mean, that's just a beautiful thing.

JIM ABBOTT

JIM ABBOTT CAME to a couple of our shows. We met and hung out because he was on the same team as Mark Langston and all those great Angels guys who were so nice to me. He was just a super guy. I was so privileged to have gotten to know him a little tiny bit.

He was born in 1967 without a right hand. "I felt the teasing and the bullying of the playground," he once told *CNN Sport*. "I keenly felt the awkward second glances in the school hallways and classrooms." Yet he developed an astonishingly deft catch-and-throw technique and ended up pitching for ten years with the California Angels, the Yankees, the White Sox and the Milwaukee Brewers. He made history by throwing a no-hitter in September 1993 (against the Cleveland Indians, 4-0), earned a career record of 87 wins and 108 losses and a 4.25 ERA, and won numerous awards for overcoming adversity. There have been a lot of pitchers with *two* hands who couldn't hold a candle to this guy.

When he was a kid he toyed with a soccer ball his parents had bought him and quarterbacked for his high school team in Flint, Michigan (throwing for 600 yards in six touchdowns!) but was most intent on playing baseball. He practiced his reflex and coordination by throwing a rubber ball against a brick wall (just like I did, but with better results), then swiftly switching his glove to his good hand to catch the rebound, standing closer and closer to the wall to make that transition faster and faster. I saw him pitch many times in the Majors, and it was incredible to watch him set up his fastball: he'd place his glove against his stump, pinning it between his right forearm and torso; then, after releasing the ball, he'd slip his good hand into the glove so fast that you might miss the move (talk about sleight of hand!), just in time to catch any balls batted back at him, throw out the runner or even start a double play. And when opposing teams tried to exploit his disadvantage with bunts and slow rollers, leaving him insufficient time to make his switcheroo, he'd discard the glove and field them *barehanded*. He was, you might say, the ultimate left-hander, but no slouch at bat either. His New York Yankees teammate Mariano Rivera claimed to have witnessed him hitting home runs during batting practice, and when he joined the Milwaukee Brewers (in 1999, at which time the National League did not permit designated hitters), he had two hits in 21 at-bats.

I'm in awe when I think about players like him who have overcome physical impediments. Can you just imagine yourself in such a situation and saying, "I want to play MLB ball?" Don't forget Monty Stratton, whose life story was made into a successful film with James Stewart, *The Stratton Story* (I have a signed ball of his, plus a copy of the screenplay and a collection of on-set photographs): after losing his leg in a hunting accident, he pitched for the White Sox on an artificial leg. They used to compare him to Grover Cleveland Alexander—in 1937 he had 15 victories—that's how good he was.

Abbott summed it up beautifully when he said, "As a kid, I really wanted to fit in. Sports became a way to gain acceptance. I think this fueled my desire to succeed. I truly believe that difficult times and disappointments push us to find abilities and strengths we wouldn't know existed without the experience of struggle."

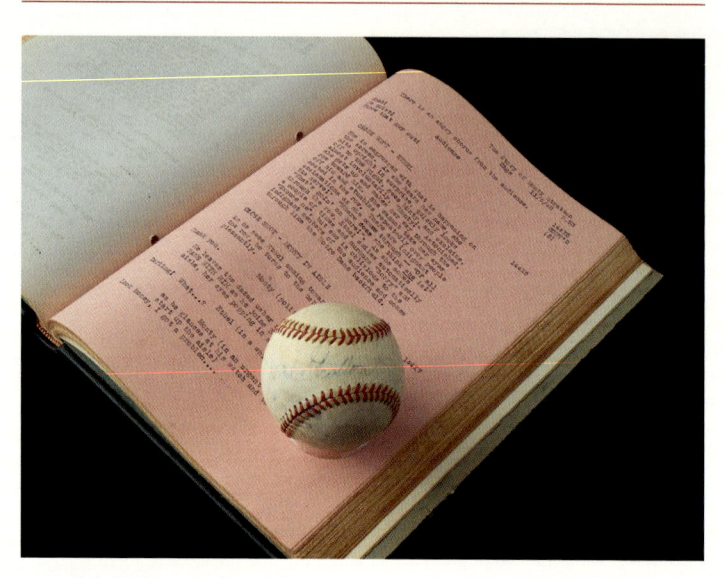

Original screenplay of The Stratton Story *starring James Stewart.*

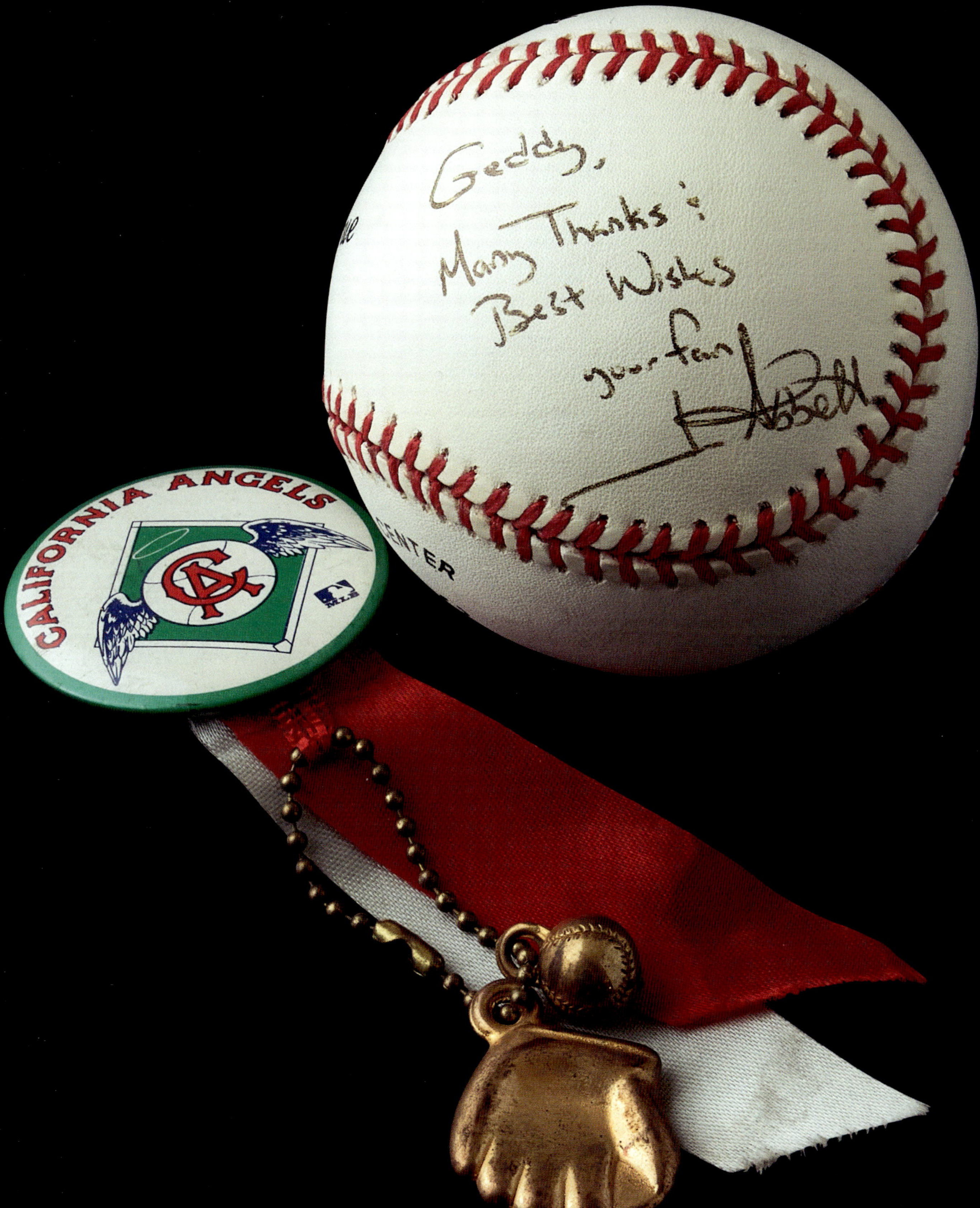
Geddy,
Many Thanks &
Best Wishes
your fan
CENTER
CALIFORNIA ANGELS

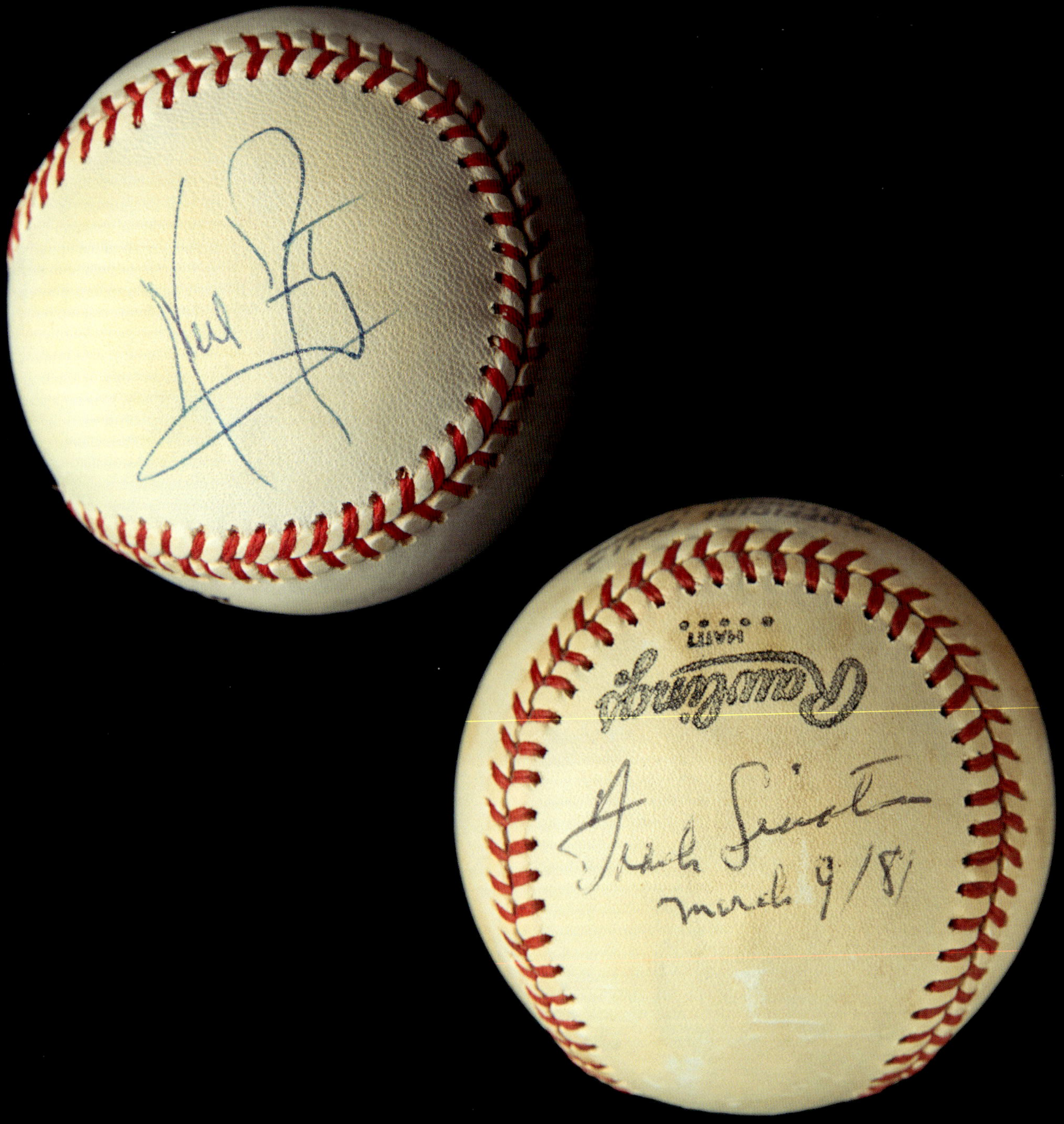
Rawlings
march 9/81

NEIL ARMSTRONG, FRANK SINATRA *and* OTHER STARS IN THE SKY

I'VE OFTEN THOUGHT of baseball as being the great social leveller. People from all walks of life are attracted to the game and can find commonality in it. So, as with my Bill Clinton/Monica Lewinsky ball, I love it when someone with a completely abstract connection to the game lands on a baseball. To me, it's great when you find an important figure in American history who becomes a part of baseball culture, if only because they signed a ball that lives on my shelf.

Neil Armstrong, the first man on the moon, didn't like to sign. Nor did Frank Sinatra (nor Lou Gehrig), but the signatures of reluctant signers end up being the most valuable by virtue of their rarity, so I had to look a long, long time for these.

I never met Neil Armstrong, but I have had the good fortune to meet a few astronauts. In 1979, Rush was the first rock group NASA ever invited to the Cape Kennedy Space Center—appropriately enough, I guess, given the number of songs we recorded about black holes and deep space—and we were bowled over. For someone like me growing up in the space race era, just the words "Cape Kennedy" (formerly Cape Canaveral) were the stuff of dreams. When Gerry Griffin, the Deputy Director, gave us our security badges, we were so genuinely thrilled that even Neil Peart (another reluctant signer!) didn't mind being repeatedly stopped for photo ops. We stood in the exhaust of a giant Saturn rocket, were taken to see a life-size mock-up of the Space Shuttle orbiter and allowed to try its docking simulator, and at the end of the day had drinks at the beach house where the astronauts hang out before a launch.

In 1981, we were taken to a VIP area about a mile from where the Space Shuttle stood steaming, looking huge even at that distance. When it took off, wow—and I mean wow—even that far away you could feel the heat and force of the explosion that boosted the rocket into space. The song "Countdown" is a description of that experience, incorporating official tapes of the dialogue between mission control and the astronauts that NASA sent us—a play-by-play of a real-life event laced with the surreal emotions of one involved or at least closely witnessing it. It's a musical time capsule so packed with my own memories that I can't honestly say how well it works as a song, but I do know that Alex received an email from an astronaut aboard the International Space Station who said that he'd taken our latest album with him into orbit.

In 1990, The Royal Astronomical Society of Canada named three celestial bodies for Alex, Neil and me; mine is "Asteroid (12272) Geddylee." So, as you can see, I have a strong fascination and fondness for outer space stuff, and in a way Neil Armstrong's signature is the pinnacle of it all.

THE BEATLES

ACCORDING TO HERITAGE AUCTIONS: "The Beatles descended into Queens in a Boeing Vertol 107-II helicopter, then transferred to a Wells Fargo armored truck for the ride to Shea. Such precautions were necessary. Two thousand security personnel were posted to corral the crowd of 55,000, comprised largely of screaming, swooning teenaged girls simply losing their collective minds at the notion of seeing the Fab Four in the dreamy flesh.

"Hearing them, however, was a different story. Upon taking the stage at the center of the Mets ballpark, it quickly became apparent that the band's specially designed 100-watt Vox amps were no match for the estrogen-fueled cacophony, and even the house amplification system proved an unworthy adversary. The Beatles found themselves unable to hear each other or even themselves, and as they closed the show with "I'm Down," John Lennon banged at his keyboard with his elbows as his bandmates roared with laughter. If there was ever a defining "Beatlemania" moment, it was August 15, 1965. This is the only known baseball signed by all four Beatles from that very show.

"Presented is one of just a tiny handful of known Beatles signed baseballs, and the only example attributed to this largest and most famous concert in the band's history. The ONL (Giles) sphere finds Paul, John, George and Ringo surviving at an average strength of 8/10 in blue ballpoint ink. A notation in an unknown hand supplies attribution: 'The Beatles, Shea Stadium N.Y.C., 8/15/65.' The signatures are authenticated by Frank Caiazzo, the most respected authority on Beatles autographs whose paperwork is considered essential by every serious Fab Four collector. LOA from Frank Caiazzo."

So, to find a ball signed by *all four* Beatles (authenticated by the hobby's premier Beatles expert Frank Caiazzo), from such a monumental concert, was a real score for me. It crossed all areas of my life: as a baseball aficionado, a performing musician, and budding young lover of music watching my sister cry in front of the television when they appeared on *The Ed Sullivan Show*. This was a baseball I *had* to have. No one was going to pay more for that ball than I did that day! It's the genuine article and one of the most coveted baseballs in my entire collection.

OPPOSITE:

JOHN LENNON • GEORGE HARRISON
PAUL McCARTNEY • RINGO STARR

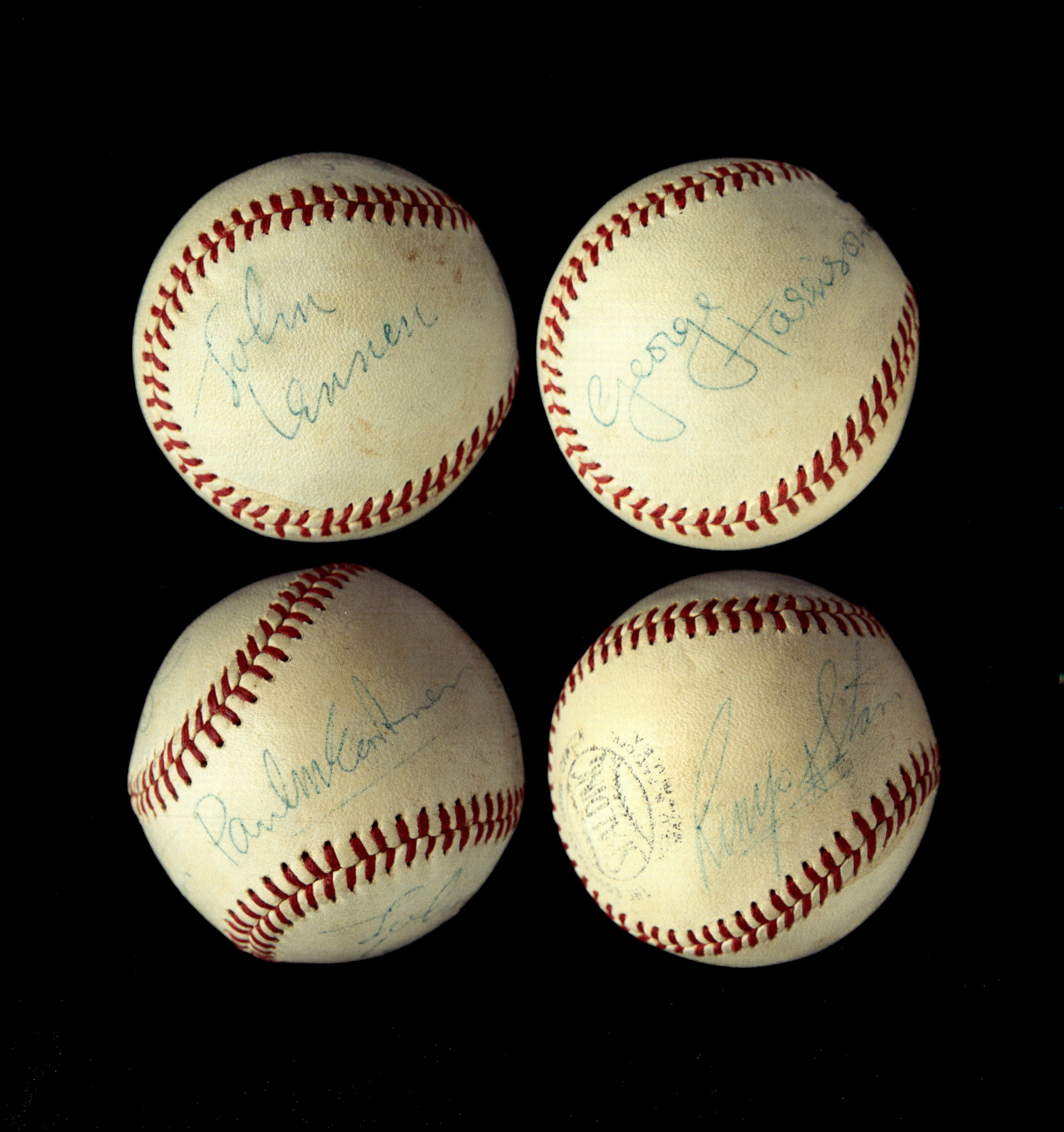
John Lennon
George Harrison
Paul McCartney
Ringo Starr

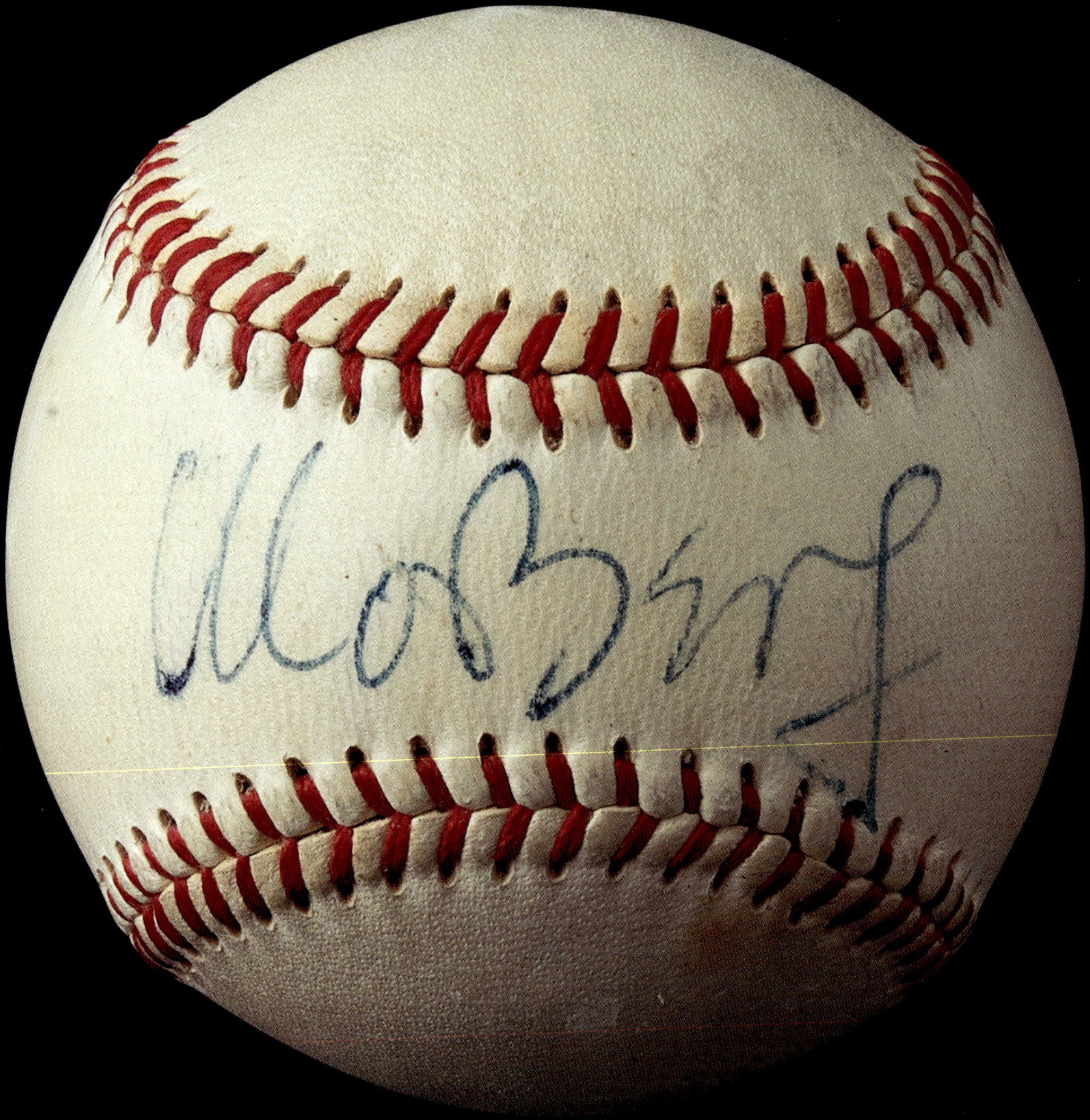

MOE BERG

I'VE ACQUIRED SEVERAL signed Berg items, including hotel notepaper on which he scribbled scientific equations during the war—serious stuff! I'm such a Moe Berg fan that I could write a book about all the books I've read about him! If you want to know where to start, I'd recommend *The Catcher was a Spy: The Mysterious Life of Moe Berg*, a fascinating account of this talented, eccentric and polymath athlete from a Jewish family, an outlier in a sport that at the time boasted very few MoTs (Members of the Tribe).

He loved languages, earned a degree in Linguistics (later helping to devise a way to teach the Japanese to pronounce the letters R and L; and like Oppenheimer, spoke Sanskrit), but his true passion was baseball. He played shortstop for the varsity team at Princeton, then turned pro, first signing with Brooklyn and eventually ending up as a "good-glove-no-hit" catcher with the White Sox. Buck Crouse, a former White Sox teammate and fellow catcher, once said to him: "Moe, I don't care how many of them college degrees you got. They ain't learned you to hit that curveball no better than me," and when Senators outfielder Dave Harris was told that Berg spoke seven languages, he replied, "Yeah, and he can't hit in any of them!"

Although his performance on the baseball field was by and large lackluster (hitting just six home runs during sixteen years in the Major Leagues, his career batting average a mere .243), he was a good receiver. He also had a larger-than-life media presence. As the *Smithsonian Magazine* tells it, "While other players were rounding the bases or waiting for their turn in the lineup, he'd entertain from the bench, telling stories about his travels, detailing the etymology of random words and chatting with the press in whatever language struck his fancy"; he became known as "the brainiest man in baseball" and was nicknamed "Professor Berg" by one admiring sportswriter (which reminds me of how in 1974, after Alex and I realized how brainy our new drummer Neil Peart was, we began calling *him* "The Professor"). And Casey Stengel once said of him, "He is the strangest man ever to play baseball"—and that was before he even knew he was a spy....

Even if he'd been a slugger, baseball was no guarantee to making a living back in the day, so Berg returned to school and got a degree in law to enhance his income in the off season.

He was quite the raconteur, holding court at social gatherings in Washington, D.C., which is how he met someone from the Office of Strategic Services, the forerunner to the CIA; that encounter led him to spy for the agency during an MLB All-Star Tour of Japan in 1934 (his baseball card is the only one on display at Langley), where he made short films of strategic Tokyo installations with a Bell & Howell 16mm camera under his kimono. At St. Luke's hospital, introducing himself in Japanese, he claimed to be a friend of U.S. Ambassador Joseph Clark Grew and his daughter, who was recovering from childbirth on the fifth floor. He never delivered the flowers, but he did capture footage of the city skyline.

His linguistics degree made him uniquely qualified to be dropped behind enemy lines during World War II, where he was tasked with luring Italian atomic scientists to America to work on the Manhattan Project and, masquerading as a Swiss physics student, snuck into a lecture by Werner Heisenberg, director of the Nazi nuclear program, to learn how close the Germans were to making their own A-bomb—and if that looked imminent, assassinate him with a gun and kill himself with a cyanide capsule, both tucked inside his jacket pocket. Legend has it that he was awarded the Medal of Merit but turned it down because he wouldn't be able to tell his friends how he'd earned it.

The 1934 team standing in front of the Imperial Hotel in Tokyo.

BARRY BONDS

"**60. COUNT 'EM,** 60. Let's see some sonofabitch match that." Babe Ruth famously uttered those words following his own record drive in 1927, and was surely watching from above when the controversial Barry Bonds did just that, smacking this official Major League orb onto the walkway of Pacific Ballpark on September 6th, 2001. With that swing Bonds became just the fifth man to reach that lofty plateau, joining The Babe, Maris, McGwire and Sosa in an elite brotherhood...there is every reason to be fascinated by this milestone ball, and its historical connection to the great Bambino makes it particularly special." (Quoted from the letter of authenticity supplied by the James Spence Authentication Company.)

Barry was the son of the well-loved Giant, Bobby Bonds, who'd played alongside the likes of Willie Mays (who was also Barry's godfather). His seemingly inherited talent showing from a young age, he made his debut in 1986 with the Pirates, exhibiting power and speed that would distinguish his career, and finishing the season sixth in the Rookie of the Year tables. But he had an attitude. He eschewed the limelight, displayed a disdain for the media and left fans with the feeling that he wasn't trying his hardest. One of his coaches, Jim Brock, said, "I don't think he ever figured out what to do to get people to like him." Still, in the 1990 season he hit .301, took 33 home runs and 114 RBIs, and won his first MVP award—and quite rightly, was soon making demands to be the highest paid player in baseball. Pittsburgh couldn't or wouldn't match the salaries that wealthier teams were, and in 1993 he was signed to the Giants for a record-setting $43.75 million.

But Bonds alienated the Giants fans too. They kind of freaked out when he announced a desire to wear Mays' retired number 24, though he settled for 25 and in the end won their admiration with his spectacular performance: he hit 46 home runs and 123 RBIs in his first year, finished 1993 with a .336 batting average and his second MVP, and in 1998 got one of the ultimate honours, being intentionally walked when the bases were already loaded—just the fifth time that it ever happened in the Major Leagues.

He soared to greater heights than ever, hitting a single season record of 73 home runs in 2001, but the cloud of PEDs, which he never quite admitted to ingesting, would forever hang over him (as well as fellow sluggers McGwire and Sosa). He's still not in the Hall of Fame, which is a shame, because before all of this, he was *already* a viable Hall of Famer.

I met Bonds when John Silverman, the clubhouse manager for the Florida Marlins and a friend of mine from the Expos days, introduced us. (I was also introduced to a few other Marlins that day, including one of the greatest hitters of our age, Ichiro Suzuki, who'd come over from Japan to take the major leagues by storm; and who graciously signed my 3,000-Hit ball; see page 13). Bonds towered over me, gave a sort of smile and signed my baseballs, and in return I gave him a Rush-signed ball. We had a short but very nice conversation and that was that. But my better Bonds story is this: another MLB clubhouse manager, a good pal of mine, once gave me a bag of signed balls. Now, at the end of the season, players always tipped the "clubbies"—mostly in cash—for taking care of them all year, but included in this bag was a framed blank check Bonds had given to one of them. So, as I write this, staring back at me in my office is...a blank check from Barry Bonds!

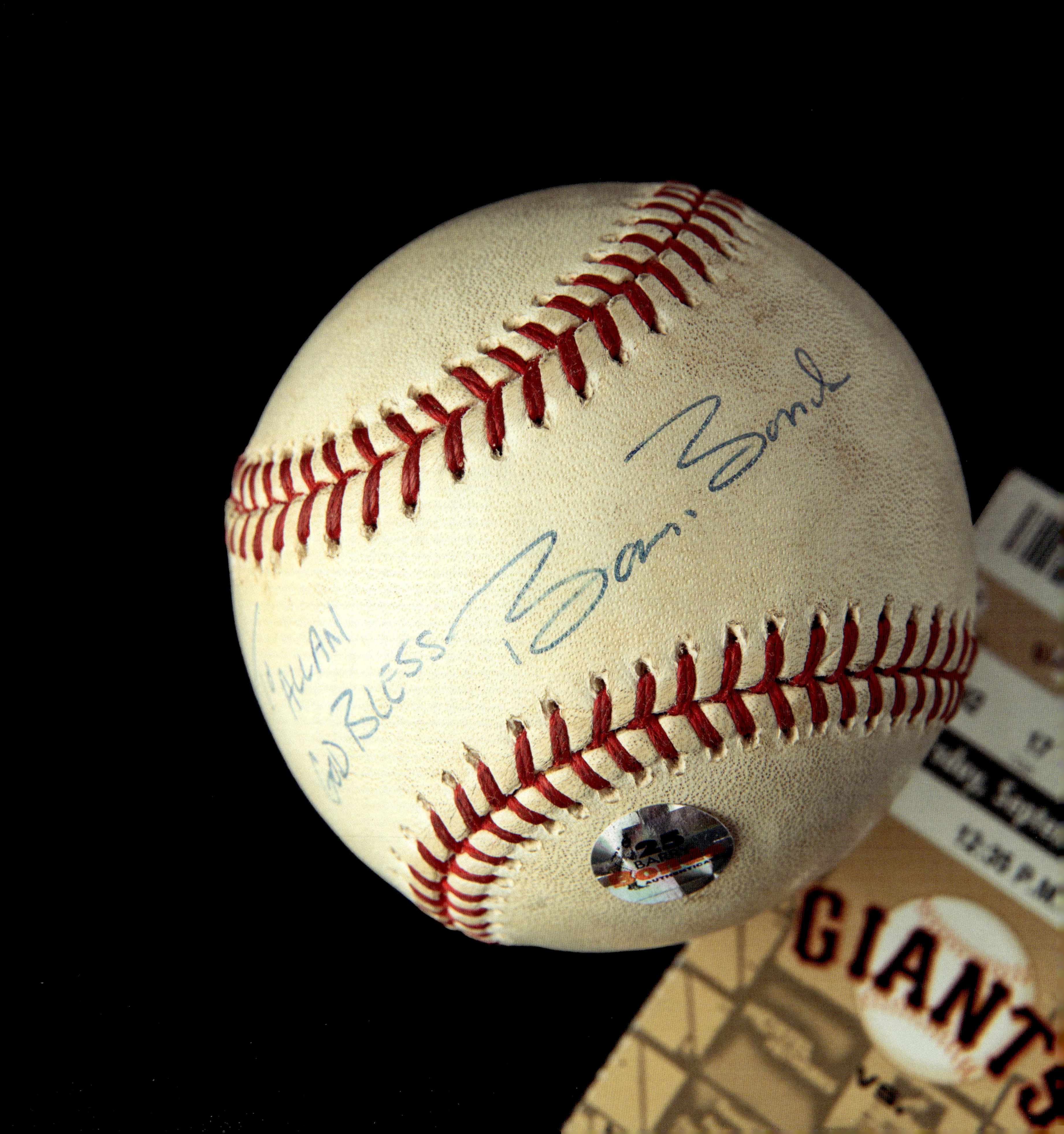
ALLAN
God BLESS
25
BARRY
12:35 P.M.
GIANTS

BOB CAIN VS. EDDIE GAEDEL

FROM GEDDY LEE'S *Believe It Or Not*, this ball features in one of the most famous, if silliest, showdowns in professional baseball history. *In one corner: Eddie Gaedel, number 1/8, at three-foot-seven the shortest batsman ever! In the other corner, the exasperated Bob "Sugar" Cain, Major League pitcher from 1949 to 1954....*

So, it was late in 1996 that I was approached by my guru J.W. Jones, who knew a gentleman, who knew a middleman, who knew Cain, who was getting on in years. The middleman said he had a ball on which Cain had written the whole story of the time he pitched for the Detroit Tigers against Gaedel. I said I was interested in buying it, but wanted a letter from Bob himself avowing that it was from him. He replied that Bob was ill, but that he'd work on it.

We bought the ball, but the letter never came, and then Cain passed away. Still, I trusted that the middleman had known Bob and that the ball was authentic. Then years later, I found another ball, one that looked like a reproduction of the first but inscribed in a slightly different script. Mine has been through the mill. You can see that the handwriting is a bit shaky and blotchy but has an air of authenticity about it. No way the second one (which I bought at auction in 2011 for seven hundred bucks, for comparison's sake) is a used ball. It's a very different animal, and I've seen a couple more just like it. Somebody obviously talked Cain into reproducing the original, which was still in his possession before he died.

But was my original an actual game ball, as the middleman claimed it was? I don't think it's possible to verify. It sure looks like a game ball, but we don't know if it's the first, second, third, fourth, or *any* of the balls that walked Gaedel that fateful day. Everyone involved in the sale has now passed away, so I have only my memory to rely upon.

That's a bit of the mystery and magic of collecting. You believe what you want to believe. You have to remember that this was an embarrassing moment in Cain's life, that became the *defining* moment in his life. What is Bob Cain known for? He was a decent pitcher who deserved to be recognised for more than throwing to a midget who'd popped out of a cake, stood in at bat and presented such a tiny strike zone that he got walked with four straight pitches, all high! I would assume that Cain sheepishly exploited this moment for his own benefit from time to time, keeping the original until he was old and frail; I'm sure that he showed it off to lots of people who came to visit him, and it became faded over the years, so then he cleaned it up a bit and retraced his own signature. That's what I choose to believe.

OPPOSITE:

BOB CAIN

As you may know Eddie Gaedel stepped out of a big birthday cake wearing a Brownie uniform, number 1/8. We all thought it was a big joke until the umpire asked for his contract which the Browns manager then produced. When he was announced to bat our catcher laid on the ground to give me a low target. The umpire made him get into his usual squat position and yelled play ball. I walked him on four pitches high. Bill Veeck was on the roof of the stadium and said that he would have shot Eddie if he had swung at any of the pitches. Midgets were barred from baseball the next day. We did win the game 6 to 1. Catcher Bob Swift. Umpire Ed Hurley. Pitcher Bob Cain.

ROD CAREW

ONE AFTERNOON IN 1992, Mark Langston invited Alex and me to hang out with the California Angels (as the Los Angeles Angels were then known). A genuinely likeable bunch, they treated us like royalty, put us in uniform and shagged us flies in the outfield. Then their legendary ninety-one-year-old honorary coach Jimmie Reese threw down a challenge: if I failed to snag just one of ten ground balls he'd hit to me with his fungo bat, I'd owe him a cigar. When I accepted, he loudly proclaimed, "I got me a lamb!" Of course, the smoke was his and the humiliation of defeat all mine.

Next up was a session in the cage with their new batting coach Rod Carew, a sensational hitter in his day. Al (who I nicknamed Big John Ball, after a big, muscular, baccy chewin' ballplayer in Philip Roth's *The Great American Novel*) flailed pop flies left and right, while I, er . . . *thwacked* line drives best I could. When we were done, Rod paused for a moment, then said generously, "Well, Alex is more of a power hitter. Geddy is like a hits-to-all-fields kinda guy." Just so kind. Alex and I were floating on air.

Every batter has a flaw that pitchers like to feast on—a hole in his swing, an area of the strike zone that he cannot get to with any authority—but as the Yankees pitcher Catfish Hunter said of Carew, "He has no weakness as a hitter inside or outside. High, low, fast stuff, breaking balls, anything you can throw, he can handle. He swings with the pitch. That's why he's so great. He has no holes." He was inducted into the Hall of Fame in 1991—the 27th player in history to be elected in his first year of eligibility.

Playing for Minnesota in 1977, he was batting over .400 and had America in his thrall, appearing on the cover of both *Sports Illustrated* and *Time*. He ended the season at a still stellar .388, but the Twins ceded the AL West Crown to Kansas City. While disappointed, he kept his chin typically up, saying, "Even when I was getting all that publicity . . . I knew that when the weather got hot, my arms would get tired and I'd have some injury or something and I'd hit the ball hard and still make outs. But hitting .400 *would* have been an individual accomplishment. Winning games is everyone's main goal. When you win, it's exciting to be in the clubhouse. When you win, you don't hear players mumbling or grumbling. It's fun." He's that kind of guy.

In 1985, after Rod's retirement from the diamond, the *L.A. Times'* Mike Downey wrote, "His bat control was amazing; he was like a kid with a video-game joystick. With a baseball bat he is Leonard Bernstein with a baton, Alan Ladd with a gun, Glenda the Good Witch with a wand, Luke Skywalker with a laser. He is a dangerous man with a blunt instrument, so be careful around him."

Since that day in Anaheim, Rod and his family have had to endure the unfathomably painful loss of their daughter Michelle to leukemia. Despite the grief, he carried on nobly and went on to become an advocate for pediatric cancer research who gives talks not only about baseball, but on organ donation and child abuse as well. He'd overcome a lot in his life but grew to be an upbeat, good-humoured, generous and wise man. In other words, a real class act. I feel privileged to have met many players in this game, but few if any more than him.

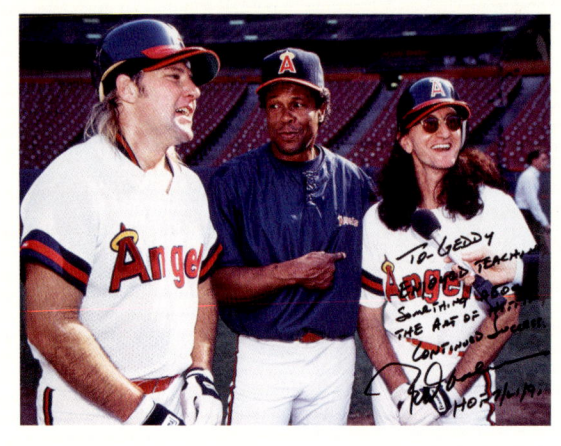

TOP: *The talented artist and renowned pothead Alex Lifeson painted this wine bottle for my 40th birthday, based on the photo above.* ABOVE: *Every person should be so privileged to have a batting lesson from this incredible dude!*

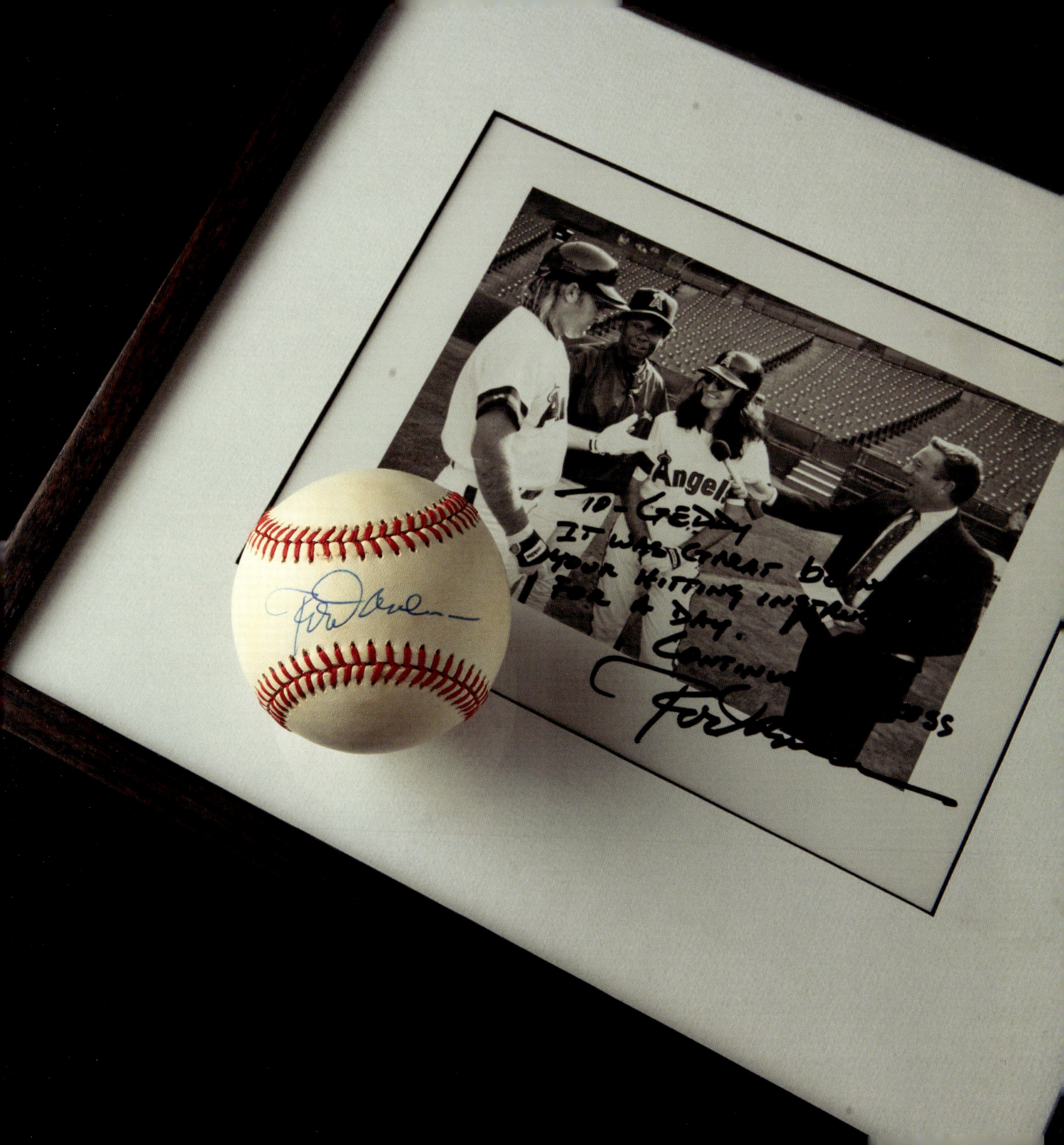

TO- GEDDY
IT WAS GREAT
YOUR HITTING
FOR A DAY.

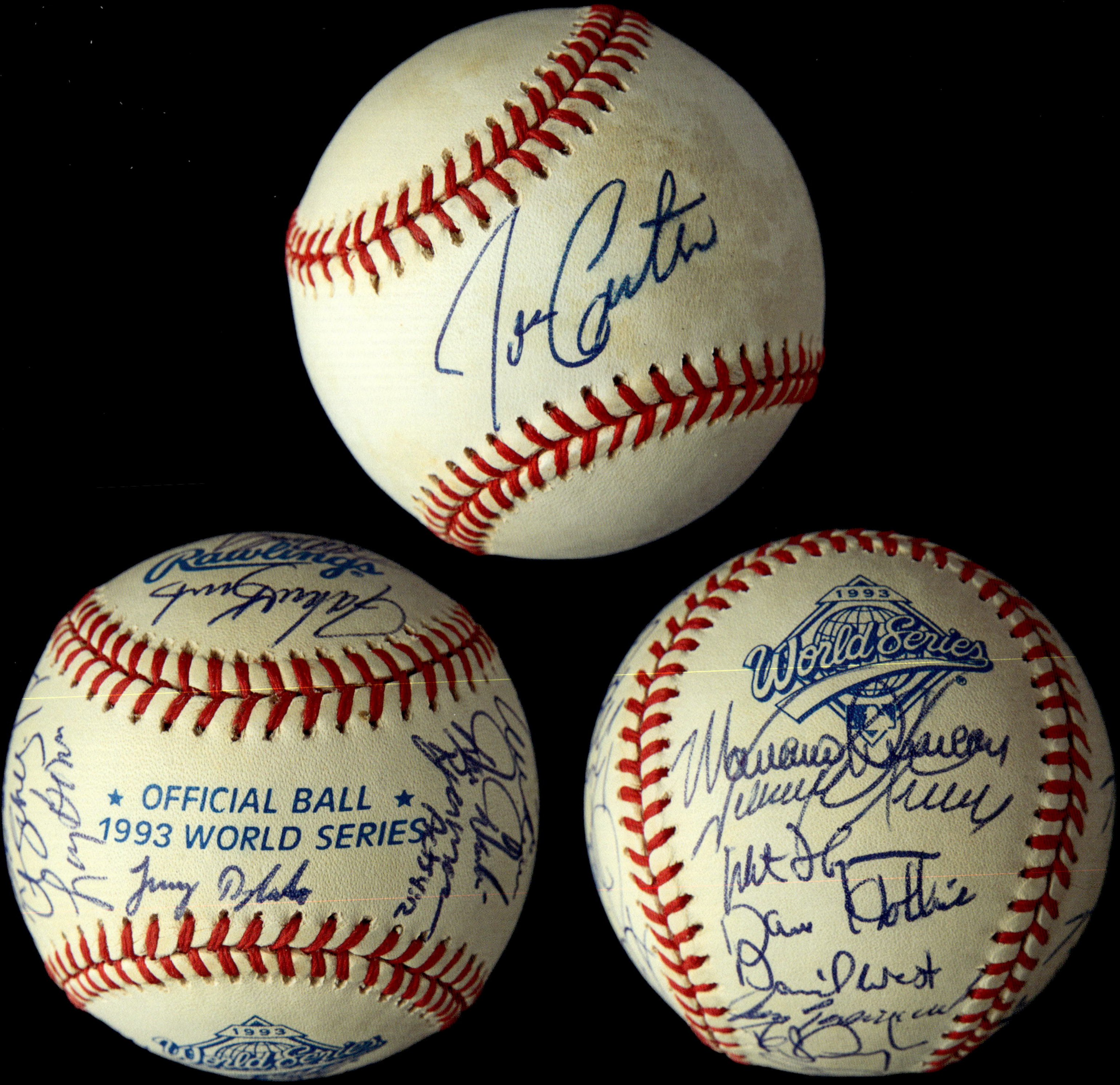
Rawlings
★ OFFICIAL BALL ★
1993 WORLD SERIES
1993
World Series

JOE CARTER

THIS IS ONE of those balls I would never sell. It's so meaningful to me because I was there when Joe Carter hit that home run for the Blue Jays to win the 1993 World Series in such a spectacular fashion, giving me my most triumphant baseball memory ever. It was the walk-off to end all walk-offs!

For years at old Exhibition Stadium, I sat beside a lovely gentleman named Roy (a retired air traffic controller, I believe) who loved the game so much that he almost never missed one. I enjoyed his company so much that I'd sometimes go alone, knowing he'd be there, and we'd have a fine time talkin' baseball. He'd been a subscriber since Day One (I came along two years later), so when the team moved to the Skydome, quite rightly he got first pick of the new seats and chose the front row right behind the dugout, while I landed seven rows behind him. We were a bit miffed not to be sitting together anymore, but I was happy for him....

Now, at the bottom of the eighth of this World Series game, the Jays had missed several opportunities and were trailing the Phillies 5 to 6. They had the bases loaded, but Pat Borders popped out, and I saw Roy, out of sheer frustration, leave his seat and stomp up the stairs. I'd thought, *He can't be leaving during Game Six of the World Series*, but because he didn't see me waving to him, I had to wait till the following season to confirm if he'd relented and come back in. When we did meet again next season, I said, "Tell me you didn't leave," and he looked at me dolefully and said, "I was on the subway when they won." Say it ain't so, Roy! This was the moment he'd been waiting for his entire life, and *he missed it*.

That was the only time a home run has been hit by a player whose team was trailing in the bottom of the ninth in a potential championship clinching game. As Carter rounded first base, jumping up and down and losing his helmet, CJCL's radio announcer Tom Cheek called out, "Touch 'em all Joe! You'll never hit a bigger home run in your life." And poor Mitch Williams, closing for the Phillies! You never knew if "The Wild Thing" was going to strike a guy out or walk him, hit the guy or give up a home run! In the dugout you could see the tension on his teammates' faces: some of them couldn't even bear to watch him pitch. This one had been especially excruciating for Phillies fans, but pure heaven to us Jays fans.

No, it wasn't our first WS win, but in '92 we'd won away in Atlanta; this time the entire stadium, the entire *city*, exploded. I've never seen Toronto go as apeshit. We thronged the streets for hours, partying in the bars and roaming around like it was Mardi Gras. Everyone was buying everyone else a drink, and at a time when professional sports had been marred by some fans' overreaction, there was zero violence, just pure, unadulterated, sports joy juice. It was a fantastic night, the ultimate for a Blue Jays fan, and I will love Joe Carter forever for it. That three-run home run was a lightning bolt. He won it for himself and for the team, of course, but he gave it to *us*—and who knows, we may never see another like it.

I've met Joe a couple of times. He's a super friendly dude, but I don't think he gave this ball to me directly; it was more likely from one of my pals in the clubhouse. Nor may he ever be in the Hall of Fame, but with that 8-5 win, he's in my heart. It was epic, believe me. You should see the smile on my face as I type this!

FIDEL CASTRO

THE DESCRIPTION ACCOMPANYING this Batos baseball's certification says, "An incredibly rare Cuban baseball signed by failed southpaw Fidel Castro. One can only wonder how history would have been altered had Fidel succeeded in his first dream, that of playing Major League ball in the States."

According to legend, he was a star pitcher at the University of Havana (or, in fact, was not good enough to make the varsity team?); he had an especially wicked curveball (or was it a fastball?); and it's said that he had tryouts with the Yankees, Senators and Pirates (though a Pirates scout wrote in his report that the kid "has nothing on his fastball" and judged him to be "Double-A talent at best"); another story, at least from Fidel himself, is that he rejected a $5,000 bonus to play with the Giants, but rather than try his luck in the Majors, he turned to his other dream to become a lawyer ... and then the dictator of Cuba, with which, as history has shown, he had far more success.

Still (and this is *not* apocryphal), he didn't completely give up baseball. In July 1959, he pitched two innings of a pickup game with his team, Los Barbudos ("The Bearded Revolutionaries," a moniker coined to describe the rebel forces of the Cuban Revolution), against a military police team—his only recorded appearance in any game. "Perhaps the last straw for Castro," the certification continues, "was when baseball moved the Minor League Havana Sugar Kings to Newark after the 1959 season. Maybe the gunshots fired by Fidel's mob during the game, wounding two players, had a little to do with it."

Like Kennedy, Castro is a figure that loomed large in the news during my childhood—again through the biased American lens, according to which Cuba was a place basically controlled by the devil. As an adult, I don't take quite as harsh a view of him. Perhaps it's not my place to say whether he was an evil man or not, but as I mention elsewhere in this book, after the revolution, he *did* appoint the All-Star U.S. Negro League player Martín Dihigo as Minister of Sports; anyone who appreciated baseball that much surely couldn't be *all* bad....

I also have this picture of Castro signing the ball. Of special note is the woman, Castro's taster, whose sole duty was to sample his food and drink in case it was poisoned.

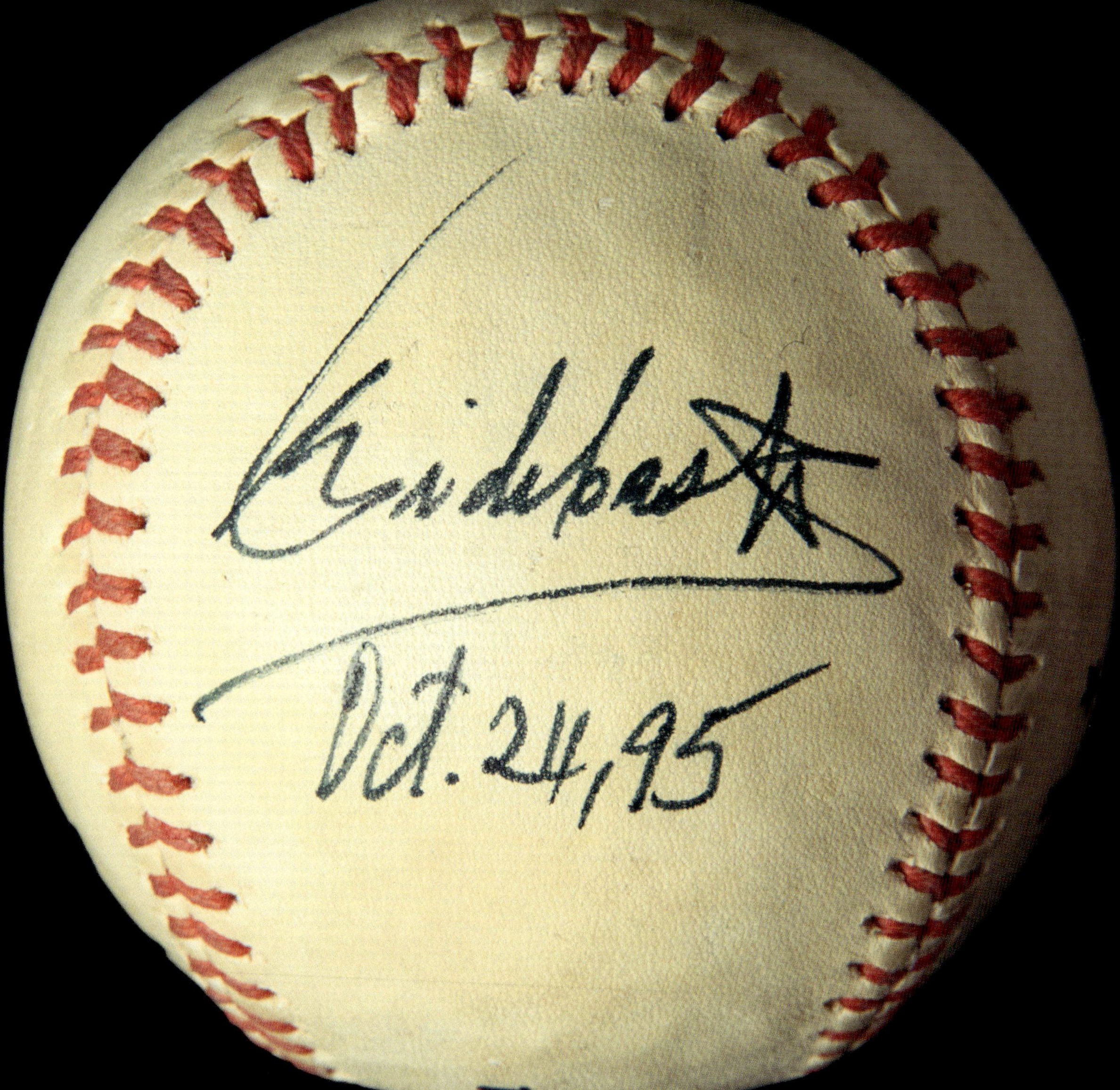
Oct. 24, 95

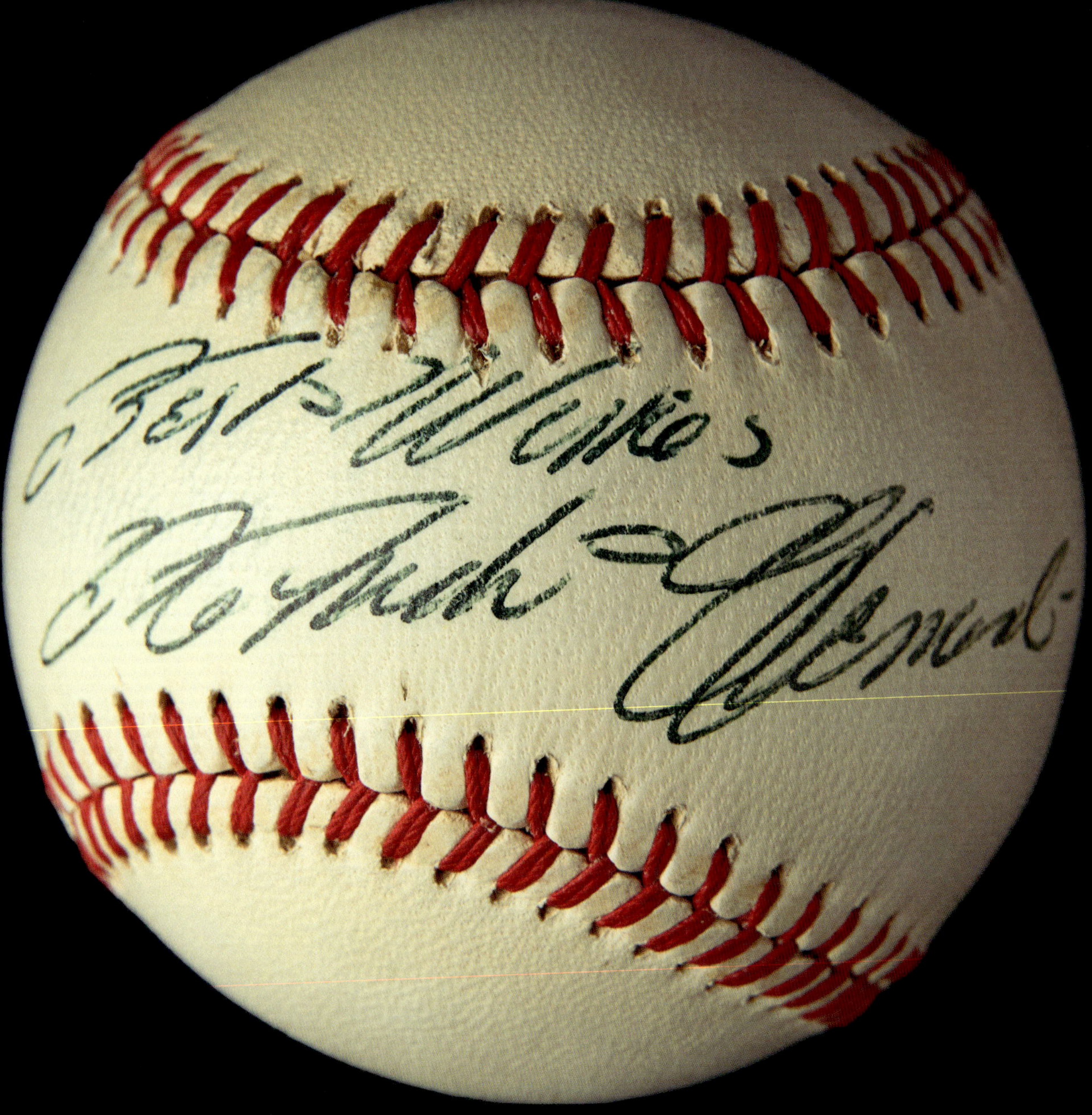
Best Wishes

ROBERTO CLEMENTE

I DON'T RECALL WATCHING Roberto Clemente when I was a kid. I was too young and American League-centric to grasp his greatness; I only later discovered that he was one of the finest Puerto Rican players of the Sixties and early Seventies, a marvellous outfielder and terrific hitter (a member of the 3,000-hit club, leading the National League in batting average in 1961, 1964, 1965 and 1967), a great all-rounder and perennial All-Star, and a humanitarian whose commitment to charitable causes would lead to his untimely demise.

He got his 3,000th hit on September 30th, 1972—thus becoming the first Latin-born player ever to enter that elite club—after which he rested for the playoffs. The Pirates looked like they were on their way back to the World Series, but failed to make it, so he returned to Puerto Rico where he managed the team that went to the amateur Baseball World Series in Nicaragua. He'd made numerous friends there and developed a particular fondness for the country, so when on December 23rd Nicaragua's capital Managua suffered a massive earthquake, he threw himself into arranging emergency relief flights, working through Christmas to raise money for medicine and food. When he learned that aid packages had been diverted by corrupt officials of the Somoza government, he decided to accompany the fourth relief flight, hoping his presence would ensure aid would get to the survivors. His wife Vera begged him not to board the airplane, which had a history of mechanical problems, but he said, "When your time comes, it comes; if you are going to die, you will die. And babies are dying. They need these supplies." The Douglas DC-7 cargo plane crashed into the ocean. He, the pilot and three other men died in the water just a mile off Puerto Rico's coast.

In 1971 the Commissioner's Award had already been established to recognise players who "best exemplify the game of baseball, sportsmanship, community involvement and the individual's contribution to his team"; in '73 (the same year the Pirates retired his number 21), it was renamed the Roberto Clemente Award. He'd long dreamed of making Puerto Rico not just a sports city for young people, but a place where they could learn other life skills. Since then, a number of schools have indeed been named after him, but not just in his hometown—in Chicago and Allentown, Pennsylvania too. In 2012, the Puerto Rico Professional Baseball League was renamed "Liga de Béisbol Profesional Roberto Clemente."

Normally a player cannot be inducted into the Hall of Fame until five years after he's stopped playing, but a special election was held for him, and in the summer of 1973 he became the first player from Latin America to be inducted into the Hall of Fame. And of course, Major League Baseball has celebrated a Roberto Clemente Day since 2022. It's one thing to admire the great players of the game, another to single out those who've done honour to their uniforms by being model citizens; when you consider how many children love the game, that's an ideal well worth pointing out. When I take my grandson to the ballgame on Roberto Clemente Day, it's an opportunity to retell this hero's story.

As a boy himself, Roberto liked to squeeze rubber balls to strengthen his hands. He used to say that hurling the javelin in high school (where he performed so well, he was considered good enough to represent Puerto Rico in the Olympics) was only part of the reason he developed such a strong throwing arm; "You know," he said, "my mother has the same kind of arm, even today at 74. She could throw a ball from second base to home plate with something on it! I got my arm from my mom."

A magnificent player. A magnificent person.

TY COBB

SIGNED BY "THE Georgia Peach" himself, here's a photograph of the monumental Ty Cobb on the bench at his very first Major League game with the Detroit Tigers, receiving a pep talk from his manager Bill Armour. On the back he describes the moment:

Rev: - here is a reprint, best I can do, per many demands. I have other reprints but thought this would be a little unusual, for only a very few of these are held by anyone. This is about five minutes before my first game of Major League, in Detroit, August 1905, my manager then was Wm Armour and he is telling me to go out there and be calm and not over awed by stands or crowd. New York Highlanders then, Chesbro a great spit ball pitcher, first time at bat, two bases, help from above I feel even now. Luck also. I was 18 years of age. Ty Cobb.

I love this letter! It's signed April 18th, 1960, only a year before his death at 74 years of age, long regarded as one of the most dynamic players of all time and still frequently approached for autographs—in this instance, apparently, by a reverend—but the photo itself sets the scene of his entry into the Major Leagues *before* he had any reputation. It's just so rich to me, seeing this man-boy on the brink of a great journey, and it tells you something of what the game was like then. These days, of course, a pitcher's glove is checked for foreign substances after every inning, but in 1905 spitballs weren't yet banned. Back then you could smear pine tar on the ball, spit on your hands, whatever it took to give your slider or curveball that extra spin, and here Cobb actually expresses *respect* for Jack Chesbro's spitballing skills.

Cobb was a fierce, tough-assed player and not without controversy. There were claims that he was a racist (some of the best known incidents of his road rage and other violent altercations involved African-Americans) and an antisemite, though some of these are now discredited. Daniel Ginsberg writes on SABR.org that while his reputation has been diminished, and "all evidence shows that his attitudes were typical of his times and Georgia upbringing" but that "he certainly did not oppose racial segregation in baseball or elsewhere."

A story also circulated that he'd make a show of sharpening his spikes before every game to intimidate his opponents as he slid into base; his bat boy Jimmy Lanier insists he never did, although in an interview published in *The National Pastime: Baseball in the Peach State*, Lanier *did* allow that Cobb "used the 'sharpening the spikes' rumor as an advantage, making the opposing players fearful of getting cut trying to tag him." As player/manager, Cobb was famously rigorous and relentlessly demanding. While no one denied his athletic abilities, he was personally disliked in the baseball community—by his own teammates, even—but in this letter you can see a kinder and more sensitive Cobb, a religious man, telling this reverend that he feels he's been blessed and watched over throughout his life.

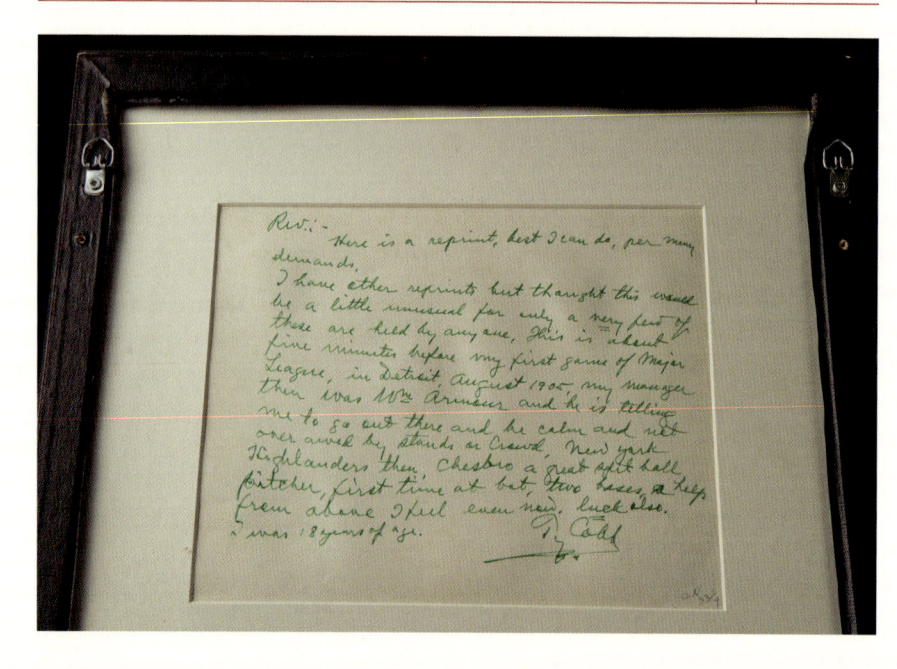

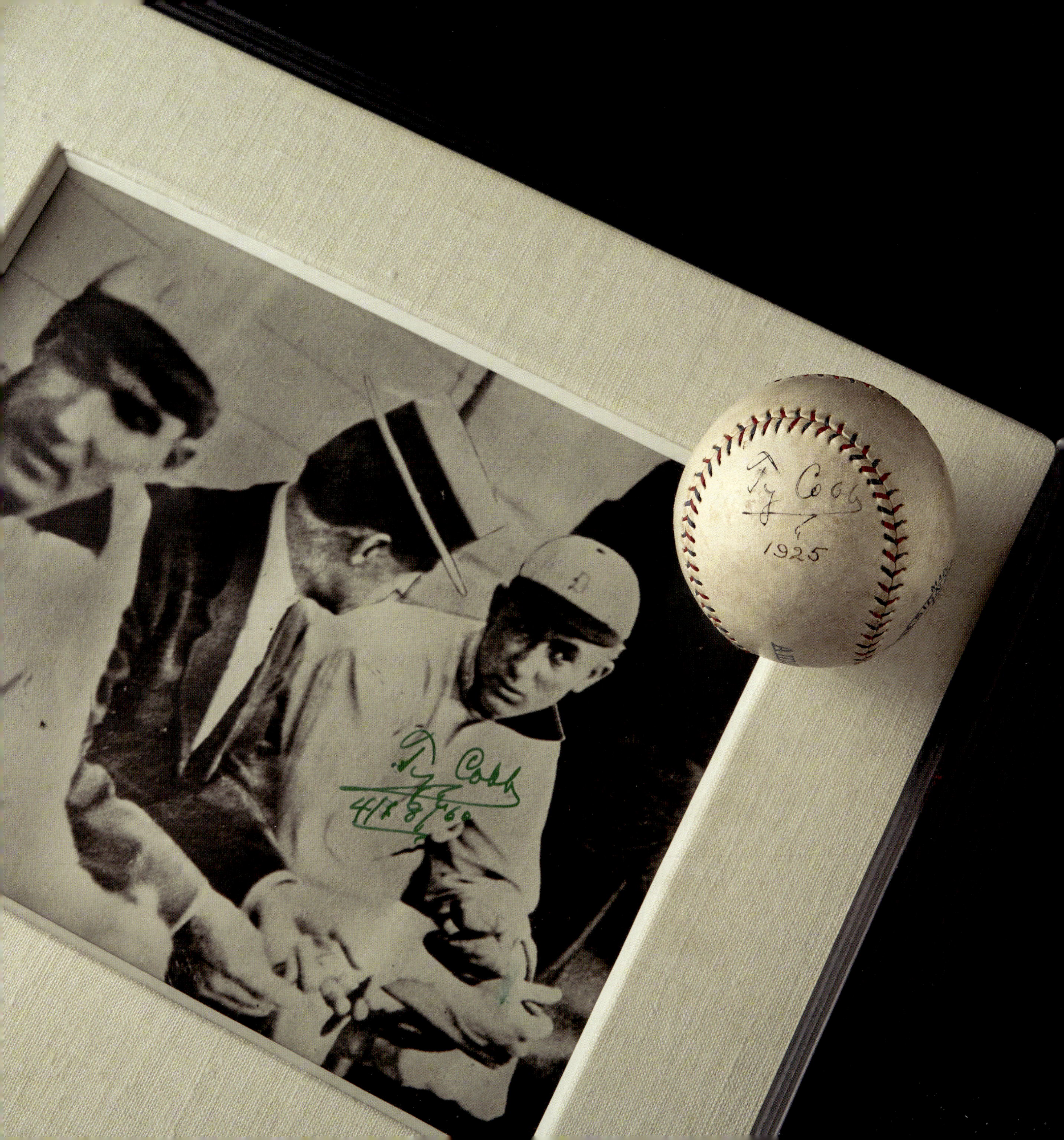
Ty Cobb
Ty Cobb
1925

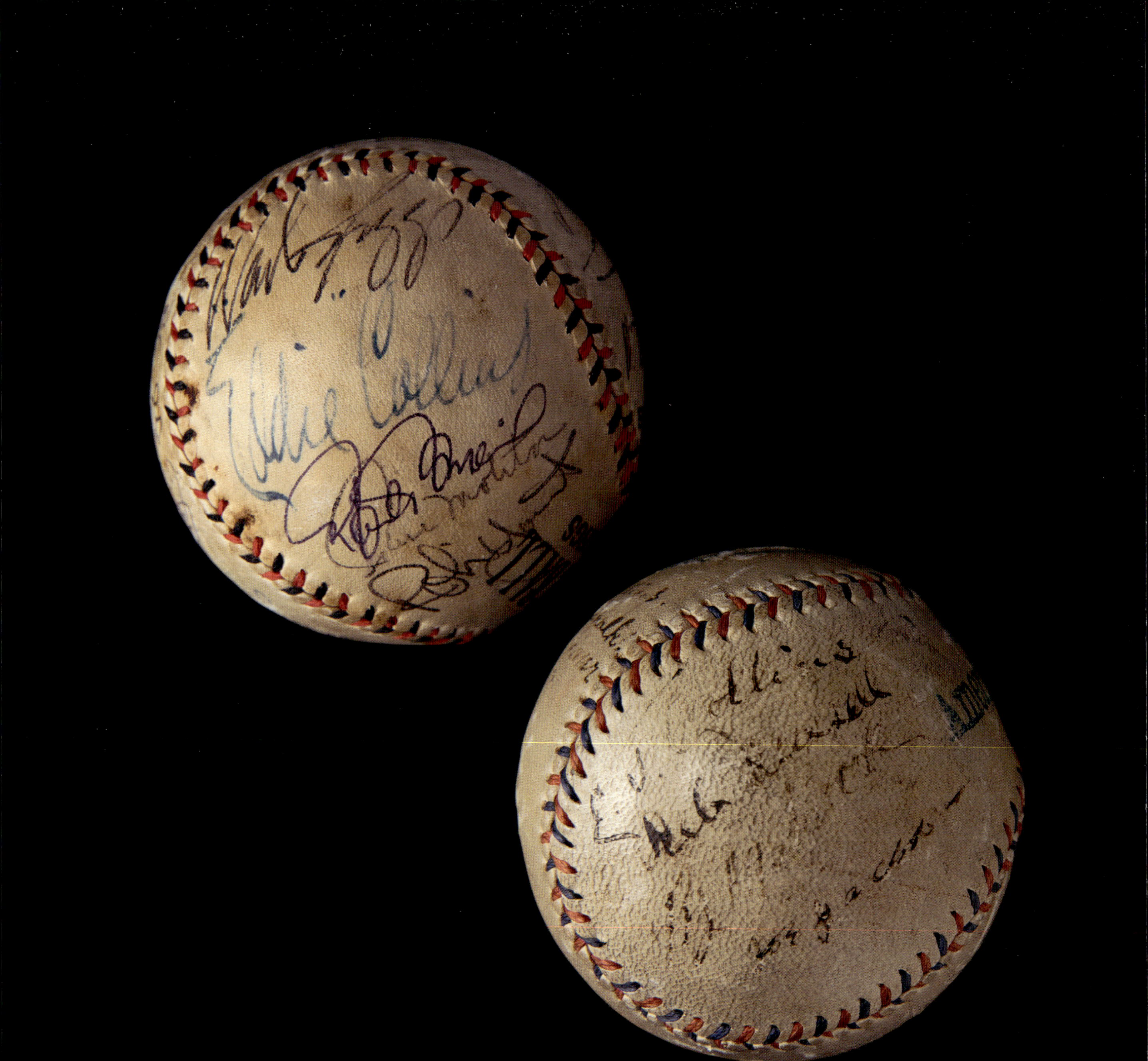

EDDIE COLLINS

IT TOOK ME eight years of searching to find a good "Fast Eddie." His signature sits proudly amongst the other elite hitters on my 3,000-hit club ball and is present on a rare 1917 White Sox ball I own, but a single-signed one displaying his distinctive loopy style is a special find. Even Heritage Auctions confirms their tremendous scarcity, stating "It's a bit of a mystery that so few exist." (His paper signatures are also rare.) Collins was a bright, educated dude, an Ivy League graduate like Moe Berg—unusual in a time when many players didn't go to college at all—this was a rough and tumble crowd, and he was a smarty pants! Paul Mittermeyer on SABR.org writes, "Saddled with the nickname 'Cocky' from early in his career, Collins drew the resentment of teammates for his self-confidence and good breeding that at times seemed as though it belonged more in a ballroom than a baseball clubhouse."

He made his Athletics debut in 1906 under the alias of Eddie T. Sullivan to protect his collegiate status while still quarterbacking for Columbia's freshman team, but was soon recognised in the Major Leagues under his own name—and how: in 1923 John McGraw, then manager of the Giants said, "I doubt if anyone will dispute my selection of Eddie Collins as the greatest second baseman of all time." Connie Mack concurred, as did the Senators' player-manager Bucky Harris, writing "Plays which were difficult for even a finished infielder were made to seem easy."

Like Moe Berg (who wouldn't let anyone touch his newspapers because he believed they were alive), Collins was beset by superstition, although he insisted he wasn't—he just thought it "unlucky," for instance, not to get base hits. Yet he feared black cats; finding a hairpin was a portent that he'd hit a single that day; finding two meant a double; in winter he soaked his bats in oil, dried them out and rubbed them down with a bone, and buried them in cow dung "to keep 'em alive"; he was driven to distraction by litter in the dugout; at bat he kept his chewing gum on his hat button for two strikes, only then putting it in his mouth; he'd not change game socks on a winning streak, and as player-manager for the White Sox apparently fired a clubhouse man for not doing the same. We all know that athletes are often superstitious, but he took the biscuit!

But as someone who in 1939 was inducted into the Baseball Hall of Fame on the strength of his defensive exploits and 3,315 career hits (or safeties, as they used to refer to them), in the end his career stats must tell the story: he still holds the Major League record of 512 career sacrifice bunts (over 100 more than any other). He was the AL MVP in 1914, a three-time AL run scored leader from 1912 to 1914, the AL bases-on-balls leader in 1915, and the AL singles leader in 1913. With a career batting average of .333, he was not the all-time greatest slugger, but a bunter *par excellence* and a masterful base stealer: he had one 200-hit season, seven 100-run seasons, and was a four-time AL stolen base leader with six 50 stolen bases seasons. He won five World Series with the A's and one with the Chicago White Sox—and while captain of *that* infamous team in 1919, was one of the few players who was not only on the level, but actually spoke up about what was going on—a fact, I'm sure, that won him no favour amongst the "Eight Men Out."

OPPOSITE:
Lurking at the top of this ball from 1917 is the scrawl of young Eddie a.k.a. E.T. Collins (and speaking of chicken scratch, at the bottom of the same panel is none other than the great Joe Jackson).

SAM E. CRAWFORD

SAMUEL EARL CRAWFORD was born April 18th (my wife's birthday, for what it's worth), 1880. Bill Lamberti on SABR.org writes that he "sprung from fertile Midwestern farm soil, and like a storm blowing across his native Nebraska's prairie swept over the major league baseball landscape for nearly two decades. One of the Deadball Era's most consistent performers, the powerful Crawford never led his league in slugging percentage, but finished in the top ten in that category every year but one from 1901 to 1915. During that span the left-hander paced the circuit in triples six times, on his way to establishing the career record for three-baggers that has not been eclipsed in the more than 85 years since his historic career came to an end."

In 1916, F.C. Lane of *Baseball Magazine* pronounced, "While we are no sculptor, we believe that if we were looking for a model for a statue of a slugger, we would choose Sam Crawford for that role. He had tremendous shoulders and great strength. That strength is so placed in his frame and the weight so balanced that he can get it all behind the drive when he smites a baseball." (Don't you just love the writing? I can hear the announcer on the radio in Biblical times, broadcasting from the stadium in the Sinai Desert: "And lo, that baseball was *smote!*")

He had a devastating combination of power and speed that elevated "Wahoo Sam" to a career record for triples with a total of 309—fourteen better than his closest rival and Hall of Fame teammate Ty Cobb. Much like Lou Gehrig's experience with Babe Ruth, Crawford often found himself in the shadow of the more famous Georgia Peach, and his single-signed baseballs are rarely seen. Only a handful date to the pre-war era, as does this fine official AL ball in the style used from 1910 to 1925—which, "with its gorgeously applied signature in black fountain pen on the side panel," says its letter of certification, "rates a stunning ten out of ten. A simply unimprovable example with only a single pinprick to the letter M that is really too minor to mention" (but they have to mention it anyway). But seriously: this is not merely a signature; it's *calligraphy*. Look at the penmanship: the elegant majuscules, the control of the nub width, the perfect base line. Signed *circa* 1915 and in immaculate condition, it's one of those balls that is the veritable apple of any collector's eye.

Like so many players of his time, he was forced to quit school as a boy. He worked as an apprentice barber, but grew into an articulate, well-read and eloquent adult. "I don't have a telephone," he said. "If I had a lot of money I wouldn't have one. I never was for telephones. Just don't like them, that's all. Anybody wants to talk to you, they can come to see you. I do have a television over there, but I never turn it on. I would rather read a book."

That's sage advice for our frenzied, hyperdistracted age, and maybe how he grokked the Zen approach to expertise long before his time: "My idea of batting," he said, "is a thing that should be done unconsciously. If you get to studying it too much to see just what fraction of a second you must swing to meet a curved ball, the chances are you will miss it altogether." I can relate to Crawford, because that's as true in sports as it is in music: during a live performance the sweet spot, so to speak, is when you're in the moment but not *over*concentrating, because overconcentration will make you tense up. It hearkens back to Malcolm Gladwell's 10,000 hours of practice theory in his book *Outliers*: those hours are baked into your *wa*, the harmony that you take with you on stage or in this case, to the plate, so that the performance just *happens*.

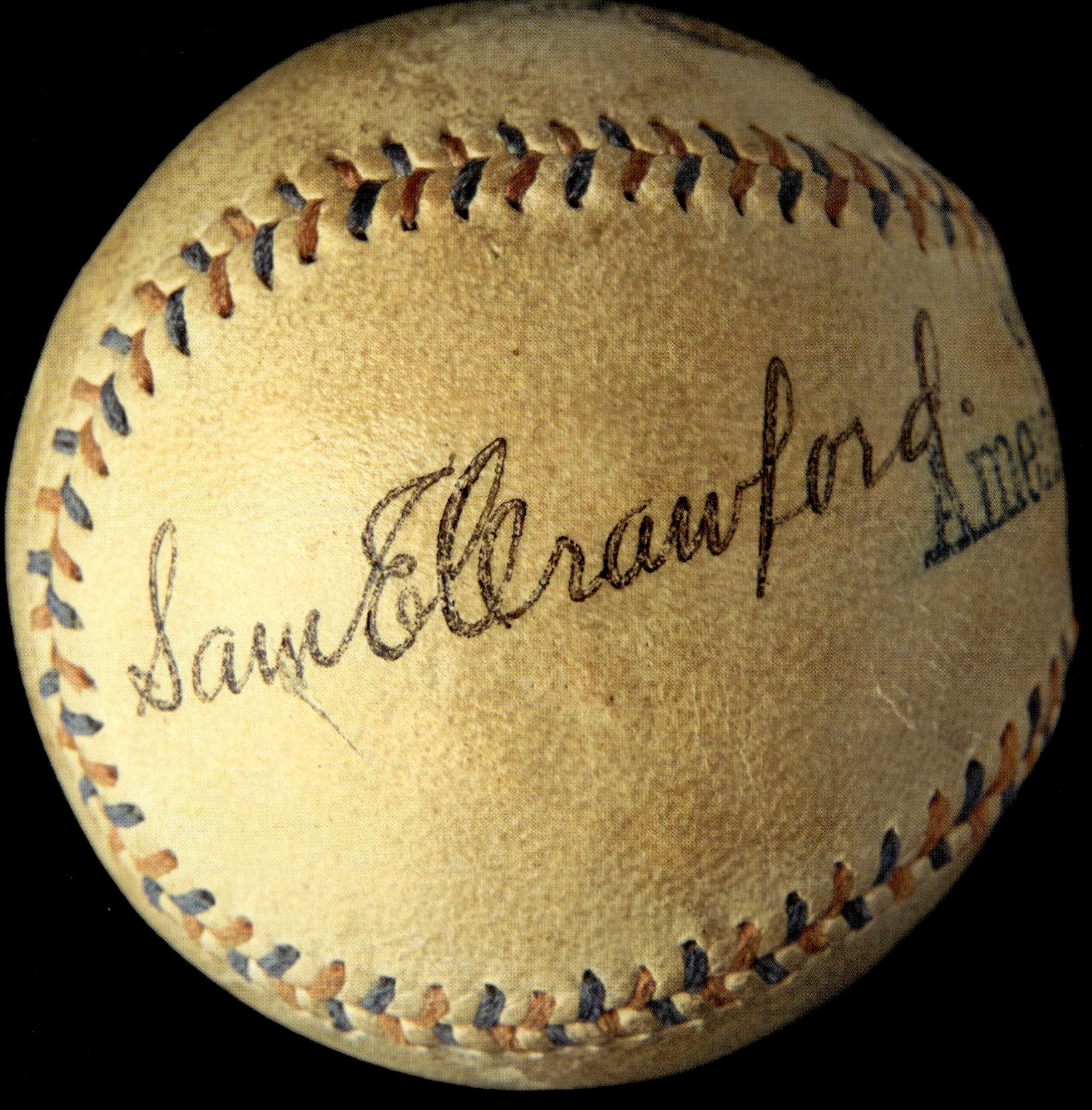
Sam E Crawford

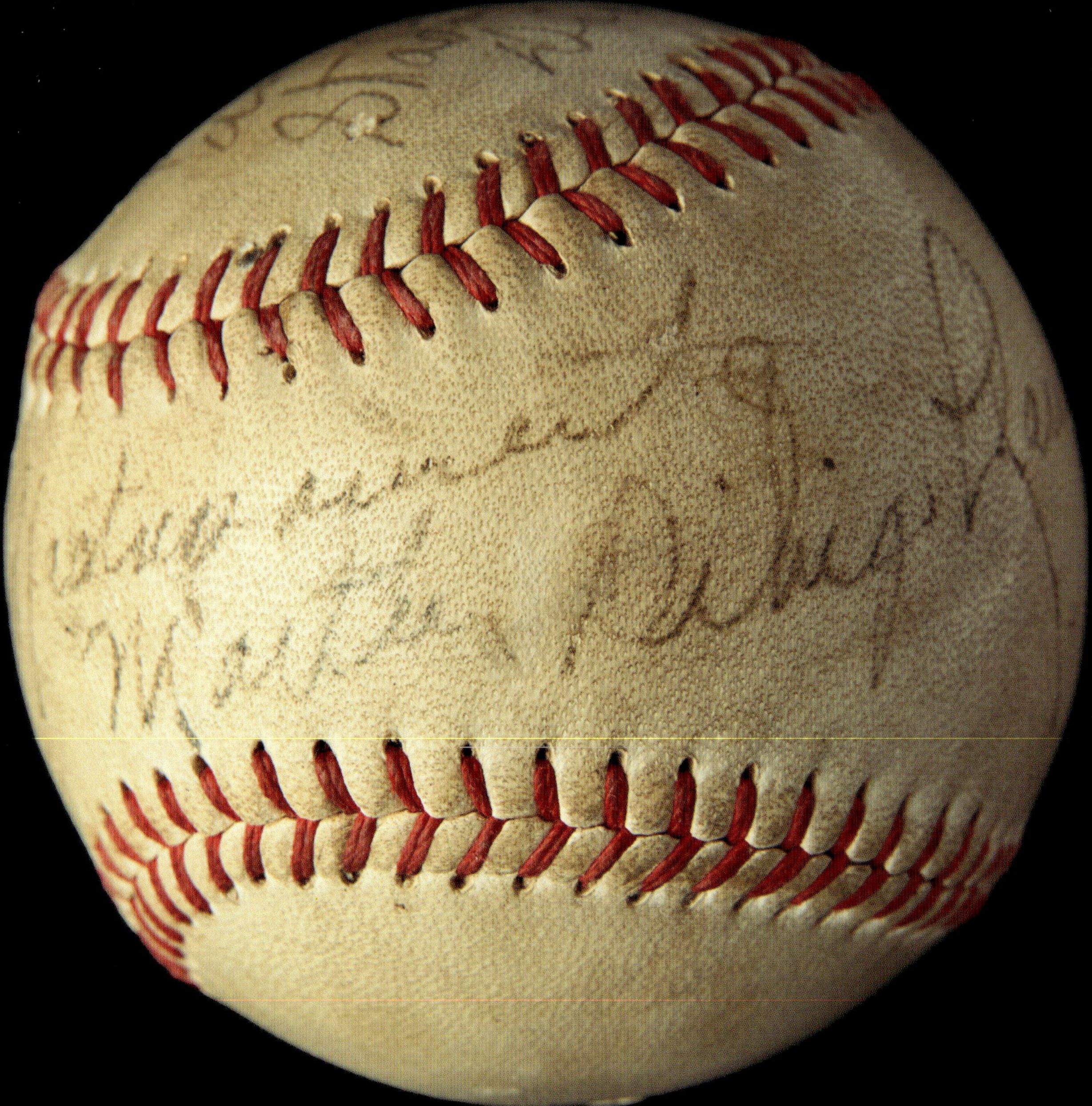

MARTÍN DIHIGO

MARTÍN MAGDALENO DIHIGO LLANOS—"El Inmortal," "El Maestro"—was one of just two players inducted into the American, Cuban, Mexican, Dominican Republic and Venezuelan Baseball Halls of Fame. (The other is another Negro League star, the shortstop Willie "El Diablo" Wells.) Buck Leonard called him "the best player of all time, black or white . . . If he's not the greatest I don't know who is. You take your Ruths, Cobbs, and DiMaggios. Give me Dihigo and I bet I'd beat you almost every time."; Cumberland Posey said that his gifts on field "have never been approached by any man, black or white"; and the Dodgers' GM Al Campanis called him "the best player I have ever seen in my life." What a pity I was never able to see him play!

Dihigo was born in 1906 in Matanzas Province, Cuba (as was the American and Cuban Hall of Fame right-hander José "El Diamante Negro" Méndez; was there something in the water?). In the summer of 1923, still only eighteen, he broke into the American Negro League as first baseman for the Cuban Stars. In time he became the New York Cubans' player-manager and, over a twelve-year career, two-time All-Star. He played in the Negro and Latin American leagues from 1923 to 1936, primarily as a pitcher and second baseman but also, in the view of the Negro League's historian John Holway, as one of the greatest-ever Black sluggers. The most versatile of Negro League stars, he's considered one of the greatest two-way players in baseball history, holding nine positions and excelling at several, batting on average well over .300. On SABR.org, Peter C. Bjarkman describes him as having "wrists of steel" and relates one of many legends surrounding the Cuban: "One ex–blackball ace, Schoolboy Johnny Taylor, witnessed a Dihigo line drive that nearly decapitated a paralyzed shortstop, then slammed against the outfield fence before the amazed infielder could raise his hands in apparent self-defense. A foot lower and it would have killed the panicked infielder." After hanging up his spikes, Dihigo became a radio announcer for the Cuban Winter League and was appointed by Fidel Castro (having reputedly helped fund Castro's revolutionary "26th of July" movement) as an unofficial Minister of Sports.

Dihigo is little known to the wider world of baseball fans, he doesn't have the allure of a Babe Ruth or the larger-than-life white characters (although he stood six-foot-four!), but he's in the pantheon of the greatest players that ever graced the diamond. I admit that for many years, until I started learning about the Negro Leagues, I had no idea about him either. Then I paid a visit to the Negro Leagues Museum in Kansas City, where I saw the Field of Dreams they'd built, featuring life-sized figures of some of the best players in the game—and the gentleman standing at the plate was Martín Dihigo.

One of the many things I took away from the museum was the rich culture in and around the league, and the variety of characters that hailed from so many different countries to play in it. Segregation notwithstanding, several of the league's teams were financially successful and produced some of the sport's finest but unsung heroes. In 2011, when I was told that there'd be an auction selling an actual baseball signed by Dihigo—in his hand, verified—I could hardly believe it. It was magic for me to find a ball that he, one of the greatest players ever, had actually *held*. And let's face it, that is the connection. It's one thing to collect signatures, but to me—and I know I have a romantic notion about this—by holding a sphere a player had in his hand, you're touching the hem of *his* DNA! Every time I put on my white gloves and look at any one of these baseballs, in some tiny way I sense the spirit with which it's imbued.

JOE DIMAGGIO

He started baseball's famous streak
That's got us all aglow
He's just a man and not a freak
Joltin' Joe DiMaggio

"Joltin' Joe" DiMaggio—Betty Bonney w/Les Brown & his Orchestra (1941)

BECAUSE HE RETIRED two years before I was born, I grew up watching Joe DiMaggio shill for Mr. Coffee electric drip coffee maker on TV before I learned that he was one of the greatest centre fielders to ever play the game. But I found out soon enough....

As Lawrence Baldassaro writes on SABR.org: "Joe DiMaggio was the undisputed leader of New York Yankees teams that won nine World Series titles in his 13-year career that ran from 1936 to 1951, with three years lost to duty in World War II. He was three times the American League's Most Valuable Player and he holds what many consider to be the most remarkable baseball record of all, a 56-game hitting streak in 1941. As the son of Sicilian immigrants, he was the embodiment of the American Dream, a rags-to-riches story played out in pinstripes, one of the popular and recognizable figures of the mid-20th century, celebrated in both song and literature. He married the nation's number one glamor girl, Marilyn Monroe. In 1999, the House of Representatives passed a resolution honouring him for his storied baseball career."

Honestly, what can you say about him that hasn't already been said? I'm going to have to leave it to those who've already put it so well:

- "He was in a world by himself. There was nobody who could take over a ballpark like he could . . . if you told me in 1938 that I would be Secretary of State, and I would be friends with DiMaggio, I would have thought the second was less likely than the first." – *Henry Kissinger*
- "Baseball isn't statistics. It's Joe DiMaggio rounding second." – *Jimmy Breslin*
- "There was a majesty in his swing, and a self-assured confidence in style and conduct that was uniquely Joe DiMaggio's. In the eye of his public, he was more than a sports hero. He was among the most cherished icons of popular culture." – *Ernest Hemingway*
- "Heroes are people who are all good with no bad in them. That's the way I always saw Joe. He was beyond question one of the greatest players of the century." – *Mickey Mantle*

I have a couple of DiMaggio items. Joe had two brothers who were also in the game, and I have a baseball featuring all three of them! I like his whirligig signature. We sometimes get this image of ballplayers from the period being ruffians, drunks and liars, and yet they had incredible penmanship and such creative use of the English language....

He was the classic five-tool player. He hit for average and power, he could run, throw and field. Joe McCarthy, the Yankees manager called him the best baserunner he ever saw. His all-round play led the '36 Yankees to the first of four straight World Series titles—only to be matched by the four titles that won by my own rotisserie league team, The Flying Heimishes.

Vince, Joe and Dom DiMaggio

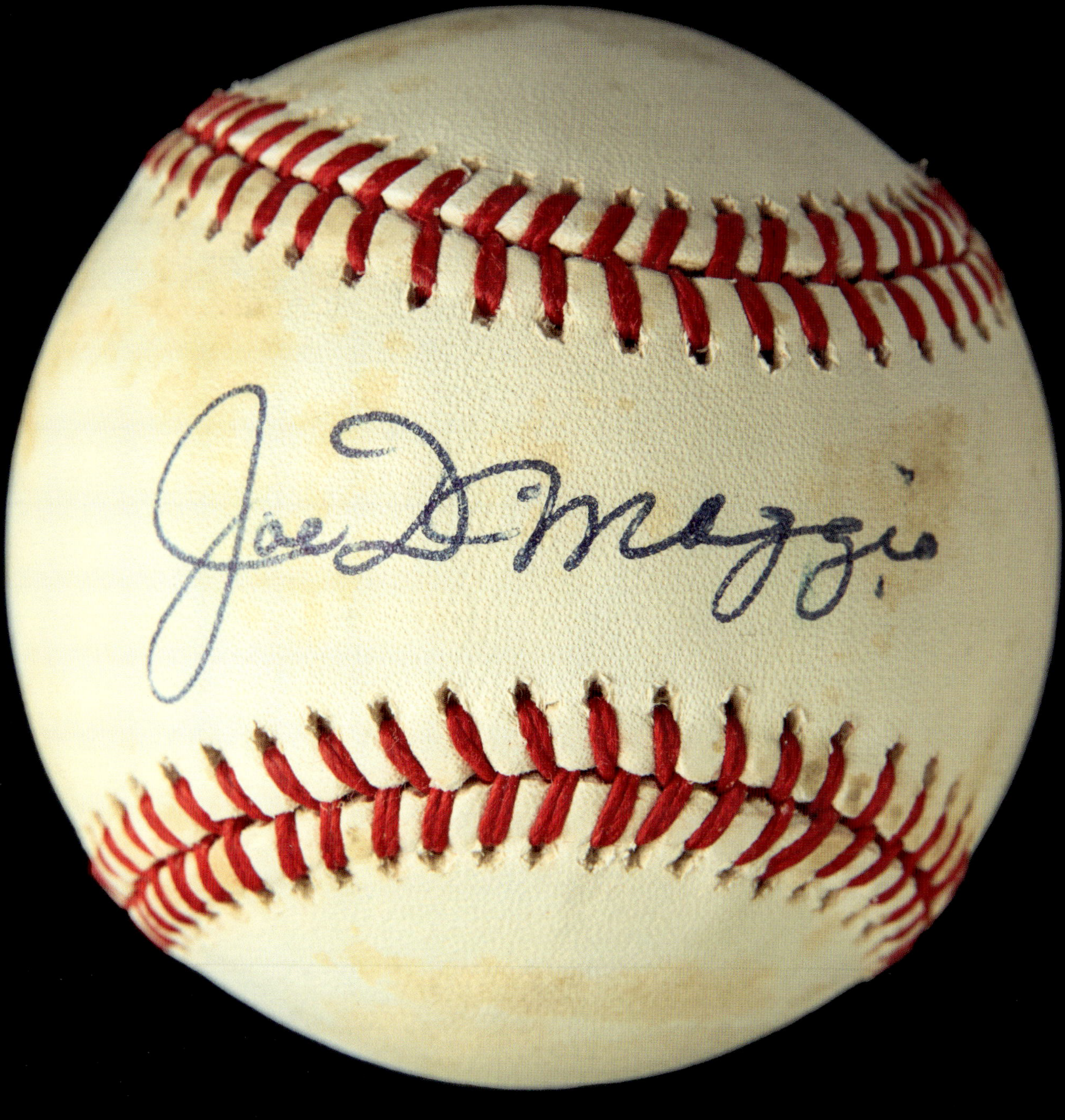
Joe DiMaggio

USED TO AUTOGRAPH
FIRST PITCH
NATS VS YANKS

DWIGHT EISENHOWER

I JUST LOVE THIS SET. It has special meaning to me not least because this was an opening day between the Washington Senators and the New York Yankees in the year I was born: 1953. (*Yikes*. Did I say that out loud?)

Eisenhower actually had a pen made for the signing. It had only one purpose, and that was to sign that ball, as you can see pictured here. (On its other side is printed the full date, April 16th, 1953.)

Ken Wood, left fielder for the Washington Senators who caught the ball in the customary free-for-all, wrote this letter to the original auction house: "I was lucky enough to be standing in the right place at the right time. For 52 years, I have tried to keep this ball in a lockbox at the bank most of the time so the signature would still be legible. It is still in the box that the new balls came in at the time. I believe the Reach wrapper is in the box as well . . . I have read about baseballs auctioned off for a lot of money. I would like to get a fair amount for it, and I would like to have the right to say yes or no."

I also love the auction house's letter of authenticity for its dignified and slightly quaint language, which I give you here in full: "As the newest resident of 1600 Pennsylvania Avenue, Dwight Eisenhower shortly fulfilled one of the President's time-honoured traditions. William Howard Taft threw out the first ceremonial pitch on baseball's opening day, April 14th, 1910. Baseball is reaffirmed at the beginning of every season as the National Pastime, and witness thereof is the Chief Executive's tossing the first ball. For years, this brief gala took place in Griffith Stadium, where the President, from his selected seating assignment, delivered his best to an awaiting senator. Now Dwight D. was a soldier by career and a golfer by leisure and a U.S. President by *vox populi*, and it's presently unknown how accurately or energetically he delivered the first pitch. We do know, however, that the ball was secured for posterity, duly signed by the President and maintained a half a century that it may now become hobby available. The date was April 16th, 1953. The instrument at hand was an OAL (Harridge) baseball. Its stampings are now somewhat faded as it should be anticipated. The ball was actually umpire mudded, accounting for its mild toning. [That means it was a game ball; the umpires rubbed down all the game balls with mud.] Providing a target for the spherical projectile was outfielder Ken Wood who, upon corralling the President's throw, prevailed upon Eisenhower to sign the souvenir. The president consented, as is illustrated in the attending photo, and that presidential signature radiates from the sweet spot. We don't know how many baseballs Eisenhower signed during the course of his two terms. This one, however, is profoundly unique—not just a standard acquiescence in an autograph request, but instead the baseball initiating the 1953 season and Eisenhower's first as Commander-in-Chief. As for the Senators, they lost the home opener to the Yankees en route to a resounding fifth place in the American League."

How about that for coolness?

JOHNNY EVERS

THERE'S A FAMOUS poem written by Franklin Pierce Adams, in 1910 for New York's *Evening Mail*, called "Baseball's Sad Lexicon."

These are the saddest of possible words: "Tinker to Evers to Chance."
Trio of bear cubs, and fleeter than birds, Tinker and Evers and Chance.
Ruthlessly pricking our gonfalon bubble, Making a Giant hit into a double–
Words that are heavy with nothing but trouble: "Tinker to Evers to Chance."

A gonfalon is a pennant or flag—referring in this context to the National League title—but what does the poem mean? Its original title was "That Double Play Again" (Adams rewrote some of that first draft and changed it to "Baseball's Sad Lexicon," but most fans know it as "Tinkers to Evers to Chance"), celebrating the Cubs' incredible turn-of-the-century infield: shortstop John Tinker, second baseman Johnny Evers and first baseman Frank Chance. They first appeared in that configuration on September 13th, 1902, and turned their first double play on the 15th of that month.

This ball, courtesy of the Johnny Evers Sporting Goods Company, is from just over twenty years later. Written in his own hand, it reads "Cleveland 6, White Sox 6, 10 innings. My last game, April 29th, 1922." Its certification says it "has been in the possession of the Evers family since it was obtained by my great uncle, John J. Evers. Signed, Joe Evers."

He didn't hit his first Major League home run until almost three years into his career—his lifetime batting average was just .270—but what he lacked in power he made up for with a mastery of inside baseball. In 1906 he stole 49 bases, 46 in '07, putting him in the National League's top five in those years. He was also a walk magnet, drawing in 108 in 1910 (marking his third straight year in the NL's top five). "I am convinced that in my own career I could usually have hit 30 points higher if I had made a specialty of hitting," he said. "Some lumbering bonehead who does make a specialty of hitting and nothing else may forge well across the .300 line and everybody says, 'What a grand hitter.' The fact is, the bonehead may have been playing rotten baseball when he got that average and someone else who didn't look to be in his class might be the better hitter of the two. Of course there are plenty of times when there is nothing like the old bingle. But there are plenty of other times when the batter at the plate should focus his attention on trying to fool the pitcher. In my own case I have frequently faced the pitcher when I had no desire whatever to hit. I wanted to get a base on balls."

David Shiner sums him perfectly on SABR.org, "Johnny Evers was considered one of the Deadball Era's smartest and best all-around players. He was just as well known for his fiery disposition. The star second baseman's nickname, 'The Human Crab,' was originally bestowed on him due to his unorthodox manner of sidling over to ground balls before gobbling them up, but most baseball men considered it better suited to his temperament than his fielding. A 5'9", 125lb pepper-pot with a protruding jaw that came to be a symbol of the man—for he was always 'jawing' about something— Evers developed a reputation as a troublemaker by squabbling regularly with teammates, opponents, and especially umpires. 'They claim he is a crab, and perhaps they are right,' Cleveland Indians manager Joe Birmingham once observed. 'But I would like to have 25 such crabs playing for me. If I did, I would have no doubts over the pennant. They would win hands down.'"

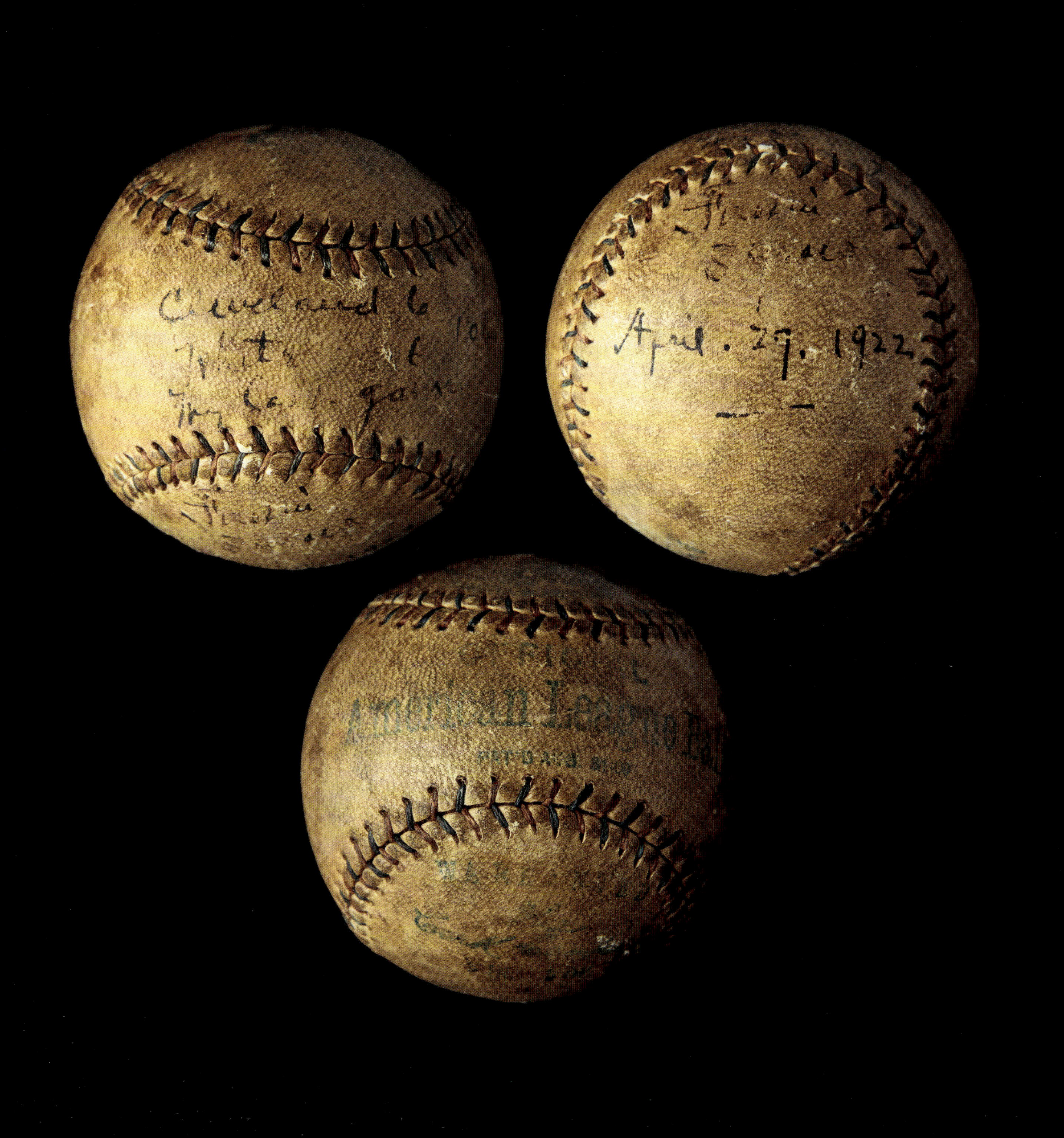
Cleveland 6
April . 29 . 1922
American League

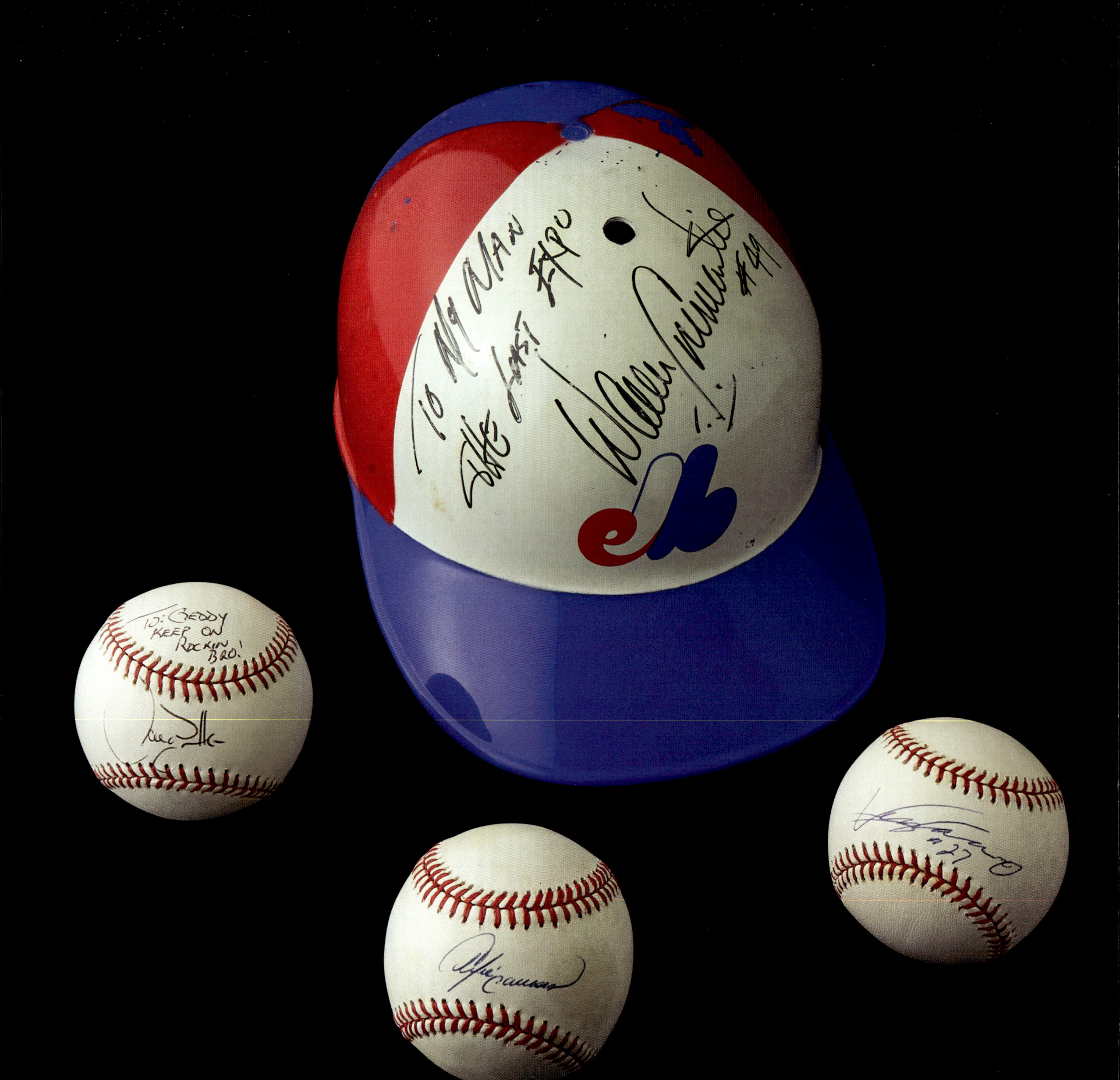

THE EXPOS

BY THE TIME I became a baseball nut the Expos were already a great team, one that galvanized the entire Canadian population—or at least all the country's sports fans, as time and again they pursued the pennant. At the end of their 13th season, on October 19th, 1981, when they played the Dodgers for the right to go to the World Series. Rush was in rehearsals and my Expos fever couldn't have been higher. But in those days there was no laptops, so how was I going to do my duty as both a musician and a fan at the same time?

I ripped the TV set out of my living room wall unit (remember how ginormous TVs were back in the Eighties?) and piled it into my car, drove to rehearsal and set it up in the warehouse beside me at stage left. You can imagine the tension: the Expos with larger-than-life characters like Andre "The Hawk" Dawson and Warren "Cro" Cromartie, are leading 1-0 in the ninth inning. I'm trying to concentrate on "The Spirit of Radio" but see that coming into pitch the ninth is Steve Rogers, so I'm, like, "*Hmm*. Rogers is a great starter but he isn't a closer? Then up to bat comes pinch hitter Rick Monday, and I begin to fret. "*Wait a second*, Rick Monday and the game is being *played* on a Monday?? I don't like this at all. What were the gods of baseball thinking?" The room goes silent but for the buzzing of the amplifiers as commentator Dave Van Horne exclaims, "Now in the stretch, here's the 3-1 pitch, and it's one long fly ball to centerfield. Dawson going back onto the warning track ... Dawson at the wall ... That ball is a home run!"

And just like that, Monday's two-run home run gave the Dodgers a lead that took all the air out of the Expos, who went down meekly in the bottom of the ninth. And I turned the TV off in agony; my first experience of the heartbreak of baseball. To all Expos fans that day would be forever known as "Blue Monday" ... *Sigh*.

The Expos had an incredibly strong team in 1994 too, with Larry Walker, Moises Alou, Marquis Grissom, Rondell White, John Wetteland and Pedro Martinez, and we all believed that finally *this* would be the year. And wouldn't you know, along came the infamous baseball strike of 1994 that put an abrupt end to the season. Some fantasy leagues got computers to simulate the rest of the season, and on many of those the Expos won, but in real life, you just wanted to cry. Shoulda-coulda-woulda.

Anyway, back during the recording of *Signals*, I became pals with "Cro" who introduced me to a few of his fellow Expos players, including the Hawk, both friends from Florida but very different people—Dawson quiet, Cromartie always talking and joking and the guy in the clubhouse giving everyone a nickname. (He called me "Unc" because, I hope, he saw me as a "wise" Jewish uncle.) Dawson was one of my first baseball heroes from that time I'd rediscovered the game as an adult. Years later, in 2016, I ran into him at a Marlins game, where he was a part-time coach, which felt like seeing an old friend, and I was delighted that he greeted me so kindly and posed for this photo together. Sometimes your heroes don't disappoint.

The other balls here are signed by two incredible Expo right-fielders and HOFers: My pal Larry Walker and Vlad "The Impaler" Guerrero, Sr. And of course the helmet is signed, "To my man, the last Expo" by Cro, who knew what a die-hard fan I'd been.

Me and the Hawk!

72 Stories 53 Geddy Lee

WHITEY FORD

AS A KID in the Sixties, I thought "Whitey" Ford was among the coolest ballplayers' names we used to bandy about the schoolyard, not just because he was the Yankees' winningest pitcher in a decade dominated by pitchers, but because his moniker was the same as Beaver's pal in my fave TV show *Leave It to Beaver*; it sounded so homespun, so all-American. (He was born Edward Charles Ford, but in 1947, while playing with the Binghamton Triplets, acquired the nickname because the team's new manager Lefty Gomez had trouble remembering who was who and called him "Blondie" and "Whitey"—and "Whitey" stuck.) So in 2008, when I saw an opportunity to have a memento as important as a 20th win—not to mention a baseball from the personal collection of Whitey Ford himself—I *had* to have it. Adding it to my collection felt like topping up the fountain of youth.

It was never written in the rules, but it was widely asserted that a pitcher stood the best chance of winning a Cy Young Award if he achieved 20 wins in a season; in doing so, he was incontrovertibly a dominant pitcher. Today that's a bone of contention amongst Sabermetrics folks, however, because we tend to view wins as a matter of happenstance more than the true measure of a pitcher's skill. Why? Because his record is as dependent on the runs his team scores as the runs he prevents. At first blush, it appears fair to argue that Whitey Ford *was* a marvellous pitcher, finishing his 1961 season with a superb 25 wins and 4 losses (and did in fact garner the Cy Young *and* World Series MVP awards), but if we look with a sabermetric eye into all the *other* pitchers in 1961 deserving of a Cy Young, it's interesting to note how he stacks up....

Now that we're armed with all these new statistics, who would he have beat out? Only three other pitchers won 20 games that year: Warren Spahn, Detroit's Frank Larry and Cincinnati's Joey Jay. Ford was certainly terrific and a gamer, as he had the best win-loss percentage, led both the AL and NL in wins, and placed third in total strikeouts. Yet he's not even in the top ten for WAR (wins above replacement), nor ERA! He's ranked 4th in Fielding Independent Pitching and 10th (behind Koufax) for most strikeouts per 9 innings. You might call this a bit of statistical revisionism, but I think it's appropriate because it reveals the pitcher's skill as opposed to his good fortune. I'm not saying you had to be lucky to win 25 games, and winning 236 games is no small feat, but you could argue that Whitey Ford benefited *greatly* from being on the '61 Yankees team. It was a good horse to tie his cart to!

Fantasy freaks are constantly gauging the drafting of either a good pitcher for a winning team or an elite pitcher for a losing team. Most fantasy leagues have gone a long way to try to equal it all out—giving points for quality starts, for example. Historically, we're also able to put into perspective the real skill level and real value of players from the past, whom we could never see in person. In the case of Whitey Ford, I get to balance out rose-coloured nostalgic memories with cold and calculating facts and figures. I know people make fun of baseball stats, but IMHO that's low-hanging fruit. Stats exist for a reason. Nowadays teams have video rooms which both pitchers and hitters can avail themselves, you'll even see players on the bench before going up to bat, analysing the pitcher's stuff on an iPad. All that information is not just for nerds; it's how smart players and managers can gain an edge and win more games.

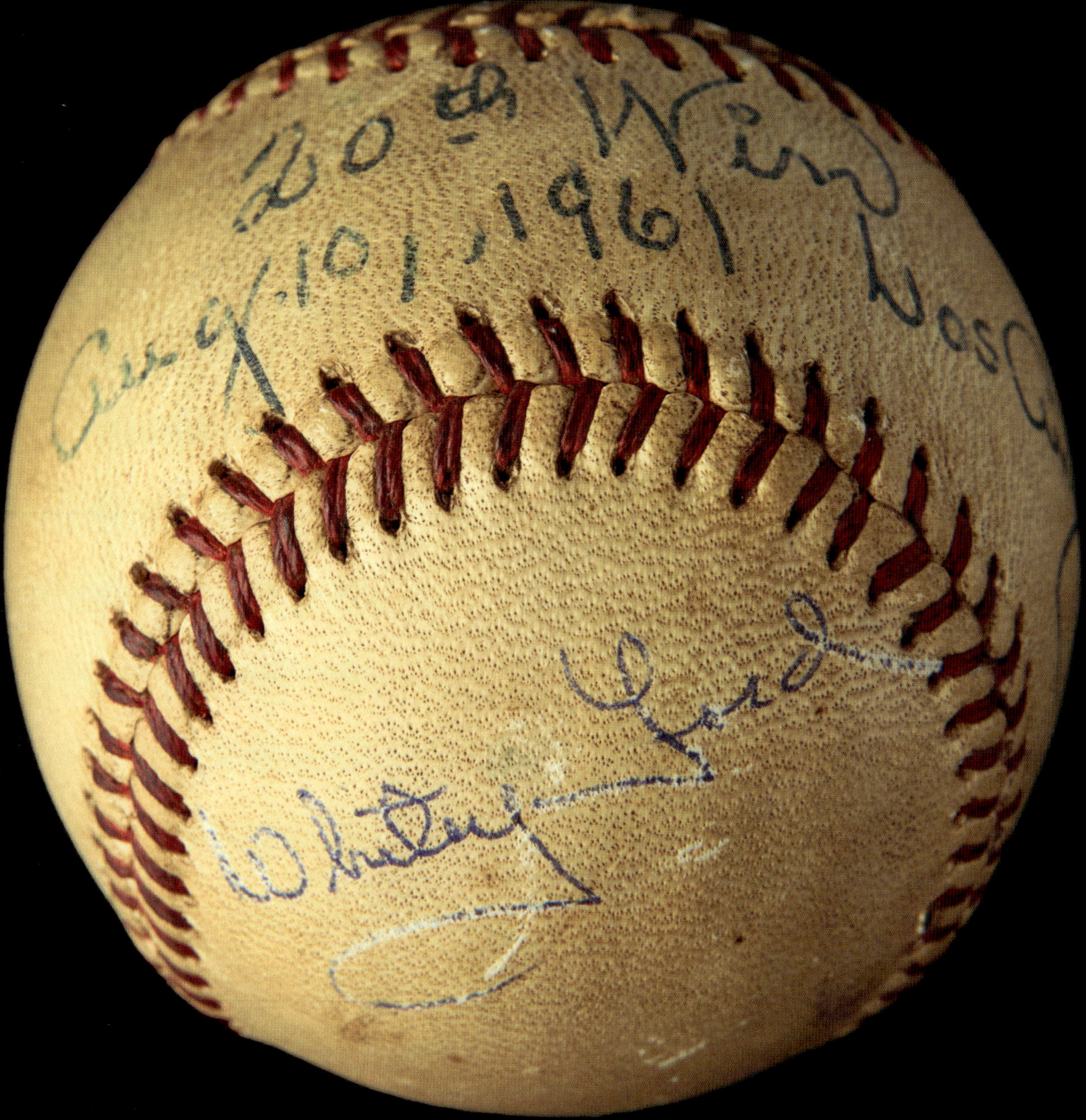
Aug. 10, 1961
Whitey Ford

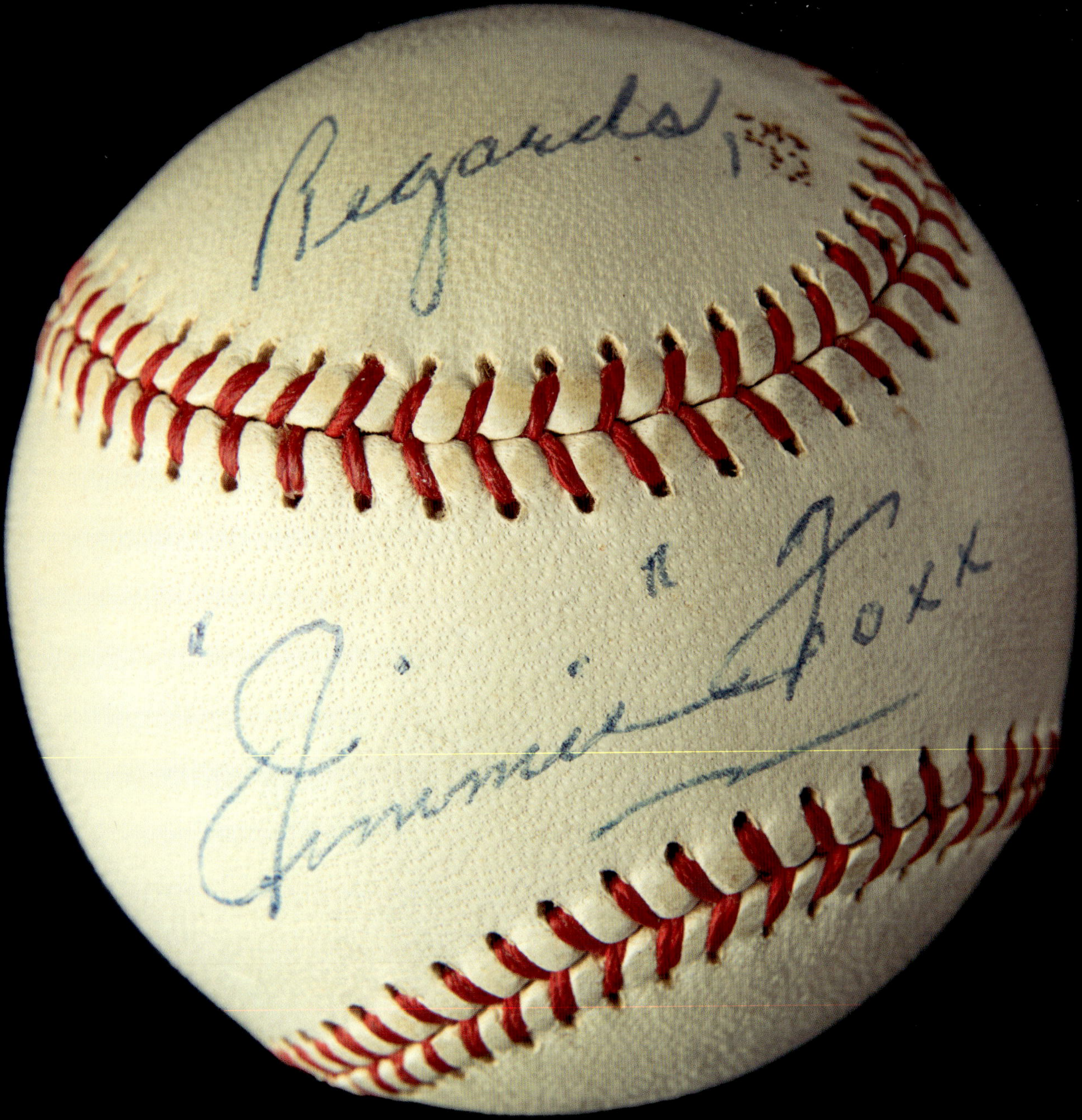
Regards
"Jimmie Foxx"

JIMMIE FOXX

JIMMIE FOXX, HACK Wilson, Honus Wagner, Urban Shocker... I love these guys' names. Their nicknames, which I used to look up in the old *Baseball Encyclopedia* when I first became a fan, were even better: "The Rabbi of Swat" (Mose Solomon), "The Yankee Clipper" (Joe DiMaggio) and "Death to Flying Things" (Jack Chapman, Bob Ferguson *and* Franklin Gutiérrez)....

Foxx was a power hitter, a beast of a slugger like "The Babe," with similar features; both were big boys with big round faces. In 1924, when he was only sixteen, Foxx played for a team in nearby Easton, Maryland. Its player-manager, Frank "Home Run" Baker, had learned of his reputation as "the most promising athletic prospect in the State of Maryland," and invited him for a try-out. The boy showed up in a pair of overalls, was quickly signed on and by the end of July, the Philadelphia Athletics had purchased his contract (although he only sat in their dugout that season). By 1928 he was a regular playing first and third, and racked up a tremendous .407 halfway through the season....

By the way, I have a Frank "Home Run" Baker ball too. To bring a little context to this period, he'd been called the "original home run king of the Majors," but led the league between 1908 and 1922 with a mere *eleven* dingers. In those days it was pretty hard to hit a ball out; playing in parks with huge outfields and a rather "dead" ball, they had to "hit 'em where they ain't" and hope it would roll a sufficient distance across the grass so they could run the bases and cross the plate. Baker hit a career 96 home runs to Foxx's 534, an enormous difference, yet (talking Sabermetrics for a moment here) calculated by WAR (wins above replacement), Baker comes in at 62.8 and Foxx at 93.0—not nearly as great a disparity. It brings out the stark difference between the Dead-ball era (which ended in 1920) and what the game was evolving into.

...After a twenty-year career with the Athletics, the Red Sox, Cubs and Phillies, dogged much of the time by sinus and vision problems (not to mention heavy drinking and an acrimonious divorce), Jimmie Foxx retired with 1,922 runs batted in, 1,751 runs scored, 2,646 hits, 458 doubles, 125 triples, 1,452 bases on balls, and a .325 batting average. And those 534 home runs were second only to Babe Ruth's 714. He was elected to the National Baseball Hall of Fame in 1951.

This ball says "Regards" (a stiff but not uncommon greeting for those more formal days). Its documentation says, "As the first baseman for Connie Mack's 1929-1931 pennant machine, Jimmie Foxx slugged an even 100 home runs, putting him in the same elite stratosphere as Babe Ruth. 'Double X' made the first serious run at Babe's hallowed 60 home run record when he clubbed 58 round trippers in 1932, and the next year he did what Babe had failed to do—win the Triple Crown... He died at the early age of 59, so anything that 'The Beast' signed is eagerly sought by collectors—since Foxx passed before the baseball memorabilia boom of the Seventies and Eighties, there's a dearth of balls bearing his solo signature, as not many people thought to seek one during his lifetime."

LOU GEHRIG

AGAIN, IT'S REALLY HARD to say anything new about people that are so famous. We all know what a superb player Lou Gehrig was, what a quiet, stoic personality he had, and how tragic it was that his career was cut short by ALS—amyotrophic lateral sclerosis, also known as motor neurone disease or—his most unfortunate legacy—Lou Gehrig's disease. Suffice it to say that you buy some baseballs because they look cool, some because they tell such a terrific story, but others purely out of respect for the player. This is a case in point. However simple the artefact, no real collection of baseball autographs would be complete without a Gehrig.

For the longest time he held the record for the most consecutive games played. On August 17th, 1933, he surpassed Everett Scott's 1,307 (I also have a ball signed by Scott from his 1,000th) but kept on going after that. 1937 was the last time he played an entire year in good health; the undiagnosed illness started to really affect him the following season. (It begins with muscle twitching and weakness in an arm or leg, trouble swallowing or slurred speech, eventually affecting control of the muscles needed to move, speak, eat and breathe. Its exact causes are still unknown today, and there remains no cure.) He was only 35.

In 1938, as James Lincoln Ray tells it on SABR.org, "for the first time in his career he came to spring training a few pounds overweight, saying that Babe Ruth [who could eat his own weight in hot dogs] 'always told me to stop eating. He warned me that when I got to my thirties I'd put weight on. But I was dumb. I kept on eating.' But Gehrig immediately went to work on his conditioning, running and working out and hitting as much as he'd done in his 20's." As he was gearing up to play his *2,000th* consecutive game, his wife Eleanor, who'd been witnessing his slow deterioration day and night and worried that the streak was taking a toll on his body, suggested, "Why not stop at 1999? People will remember your streak better because of *that* number." But the Iron Horse, as people called him, whipped himself into shape and kept on trucking. Self-effacing chap that he was, he'd then downplay his accomplishments, telling writers who inquired that ballplayers had off-days and rain delays and only worked about eight months a year! But there was no question he was breaking down. "Somewhere in the creeping mystery of that summer," Eleanor later remarked, "Lou lost the power." (Interesting that she uses that word, because Lou Gehrig's disease is commonly described as a *creeping* paralysis.)

By the middle of August 1938, he had enough. "Hell," he said. "I'm not hitting with all these changes of stance—I've tried everything." Yet he *still* put up a respectable number. Even as commentators expressed concern about his evident decline, he was hitting .295 with 29 home runs and 114 RBI's, which would be a *career year* for a lot of good players! Then in May of 1939, while putting on his uniform, he collapsed. His consecutive game streak ended at 2130.

Many years later, Baltimore's shortstop Cal Ripken (coincidentally nicknamed the Iron Man) would break Gehrig's record, but you know—and sorry if you find this controversial—after Ripken was injured, rather than sacrifice the streak, his manager would put him in the game until he'd had his first at-bat and then *pull* him to keep the streak going. Now, that's not fair dinkum. Gehrig played every inning of every game until he couldn't shoot. Yes, it's true that Lou's streak was also sustained when, just once when he was sick with the flu, the Yankees' General Manager Ed Barrow postponed a game as a "rainout" though it wasn't raining, but to me what Ripken was doing was more blatant and, though I think he was a very fine player indeed, personally I don't think his streak compares.

I also have this framed photo celebrating Gehrig's 2,000th consecutive game, signed by Lou (and Earle Combs sneaking his scrawl in there too—as, I think, a joke) and presented to the Yankees' manager Joe McCarthy.

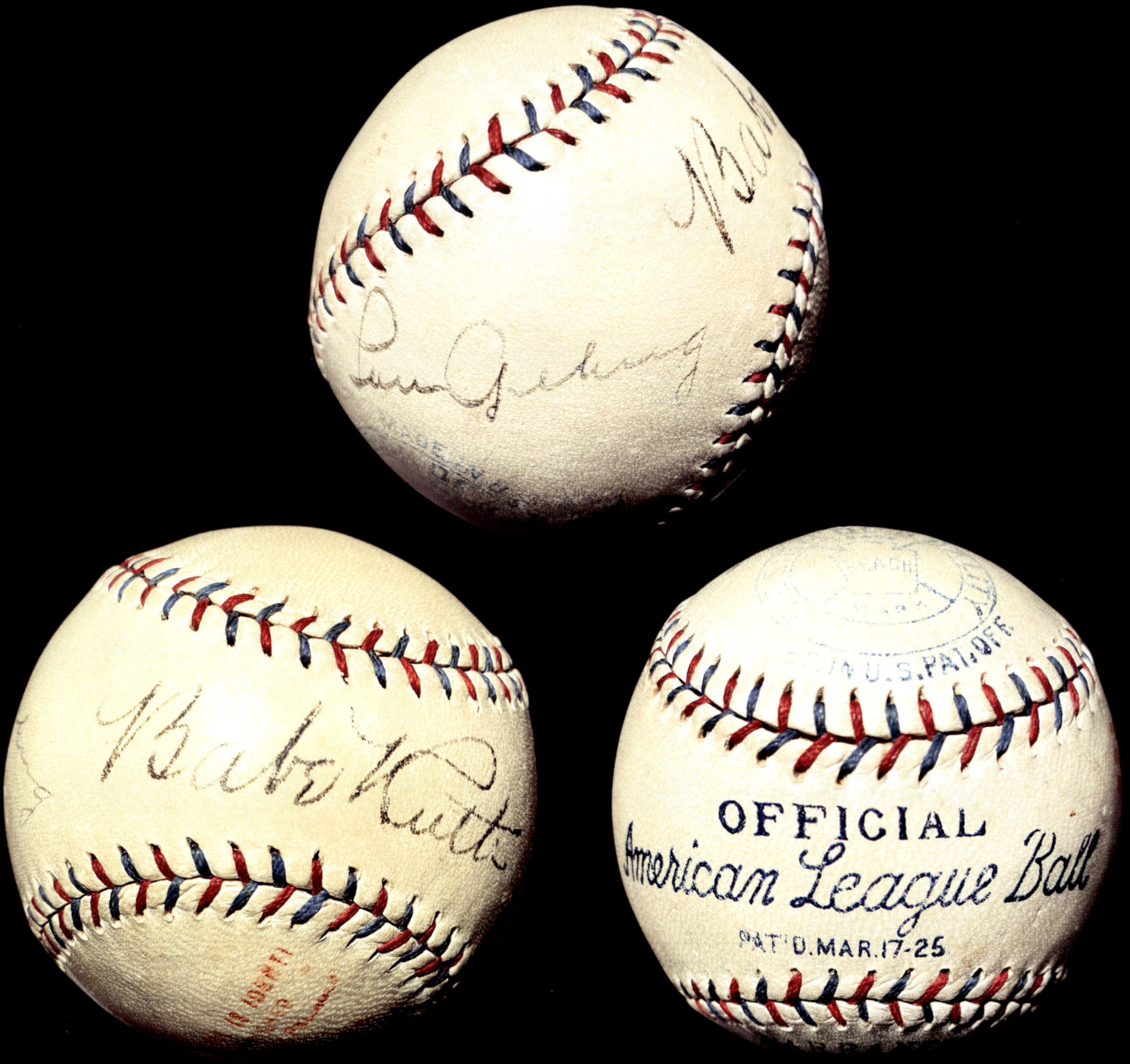
Babe Ruth
OFFICIAL
American League Ball
PAT'D. MAR. 17-25

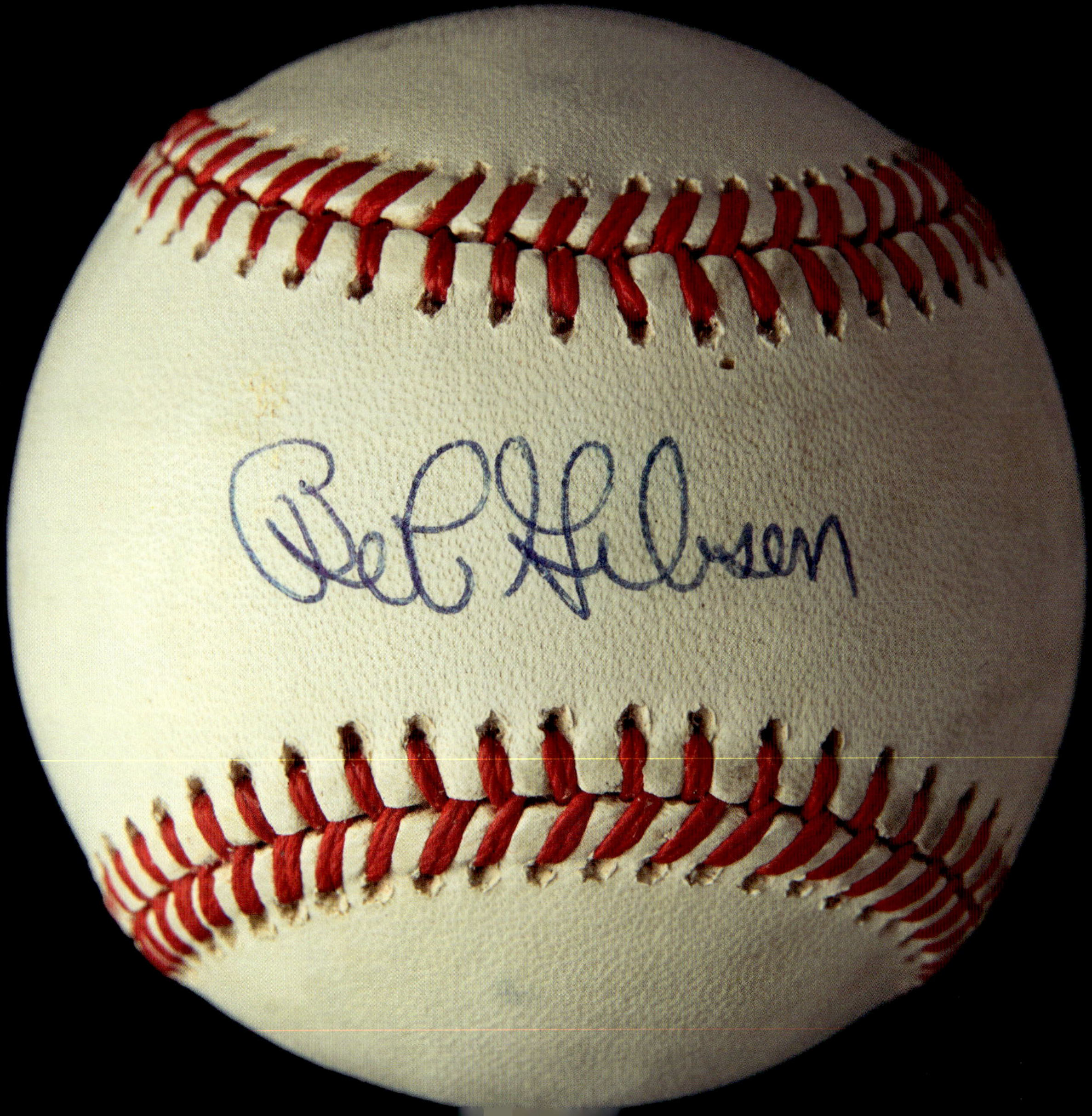

BOB GIBSON

BOB GIBSON PITCHED at a time when the ERAs of great pitchers like him were so minuscule that they lowered the mound by five inches after 1968 to make the game more hitter friendly. His ERA in 1968 was 1.12! He was the second player in Major League history, after Walter Johnson, to strike out more than 3,000 batters, and the first to do so in the National League. He was a natural Hall of Famer, one of the greatest pitchers of our time.

I had the great pleasure of meeting him at Spring Training with St. Louis, by which time he was a roving pitching coach. First spotting him across the clubhouse, I thought he cut an imposing figure. He was friendly to me, but I was in awe. When you see images of him on the mound, he looks like he could kill you with his glare, never mind a throw. I was only eleven when he pitched the 1964 World Series, but what I've read since sure fits the giant I met, a man whose character is perhaps best summed up by his own long-time backstop, Tim McCarver: "For my money, the most intimidating, arrogant pitcher ever to pick up dirt on a mound is Bob Gibson. If you ever saw him work, you never forget his style: his cap pulled down low over his eyes, the ball grip almost mashed behind his right hip, his eyes smouldering at each batter almost accusingly. He didn't like to lose to anyone in anything. Bob was a man of mulish, competitive instinct."

He was not a fraternizer, either. In the shower after 1965's All-Star Game, Joe Torre complimented him on his performance. Gibson didn't say a word—just showered, got dressed, and left. His aloofness was also felt by the press, who respected him but could never fully understand what had made him who he was. He'd grown up, as his autobiography has it, "from ghetto to glory." From his farm club days in Georgia, he'd borne the brunt of racial bigotry, forced to live and eat in the "black" part of town away from his teammates, and exposed to constant racial taunts from so-called "fans." One of the few people in the game he'd warm to was his first manager, Johnny Keane, who, he said, "had no prejudices concerning my colour. He was the closest thing to a saint that I ever came across."

He had pinpoint control of a vicious slider, two- and four-seam fastballs and fearsome brushbacks. "His delivery," writes SABR. org's Terry Sloope, "gave hitters the impression that he was exploding toward the plate... He rarely hit them deliberately, but anyone determined to reach across the plate to drive an outside pitch could count on getting shaved by an inside pitch. If the batter's body happened to get in the way of the ball, if he had to go down on his back-side to avoid getting hit, so be it. Gibson made no apologies." He once joked that the only reason he glared while pitching was because of his poor eyesight and inability to catch the catcher's signals clearly, as he did not wear glasses while pitching.

In his inimical way, Yogi Berra would have simply said, "Baseball is 90% mental. The other half is physical," but Gibson was more penetrating: "I'd like to think that the term 'intensity' comes much closer to summarizing my pitching style," he said, "than do qualities like meanness and anger, which were merely devices. My pitching career, I believe, offers a lot of evidence to the theory that baseball is a mental discipline as much as a physical one. The part of pitching that separates the stars from everyone else is about 90% mental. That's why I considered it so important to mess with a batter's head without letting him get inside my mind."

JOSH GIBSON

IN 1930, THE Washington Senators' pitcher Walter Johnson said, "There is a catcher that any big league club would like to buy for $200,000. His name is Gibson. He can do everything. He hits the ball a mile. He catches so easy, he might as well be in a rocking chair. He throws like a rifle. Too bad this Gibson is a colored fellow." Josh Gibson was known as "the Black Babe Ruth," but as Ken Burns said in his *Baseball* documentary, "There were some who thought Ruth should have been called the white Josh Gibson." Now, *that's* respect.

Bill Johnson writes on SABR.org, "A column in the *Sporting News* credited Gibson with a drive in a Negro League game that hit just two feet from the top of the wall circling the bleachers at Yankee Stadium, approximately 580 feet from home plate in the original park. 'Had the ball been just two feet higher,' the article mused, 'it might have carried 700 feet.' Jack Marshall, of the Chicago American Giants, swore that he saw Gibson hit a ball completely out of Yankee Stadium, and some accounts credit Gibson with between 800 and a 1,000 homeruns in a career that lasted only 16 years. 'There exists no official source of statistics, no compilation of scorecards. Many gaps exist in the historical record,' an authority on the Negro Leagues points out. The record keeping was incomplete and non-standardized, so the actual total is unclear and probably unknowable [but] Josh Gibson was, by so many accounts as to make the claim indisputable, one of the greatest sluggers who ever stepped into a batter's box."

During the war years, the Negro Leagues were loosely structured and featured a good many barnstorming and exhibition games; it's likely this ball comes from one of those.

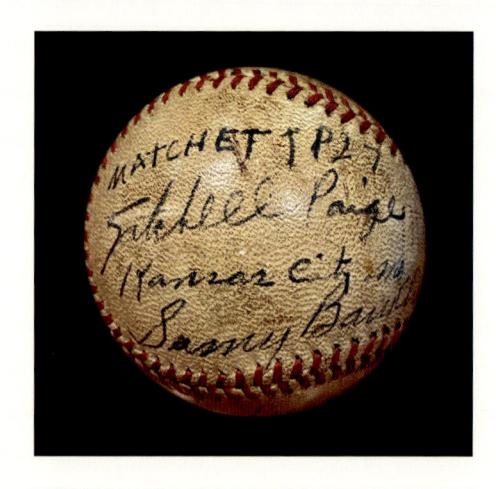

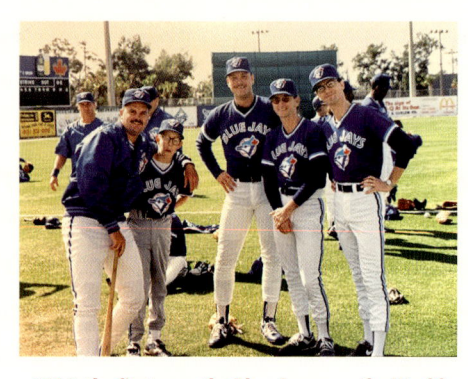

1992, the first year the Blue Jays won the World Series: hugging my son Jules is David Wells. Walking behind him is Kelly Gruber. Then Duane Ward, me looking dorky as hell, and my bro, Allan.

In 1942's regular season, the Grays, anchored by Gibson and defending the Eastern Negro League championship, and the Monarchs, led by Paige, who were the greatest draw in the game at the time, played against each other four times. They were the two best teams back then, black *or* white, and every time they met on the diamond, the contest was an epic struggle.

The auction catalogue that accompanies the ball says, "It's almost impossible to find a baseball signed by stars from the Kansas City Monarchs and the Homestead Grays from their heyday in the Forties, but to find one that features *two* men that define the storied league to this day, Satchel Paige and Josh Gibson is extraordinary. We are pleased to present this ball signed during the precise time these men anchored the best Negro League teams of the period. Our research indicates that this ball is most certainly game-used, from one of those teams' classic battles during the 1942 season." In fact, the players signed head-to-head on this ball also include James Cool Papa Bell, Buck Leonard and Sam Bankhead of the Grays (as well as their player-manager Vic Harris and coach Candy Jim Taylor); and Newt Allen of the Monarchs. It's an amazing piece of history.

I bought the ball from the collection of the great Major League pitcher and friend of mine, David Wells, so that was a double whammy for me. I have great memories of him and the Blue Jays during the Nineties. He used to come to our gigs a lot and, I believe, holds the record of staying back in the dressing room, drinking beer and telling baseball stories to our road crew long after we'd climbed aboard our bus and disappeared down the road.

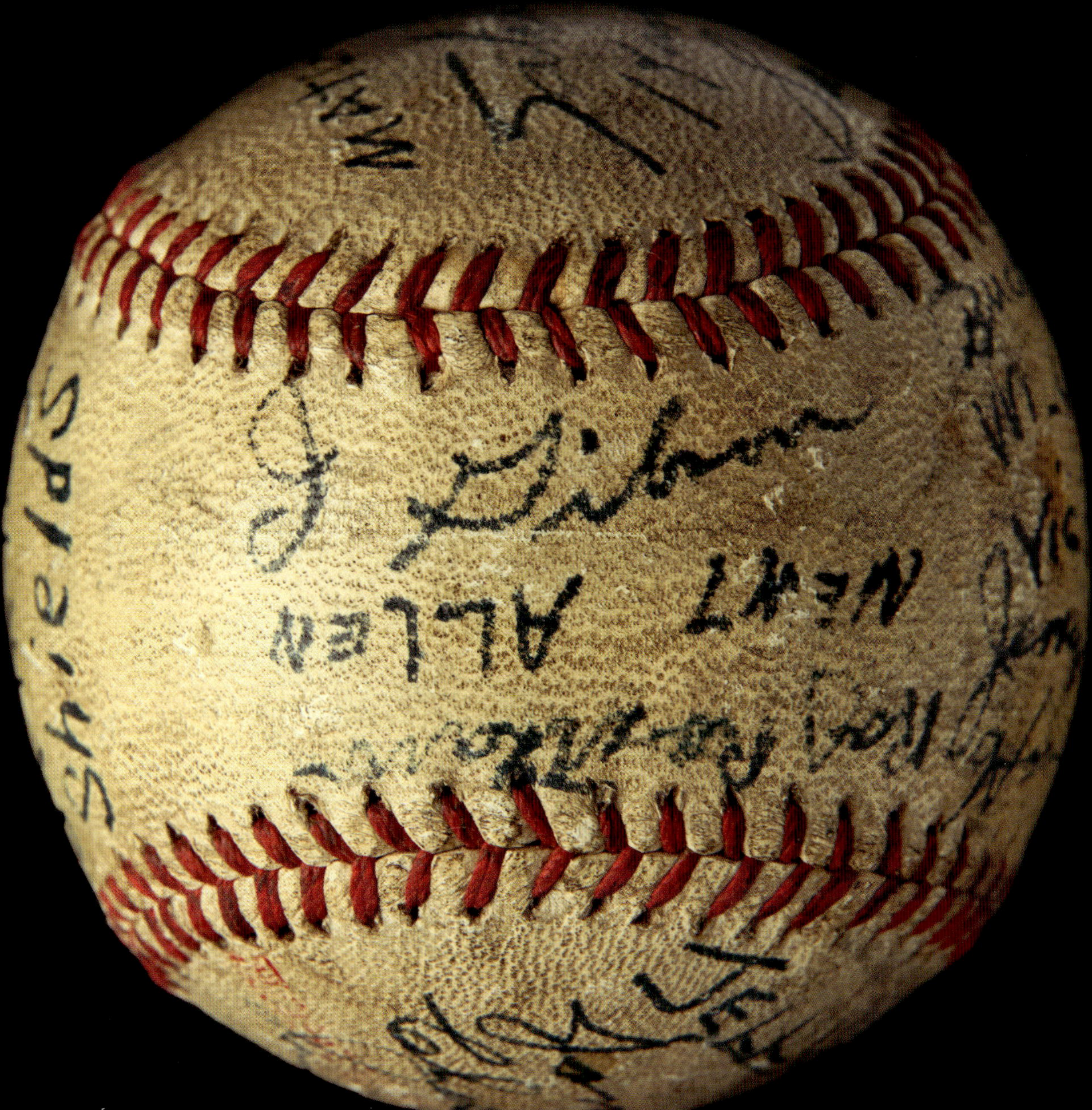
ALLEN
Shields

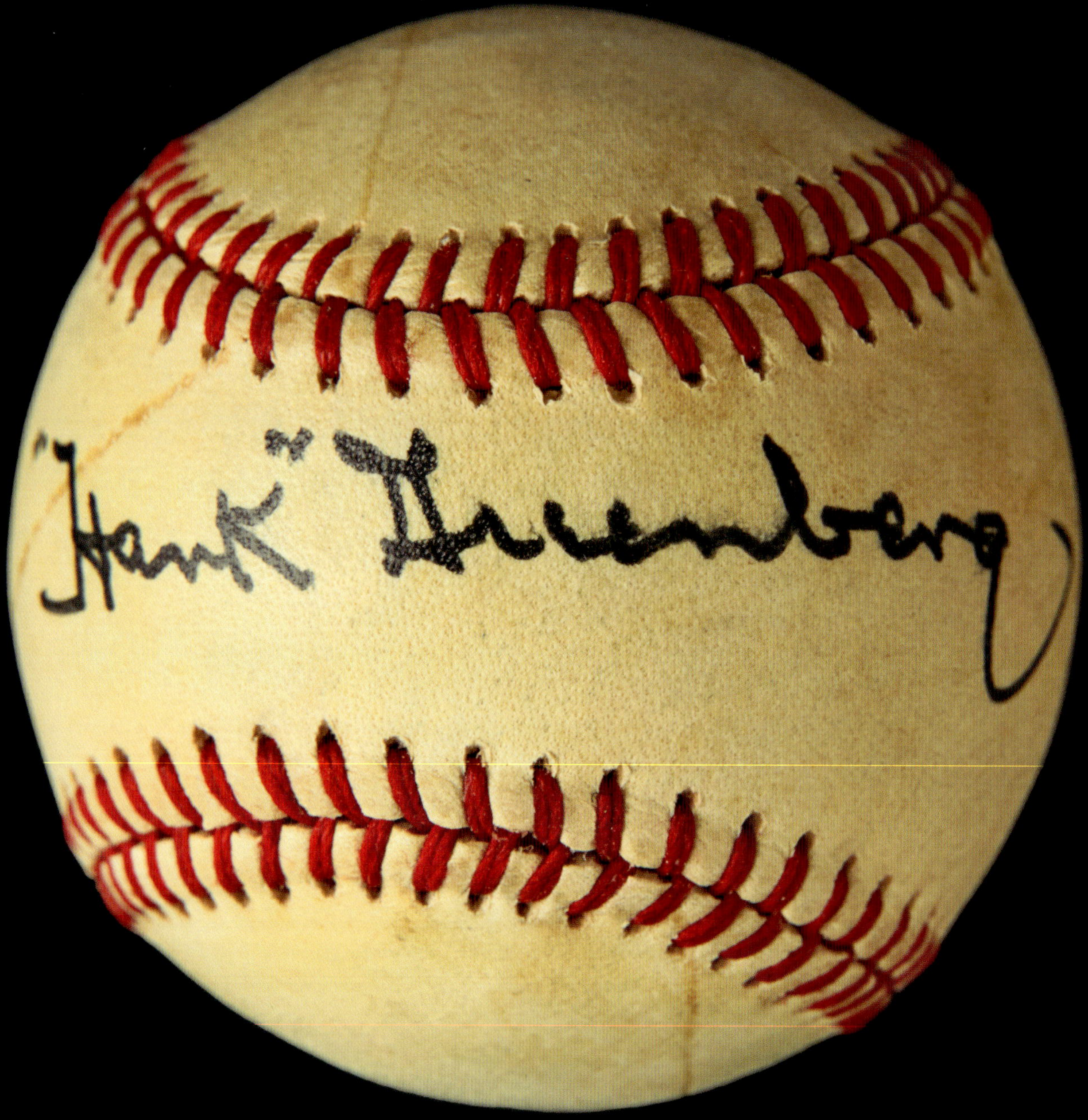
"Hank" Greenberg

HANK GREENBERG

WHEN WE WERE kids, we were always looking for Jewish athletes to admire and were flummoxed to find so few out there. Growing up in and around mostly Jewish families, we'd sometimes forget that we were a minority and innocently assumed that the wider world was as rife with Jewish talent as our own neighbourhood. In reality, Jews made up maybe 3% of the general population, so it was only normal that a tiny percentage of players were Jews, but to us it was like, "I don't get it. Why aren't there *more* Jewish ballplayers?"

The obsession persists amongst my fellow baseball geeks. Whenever the next great Jewish hope comes up—like, say, the Blue Jays' Shawn Green—we glom onto him. Even recently, when a relief pitcher named Kenny Rosenberg came up to the Majors for, basically, a cup of coffee, he was immediately known to every Jew across the land. *News flash:* "A Jew made an appearance in the Angels' bullpen today!"

I first heard references to Hank Greenberg as a boy watching the Tigers on TV, but it was only as an adult that I realized what an important player "The Hebrew Hammer" really was. As Scott Ferkovich points out on SABR.org (case in point: just now I had to furiously look up his name to see if *he's* Jewish), "Any list of the greatest sluggers ever to wear a Detroit Tigers uniform has to include Hank Greenberg. Despite losing four years of his physical prime to World War II, he still put together a 13-year career that included 331 home runs with 1,276 RBIs. A .313 hitter, he also drew a high number of walks, contributing to his .412 lifetime on-base percentage. Add to that a slugging average of .605, and his career OPS is an exceptional 1.017, a figure topped by only four other players at the time of his retirement: Babe Ruth, Ted Williams, Lou Gehrig, and Jimmie Foxx."

In 1938, he made a serious run at Babe Ruth's single-season home run record. Elsewhere in this book I refer to prejudice against African Americans and the abuse Hank Aaron and Roger Maris endured trying to break the Babe's record; you can only imagine what was hurled from the bleachers when someone named Hank Greenberg was at the plate (in his first year in the Majors he even suffered Jew-baiting from his own teammates). Hank claimed that he never strongly identified himself as a Jew, but admitted that "Sure there was added pressure being Jewish. How the hell could you get up to home plate every day and have some son of a bitch call you a Jew bastard and a kike and a sheenie and get on your ass without feeling the pressure. If the ballplayers weren't doing it, the fans were. I used to get frustrated as hell. Sometimes I wanted to go up in the stands and beat the shit out of them."

In the end he hit 58 home runs, two short of Ruth's record. There are views on this. In 1966 Mordecai Richler wondered aloud in *Commentary*, "Greenberg just possibly understood that if he shattered the Babe's record, seemingly inviolate, it would be considered pushy of him and given the climate of the times, not be such a good thing for the Jews." Interesting, but I don't buy it. For one, Hank's personality wouldn't allow it; he once stated, "If I, as a Jew, hit a home run, I was hitting one against Hitler." Plus, there's the evidence that, as "the chase" went on, Hank received more walks than he did in *any other time* in his career. No pitcher wanted to be the guy to give up a record breaking home run to one of the Chosen People.

Over the years, I have garnered a few important Greenberg artefacts. My favourite story behind one of them is this: after he and his wife established an animal welfare foundation, I once made a donation of just $10, and in return received . . . a personalized signed photo! What a mensch.

LEFTY GROVE

IN THE CASE of Whitey Ford I talked about the debate over the real significance of a pitcher's twenty wins. Well, here we have a *300th* win. July 25th, 1941 was Robert Moses Grove's last year in baseball, so he was obviously no longer in his prime, having started his career in 1925, but managing such a feat sixteen years later defies all statistical revisionism. Here was a truly dominant pitcher. He had a record nine ERA titles, led the American League in ERA nine different times, led it in strikeouts his first seven years, pitched effectively in hitters' parks like Shibe Park and Fenway Park (if you could survive as a pitcher there, you had some good stuff!) and starred in three World Series. That's no accident. That's not down to luck. It has nothing to do with the team you play for; it has *everything* to do with your skills. It speaks to durability, persistence, savvy, flexibility, learning how to overcome. (Lefty did nothing in small measures, by the way: as Jim Kaplan puts it on SABR.org, "Few if any pitchers threw tantrums on a par with the 6'3", 190-pound Lefty, He even led all pitchers by striking out 593 times as a batter.")

Baseball is known for good reason as a game of constant adjustments. No pitcher is going to reach 300 wins without understanding that concept. You can't just throw the same stuff for years and hope to keep on winning, because hitters will adjust to your stuff; to stay ahead you have to adjust, and adjust *again*; to stick around long enough, you need a willingness to learn and an ability to apply what you've learned, to evolve with the game. (I was watching a very young player who burst onto the scene this year. When he first came up, his very first hit in Major League Baseball was one of the longest home runs ever. Everyone was singing his praises, and for the next few weeks he was torturing pitchers. He was unstoppable. But then the pitchers found the holes, and while he's still dangerous, since then he's been striking out at an inordinate rate.) Over the course of his career Lefty Grove demonstrated not just raw skill but brains and an ability to be coached, an ability to learn from his mistakes. That is really the litmus test of any baseball player. I'd go so far as to say that it reflects a successful human being in any endeavor.

Kaplan continues: "Grove labored to get the big one. He had six wins by midseason. On July 25th, Red Sox manager Joe Cronin told him, 'Pop, this is a nine-inning game. I'm not coming out to get you.' Cronin didn't, and Grove survived a rock-'em, sock-'em slugfest to beat the Indians on 12 hits, 10-6, with his best friend in baseball, Jimmie Foxx, getting the decisive two-run triple. His final win was no pathetic last gasp, some descriptions notwithstanding. Grove threw only 38 balls and walked just one batter. He was the twelfth 300-game winner, the first since Pete Alexander in 1926 and the last until Warren Spahn in 1961, he had earned his place in history. He was roundly toasted at a champagne dinner party he threw for teammates that night." (He retired in December that year, an event that was somewhat overshadowed by the bombing of Pearl Harbor the same day.)

The ball is verified by Grove's daughter, but to me the nicest thing is that it's signed by the entire 1941 Red Sox team: Lefty's on the sweet spot, of course, but then there's Jimmie Fox, Ted Williams, Moe Berg, Bobby Doerr, Mickey Harris, Dom DiMaggio, player-manager Joe Cronin . . . And to top it all off (so to speak) I also have Lefty Grove's actual hat (with his name sewn on the inside band). Come on, that is one sweet combo.

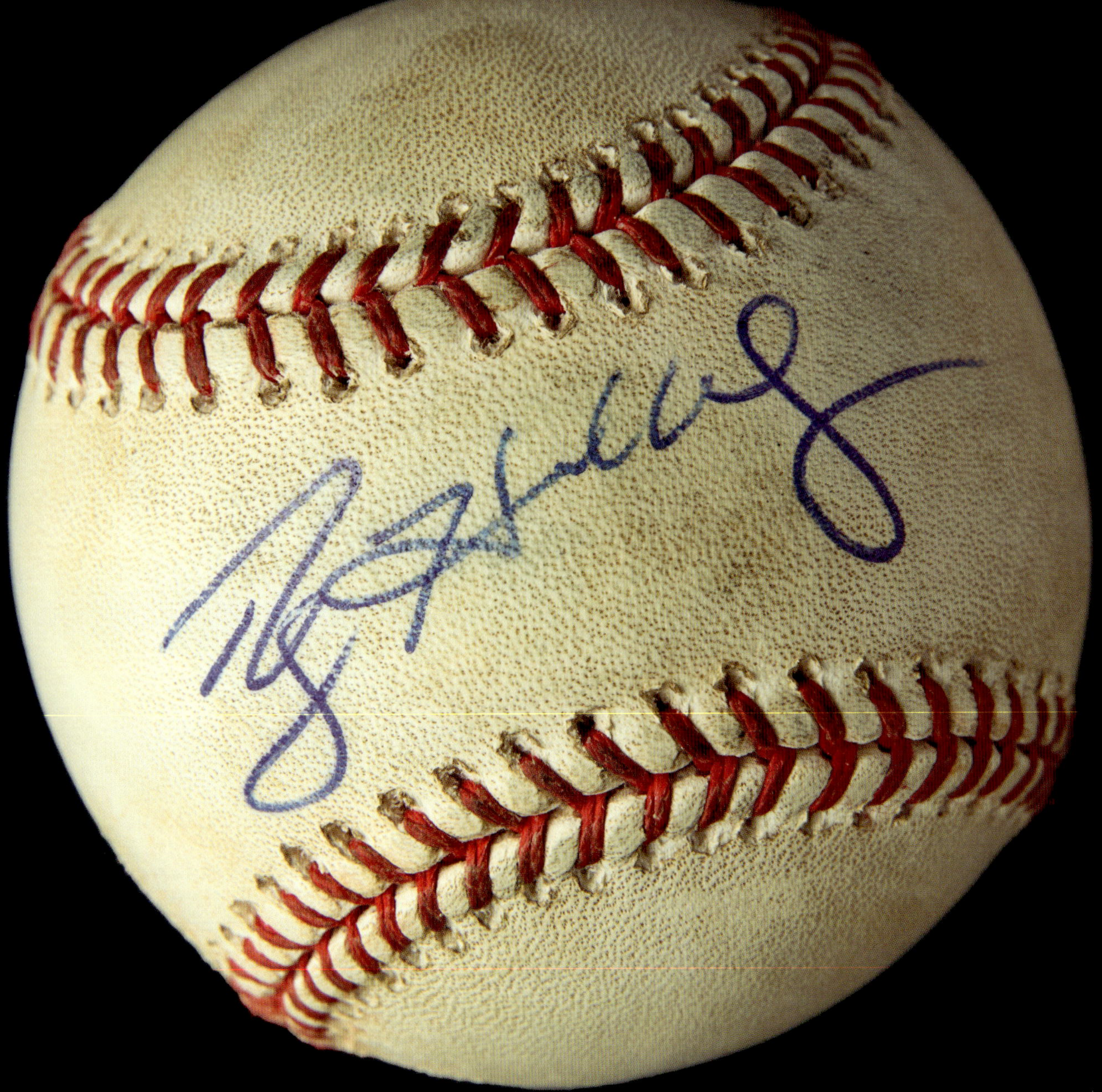

ROY HALLADAY

ROY "DOC" HALLADAY was a six-foot-six, larger than life character, what people of my persuasion call a "mensch." The day he was drafted by the Blue Jays, he made a speech to the effect of being speechless that anyone would pick him, let alone the Jays. He had this authenticity, this genuineness. He had a philanthropic mindset. He stood for something more than just being an athlete.

He came up through the Blue Jays system as a highly touted prospect; Blue Jays fans had waited patiently for the day he would come out of the Minor Leagues and pitch for them, and in 1995 he was selected in the first round of the amateur draft. He'd pitch some amazing games, but in 2001 somehow things were just going wrong for him, and he was sent back down to A-ball—quite the demotion. It was pointed out to him there that the problems that he was facing weren't physical but mental—it was a *focusing* thing—and to help him he was given Harvey Dorfman's book *The Mental ABCs of Pitching*; that and Dorfman's other book, *The Mental Game of Baseball*, became Halladay's bibles. He got his game face together and worked his way back up to the majors, and through the tutelage and the reading and sheer hard work, working as hard on an off-day as he did on on-days to keep himself in shape, he returned in 2002 as the dominant pitcher for the Blue Jays. He just *took off* to be one of their greatest pitchers ever.

By 2009, the Jays were in the dumps, not having made the playoffs since their back-to-back championships in '92 and '93, but their woes had little to do with Halladay's pitching, and although he was still happy with Toronto, he was traded to the Phillies, which was heartbreaking for us Toronto fans. "I really feel like I fulfilled a lot of obligations," he said, "but at some point you have to be a little selfish on what you want." What he was getting at, of course, was that he wanted to pitch in the postseason. "I really do hope it's here in Toronto, but I'd hate to look back and regret that three or four-year window."

He went on to enjoy a stellar career with the Phillies. On May 29th, 2010, against the Florida Marlins, he pitched the 20th perfect game in Major League Baseball history, retiring all twenty-seven batters, striking out eleven. *He* retired in 2013 (and the Phillies would hire him as their mental skills coach). On November 7th, 2017, piloting a plane near his home in Clearwater, Florida, he crashed into the Gulf of Mexico and perished. In March of 2018 his number was retired, and in 2019 he was elected to the Hall of Fame.

But here's the clincher: to show how grateful he was to have been rooted for in his darkest hour, at the very end of his career he signed a one-day contract with Toronto so he could announce his retirement as a Blue Jay. Unless you're a diehard fan of a team, you may not be able to understand how much a little gesture like that means, but it's what I meant by him being a *mensch*. He did it for the fans, for the city that gave him his opportunity and the organization that got him all the help he needed to overcome his demons. Roy Halladay was a straight ahead all-American dude, but he had attributes that Canadians could seriously admire!

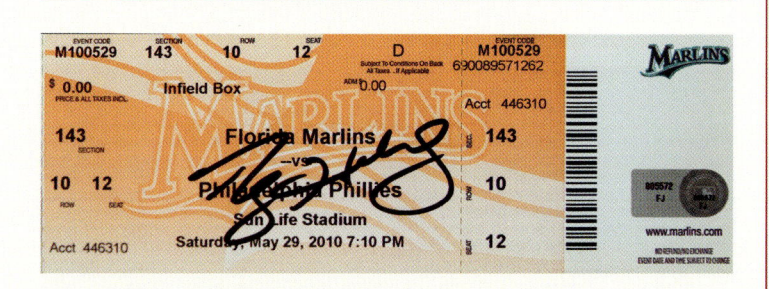

Here's a ticket from Halladay's perfect game on May 29th, 2010. The ball pictured at left is from his no-hitter in the NLDS. October 6th, 2010. Cincinnati Red Scott Rolen struck out swinging against Halladay at the top of the second inning. What a year!

GABBY HARTNETT

HERE'S A SPIFFY combo, an array of artefacts connected to a special White House reception on July 22nd, 1969, held at the behest of Richard Nixon to celebrate the anniversary of professional baseball's founding year. Nixon was a huge baseball aficionado. In the golden booklet you see in the photo, he writes about his love of the game and assembles his ultimate All-Star teams, era by era. In it, like a true baseball nerd, he methodically lists his favourite players—infield, outfield, relief pitcher, etc.—and there, in the early Live-ball era, is Gabby Hartnett.

The great Chicago Cubs catcher was invited to that reception in the nick of time—he died in 1972, on his seventy-second birthday. Top right is a ball signed by Nixon (I had three Tricky Dicky balls in my collection: one signed to Braves catcher Del Crandall, "Dick Nixon," which was unusual, and another signed on Opening Day at Griffith Stadium in 1959, when he was Vice-President under Dwight Eisenhower, who did not attend the game.) And top left is one of my George Sosnak illustrated baseballs (it originally belonged to the great Expos and Mets catcher Gary Carter), representing the Presidential opener in Washington during the same year as the Major League's anniversary; I think it's pretty cool to see his rendition of the Presidential seal beside the real embossed ones on both Gabby's invitation and the booklet. A neat bit of business here, a wonderful collection of Americana.

How good was he? Well, Bill James ranks Gabby Hartnett 9th all-time among MLB catchers, and according to Bill Johnson on SABR.org, "He carved out a career as one of the finest catchers ever to play the game." In fact, his bat and mask were the first artefacts sent to the newly constructed Baseball Hall of Fame in 1938. Not too shabby, Gabby!

One of several historic moments in baseball that he played a part in was Babe Ruth's mythical "called shot" home run off the Cubs pitcher, Charlie Root, in the 1932 World Series: William McNeil's *The Life and Times of the Cubs' Greatest Catcher*, quotes him as saying, "I don't want to take anything from the Babe, because he's the reason we make good money, but he didn't call the shot. He held up the index finger of his left hand . . . and said, 'It only takes one to hit.'" The "called shot" is an apocryphal bit of lore that has refused to die; have I now presented enough evidence in this book to lay it to rest?

Hartnett helped to make a second slice of baseball history famous in 1938, the year he'd become the Cubs' player-manager—not as catcher in this instance, but at bat: after trailing the Pirates by six games in the league's final standing, the Cubs had cut their lead to a half game, setting the stage for a nail-biting showdown. During the second of the three-game series, as the *Chicago Daily News* sportswriter John Carmichael described "With darkness descending on the lightless Wrigley Field and the score tied at 5 runs apiece, the umpires ruled that the ninth inning would be the last to be played. The entire game would have to be replayed the following day if the score remained tied. Hartnett came to bat with two out in the bottom of the ninth inning. With a count of 0 balls and 2 strikes, he connected on a Mace Brown pitch, launching the ball into the darkness, before it eventually landed in the left-center field bleachers. The stadium erupted into pandemonium as players and fans stormed the field to escort Hartnett around the bases." That walk-off home run became immortalized as the "Homer in the Gloamin" and perhaps the highlight of his career.

WASHINGTON SENATORS
SEAL OF THE PRESIDENT OF THE UNITED STATES
PRESIDENTIAL OPENER
The President
requests the pleasure of your company
at a reception to be held at
The White House
Tuesday afternoon, July 22, 1969
at 4:00 o'clock
Leo "Gabby" Hartnett
Hall of Fame 1955

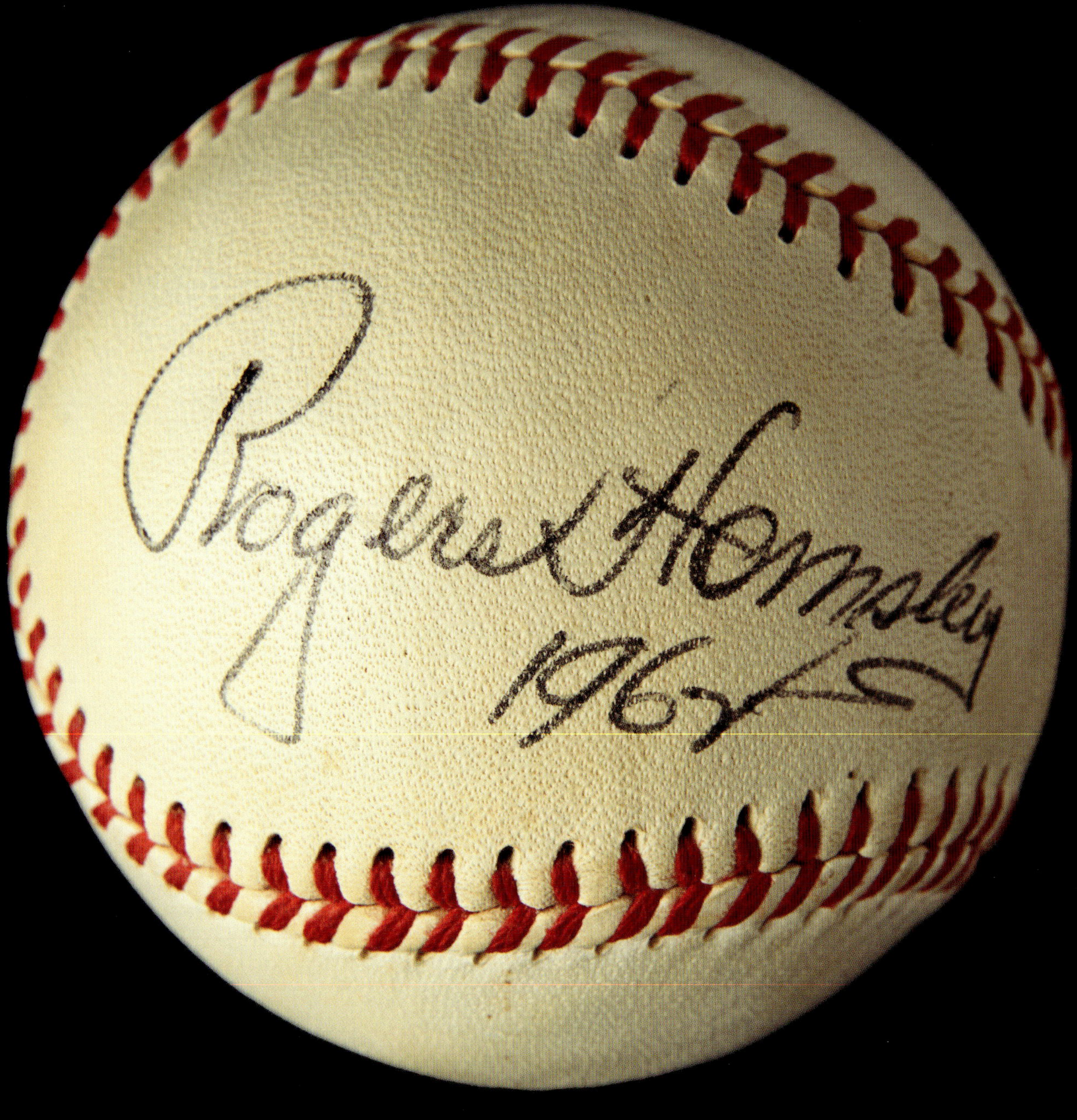
Rogers Hornsby
1962

ROGERS HORNSBY

AS WELL AS this beautiful single-signed ball, I own a rare signed first-edition book that Rogers Hornsby wrote, *My War with Baseball*—also signed in 1962, right before he started the season as the batting coach with the inaugural New York Mets. (It features a foreword by Casey Stengel, but we should probably credit the book's co-writer Bill Surface too; just as Hornsby said he had never seen a movie because they were bad for the eyes, he also thought reading weakened them!)

The memoir pulls no punches as he looks back on his forty-eight combative years as player, manager, coach and scout. As you might have guessed from its title, he was a hard-nosed, irascible type, regarded as one of the best hitters of all time but also someone tough to get along with. "He was almost as well known for his bluntness and complete lack of diplomacy as his prowess with a bat," writes C. Paul Rogers on SABR.org. "He rarely argued with umpires but said whatever crossed his mind to anyone else, including the owners he worked for. Longtime Cardinals owner Sam Breadon remarked that listening to Hornsby was like having the contents of a rock crusher emptied over his head."

"He was frank to the point of being cruel and as subtle as a belch," the sportswriter Lee Allen added, while Anthony J. Cooper wrote in *Voices from Cooperstown*, "He ran the clubhouse like a Gestapo camp. You couldn't smoke, drink a soft drink, eat a sandwich. Couldn't read a paper. When you walked in the clubhouse you put your uniform on and got ready to play. That was *it*! No more kidding around, no joking, no laughing. He was dedicated to the game and made sure you were too." Aside from betting on the nags, Hornsby was all baseball, all the time: "I could play every day," he once said. "What else is there? People ask me what I do in winter. I'll tell you what I do, I stare out the window and wait for spring."

I love how immensely quotable he was. Among my other favourite quips of his:

- "I don't like to sound egotistical, but every time I stepped up to the plate with a bat in my hands, I couldn't help but feel sorry for the pitcher."
- "Any ballplayer that don't sign autographs for little kids ain't an American. He's a Communist."
- "I've cheated, or someone on my team has cheated, in almost every single game I've been in. And I've always played hard. If that's rough and tough, I can't help it. I don't believe there's any such thing as a good loser. I wouldn't sit down and play a game of cards with you right now without wanting to win. If I hadn't felt that way I wouldn't have got very far in baseball."
- (And in what I'd call a serious understatement) "I have never been a yes man."

No, he wasn't subtle, but you could say he was only telling it like it was. As a slugger, he hit for *power*: .424 with 25 home runs in 1920; in the next year 39 home runs and a "mere" .403; in 1924 he hit .424; in 1925, 39 home runs; 39 again in 1929, hitting .380. His 450 total bases in 1922 remain the National League single-season record. My god, those stats are just insane. He was an astounding hitter.

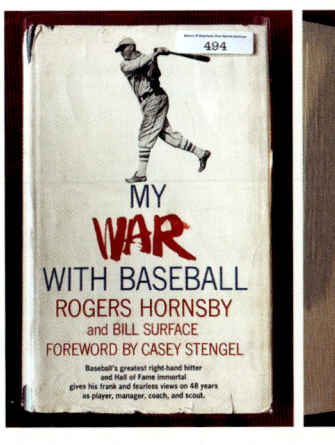

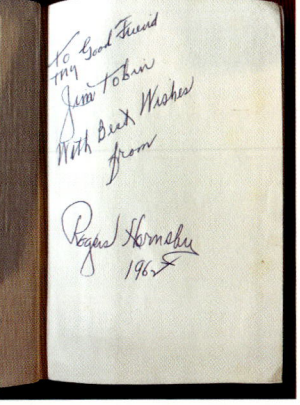

JOE JACKSON

"SHOELESS" JOE JACKSON was a simple, illiterate man who just flat out *hit*. "It don't take school stuff to help a fella play ball," he once said. "All the big sportswriters seem to enjoy writing about me as an ignorant cotton mill boy with nothing but lint where my brains ought to be. That was all right with me. I was able to fool a lot of pitchers and managers and club owners I wouldn't have been able to fool if they thought I was smarter." Nonetheless, his career was ended by his involvement in the infamous 1919 Black Sox scandal. Because of it he never won a batting title, he never got a plaque in the Hall of Fame, but he was one of the greatest natural hitters in the history of baseball. His average of .408 in 1911 still stands as a Cleveland team and Major League rookie record.

The story of the scandal has been often and memorably told in books like Harry Stein's *Hoopla*, movies such as *Eight Men Out* (it also crops up in *The Godfather Part II* and *Field of Dreams*), TV shows including *Boardwalk Empire* and *Mad Men*, and of course Murray Head's plaintive ballad, "Say It Ain't So," so I won't go into it in detail here. Suffice it to say that Jackson was among the infamous eight who were found to have taken bribes from a gambling syndicate to throw the World Series. The situation was complex, since the Sox owner Charles Comiskey was a cheapskate who barely paid these guys a living wage—it's not surprising that some of them succumbed to this bribery. Still, Jackson showed an incredible lapse of judgment in trusting the ringleader Chick Gandil, whom he didn't know very well. But I guess Jackson couldn't tell his *bat* what to do because he still hit .375!

After he was kicked out of the game, he played "outlaw ball" under assumed names around the South, where folks regarded him with kindness and still stood in awe of his ability, and in the industrial leagues (organised in workplaces such as shipyards and steel mills under a post-WWI government scheme that allowed players to work instead of going abroad to fight). He sported a sizable paunch around his midsection, but he could still knock the stuffing out of a baseball until he was 50 years old.

The bat you see in this picture is one of only *two* signature model Joe Jackson bats known to exist. After that the story gets hazy. Was this a bat he used himself? Did he take it with him after he was expelled, scratching his name out where it had been engraved because he was banned from *any* kind of baseball? Its letter of authenticity says, "There are unique circumstances relating to the signature on this H&B [Hillerich & Bradsby] bat that allow us to define it as dating from 1917 to 1920," i.e., *before* his lifetime banishment, so we can but surmise.

There is however no doubt about the team-signed ball from the 1917 White Sox. Signed two years before the scandal hit and at the bottom you can see the little chicken scratch that says "Joe Jackson." Finally, there is an actual ticket to Game Four of the infamous 1919 World Series in remarkably good condition. This little grouping is my homage to perhaps the greatest hitter that ever lived, but whose bad judgement cost him more than we can know.

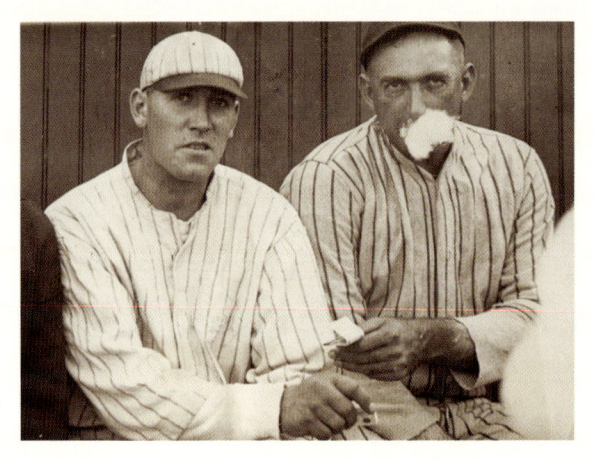

(I also own this International Newsreel photograph, originally published June 28th, 1922, of Jackson between innings in New Jersey, playing in the industrial leagues under an assumed name and breaking a league no-smoking rule to obscure his face so that he won't be recognised by a passing photographer.)

Cincinnati National League
BASE BALL CLUB
World's Series
1919
Redland Field
ADMIT ONE
Bleacher Seat
GAME 4
Bleacher Seat $1.00
War Tax Paid .10
Cost of Ticket $1.10
RAIN CHECK
If legal game is not played on scheduled date, this coupon is good for admission and same seat for game whenever it is played.
KOESSLER BROS., CINCINNATI
ENTRANCE: Western Avenue, near Findlay Street.
Gates at the Park will be opened each day during the series at 10:00 a. m. The holder of this ticket will be given choice of Bleacher seat or standing room on field in front of Bleachers, according to time of arrival.
No 1758

TRIPLE-PLAY
AT
Shimonoseki Japan
Nov. 24, 1931
KAMM-P
TO
MARANVILLE-SS
TO
KELLY-1B
Connie Mack
Cascarella
Babe Ruth
J. Foxx
John Quinn
Earl Averill
C. Gehringer
E. McNair

JAPAN 1931 *and* 1934 TOURS

AMERICAN ALL-STAR TEAMS made goodwill tours of Japan, playing top collegiate ballclubs and amateur squads, in 1913, 1920, 1922 and 1931, by which time the Japanese were so in love with baseball that allegedly more youngsters were playing the game there than in the States. The tours were organised by sportswriter Fred Lieb and former Major Leaguer Herb Hunter, a rather mediocre utility infielder who went on to bigger and better things after his playing days ended. (According to baseballhistorycomesalive.com, Hunter "had the reputation of a bit of an eccentric, and one account said he was 'the butt of almost every clubhouse joke.' Another said, 'He was so absentminded that his manager would escort him to the railroad station to ensure that he would not miss the team's road trips.' Not exactly the attributes you'd expect from a tour organizer!") More successful as an entrepreneur, he became known as Japan's Ambassador to the Orient, and worked as an advisor to a group of wealthy Japanese businessmen hoping to establish their country's first pro league.

Lou Gehrig, Lefty Grove, Ralph Shinners, Al Simmons, Tom Oliver, "Muddy" Ruel, "Lefty" O'Doul, Frankie Frisch and Mickey Cochrane were among the 1931 team, as well as the three players named on this unique ball who pulled off a dramatic triple-play in Shimonoseki on November 24th: the Dodgers first baseman George "High Pockets" Kelly, Boston Braves shortstop Walter "Rabbit" Maranville and White Sox pitcher Willie Kamm. The Major Leaguers were greeted with a tumultuous parade through Ginza as tens of thousands of fans cheered the visitors with cries of *banzai* (May you live 10,000 years!). "The enthusiasm of the Japanese for baseball just about borders on the fanatical," Gehrig told the *New York Times*. "Everywhere we played we packed them in, and after the games thousands who had been locked out still would be standing in the streets waiting for us to come out. At times it would take hours for our cars to take us from the park to the hotel." The Japanese were overmatched in the 17-game series, however, with just 30 runs vs the Major Leaguers' 149, the consensus being that they were slick fielders and good pitchers, but poor hitters.

(Kelly had made his debut in 1915 and would play his last in 1935, while Maranville retired in '35 and Kamm in '36, so you could say these guys were seasoned veterans—all-stars, but at the end of their careers; Kelly would be inducted into the Hall of Fame in 1970, but many felt he was not worthy—Bill James ranked him its worst player ever! Charges of cronyism were levelled against the Veteran's Committee that had voted him in, resulting in its powers being reduced in subsequent years.)

Unfortunately, the Americans also insulted their hosts by showboating during those one-sided games. By 1934, tensions were mounting around the globe with uncomfortable feelings about Germany and their association with Japan's imperialist government, yet the tour was still a success. This time more than half a million Japanese thronged the streets of Tokyo to welcome the team like today's rock stars to see players such as Babe Ruth, Earl Averill, Lou Gehrig, Charlie Gehringer, Lefty Gomez, Connie Mack, Jimmy Fox, and one of my favourite eccentric ballplayers of all time, Moe Berg (whose espionage for U.S. intelligence I describe in another chapter). The Americans won all eighteen games, The Bambino alone hitting thirteen home runs, but his daughter recalled how the fans would rise to their feet every time he came to bat and wave both Japanese and American flags. Less than a decade later the Japanese would bomb Pearl Harbor. That would be the last goodwill visit to Japan until 1986, so the second ball in this grouping represents not just an awesome American team but the end of an era . . . Herb Hunter would only return to Japan with the United States Navy.

ICHIRO SUZUKI, SHOHEI OHTANI *and* SADAHARU OH

IT'S HARD FOR a player to move from one culture to another. Branch Rickey chose Jackie Robinson to break the MLB colour barrier because he thought he had the personality to take the taunts and the pressure. It was an ungodly position to put any human being in, but also the greatest thing that ever happened to the game. Aside from correcting a horrible injustice, it opened owners' and managers' eyes to what other parts of the world could offer the game: Puerto Rico, the Dominican Republic, Venezuela, Cuba and more recently Japan.

North Americans have tended to look at Japanese baseball as inferior because of smaller parks, a lighter ball, yadda yadda, but there's nothing inferior about Japanese players. The thing is, making the transition has as much to do with ability to *adapt* as it has to sheer talent. When Warren Cromartie first went to play for the Yomiuri Giants, he freaked out because their practices were so exhausting that by game time he felt he had no joy juice left. It differed so from America, where you play baseball, you don't *work* it, and yet in time he thrived; the diet was a big change for him too, but he got into the best shape of his life. And games there can end in a tie... that one he could *never* figure out! A lot of little quirks got lost in translation for him, and of course it works both ways.

It's about a lot more than just having talent. The Blue Jays' Yusei Kikuchi was touted as the next great pitcher from Japan, but he struggled for a while before showing his brilliance, while others like Shohei "Showtime" Ohtani adapted easily. On the diamond he's just so confident and chill. He exemplifies the word poise. The first time I saw him play in person was when I'd been invited to meet Albert Pujols and have him sign my 3,000-hit ball. In the cage during batting practice was Ohtani with his very erect stance, just batting balls out of the park, one after the other, like he was hitting Nerf balls, and everyone was just abuzz. When he first got drafted, fantasy leagues got a headache because they had to invent new rules for a player who was actually two different people: Ohtani the hitter and Ohtani the pitcher—a true two-way player. How would you show him in the lineup? It was mad! It's very unfortunate this year that he may have to undergo Tommy John surgery a second time, because until now you could say he was maybe the greatest ballplayer we will ever see.

Sadaharu Oh, meanwhile (as Peter C. Bjarkman on SABR.org writes) "owns a leading claim to the title of baseball's greatest all-time home run slugger... Charismatic and workaholic, he produced one of the most impressive career resumes found anywhere that professional baseball has been played at the highest levels." I never met him, so I'll let him speak for himself: "I had reached the point where I simply lived to hit. How can I say it without sounding foolish? I craved hitting a baseball in the way a samurai craved following the Way of the Sword. It was my life." Amen to that.

Finally, Ichiro Suzuki, an incredible right fielder, a great defensive player, and without question the greatest batter to make the transition from Japanese to American baseball—both a power hitter who used his bat control to spray the ball around the field, *and* a master of choppers and bunts. As the *Washington Post*'s columnist Thomas Boswell said, "To see Ichiro hit is to be taken back almost a century to the hit-them-where-they-ain't technique." The result: in Japan and the U.S. combined, a record *4,367* hits. Fitting for a man whose name means "brightest, most cheerful," it couldn't have happened to a nicer guy.

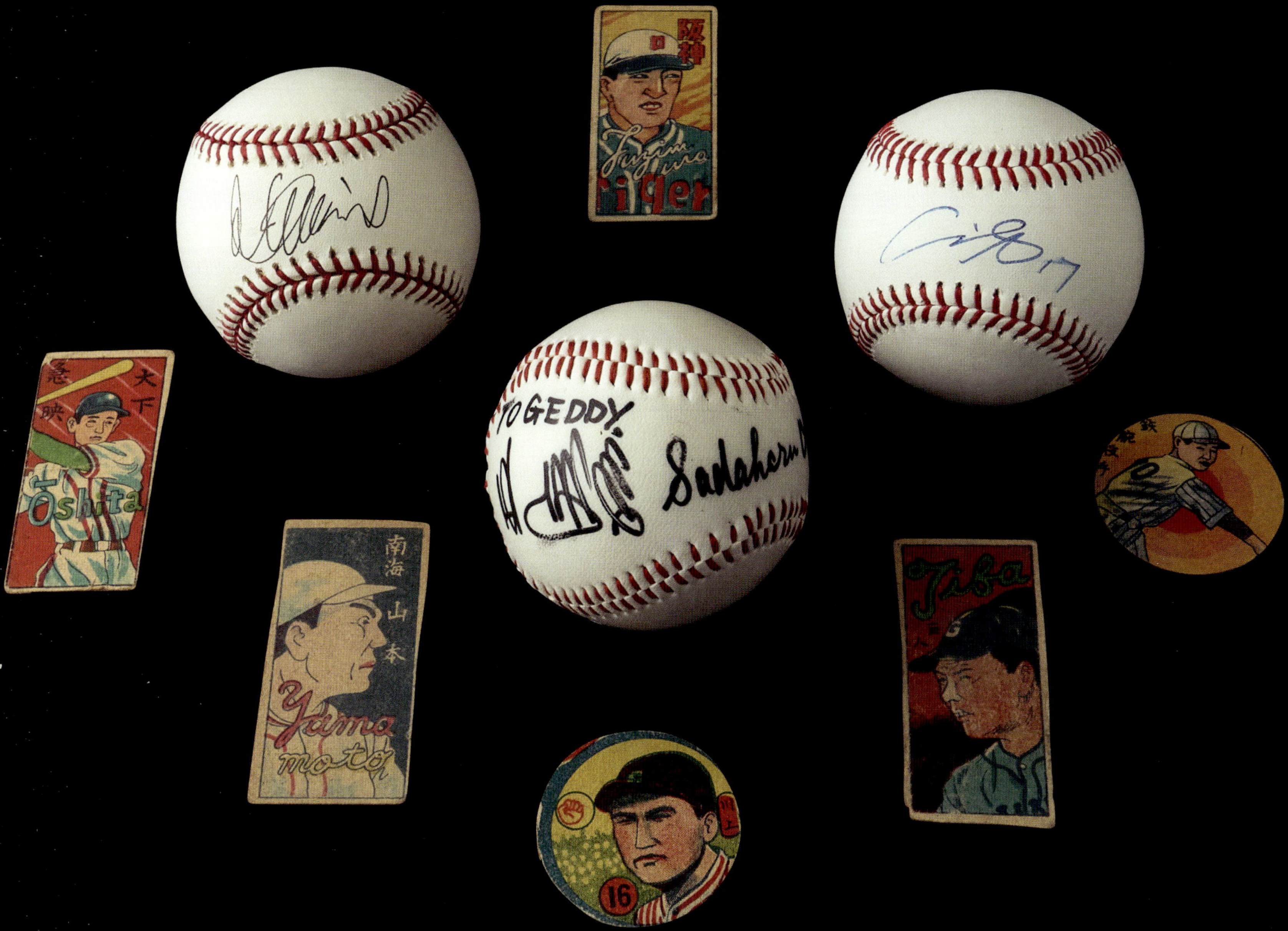
TO GEDDY
阪神
Tiger
南海
山本
Yama
moto
Oshita
大下
16

Ball Used In Game
May 18 2004
Perfect Game
Randy Johnson

RANDY JOHNSON

RANDY JOHNSON CAME up in the Montreal Expos system and in 1989 was part of a trade that sent star pitcher Mark Langston from the Seattle Mariners to the Expos. Shortly afterwards, Mark and I met and over time became friends. In an odd twist of fate, a year later I'd meet and become friends with Randy. How about that? Two new pitching buddies, both music fans, traded for each other!

In the course of his pitching career, Johnson threw two no-hitters, the first in June of 1990. On tour in March of that year, Rush was coming to Seattle, and he being a huge music fan, a drummer and a big fan of Neil Peart, reached out through his connections in the music business to ask to say hello at soundcheck. I remember him telling me then that before games he sometimes listened to "Tom Sawyer" to fire himself up—and three months later, sure enough, he listened to it in the dugout before he went out to pitch that first no-no.

He's a remarkable person, very talented and incredibly smart. He's the only athlete I ever heard talk about a sense of accountability—to the game, to the fans and to himself. Always looking for an edge, he experimented at one time with sensory deprivation tanks to see if they'd help speed up his recovery between starts and make him a stronger pitcher. He's also been an amateur photographer since college, and takes it very seriously. One time, he wanted to come to shoot a gig of ours in St. Louis, but was playing a game the same day in Detroit. It was an afternoon game, so I said, "How can you come? You're pitching!" He said, "Yeah, I know, but I'm going to pitch a fast game and then I'm going to get a flight out and come to St. Louis." I thought, "What does he mean, 'I'm gonna pitch a fast game?' Surely the Detroit hitters might have something to say about *that*." Later, I happened to tune in to the game, and he had an effin' no-hitter going through seven innings! And as soon he gave up a hit, they pulled him from the game, he went into the locker room, showered and dressed and raced to the airport, flew to St. Louis and arrived at the gig in time for the show. There he was in the middle of it, taking photos from the pit.

You can always spot him from a distance because at 6'10" (and the tallest player in MLB history when he entered the game), he's literally shoulders above everyone else. After the show, we put back a lot of wine (though he's really a beer guy), and since it had been a long day for him, he crashed on the sofa in my hotel room—and I'll always remember him with his head at one end and his feet extended well off the other end as we carried on drinking. Oh, and by the way, it's not just lip service when I say he's a great photographer. One of his shots was so good, it made the cover of the *R40 Live* recording.

He's gifted me a few baseballs from his significant games, including this one, when he retired all twenty-seven Braves batters he faced at Turner Field, clinching a 2-0 victory to become, at forty, the oldest pitcher to throw a perfect game—the Major Leagues' seventeenth. It's part of a little homage to Randy that I keep in my office that includes a signed uniform, a ball from his first no-hitter, another from his 300th win and one from a game in Seattle where he struck out nineteen Oakland A's. Thank you my friend, I shall never part with them.

Hall of Fame pitcher and Hall of Fame photographer, and the hall of fame of damn fine fellows.

WALTER JOHNSON

TY COBB ONCE said about Walter Johnson's fastball, "It made me flinch and hissed with danger," while Ring Lardner wrote of him, "He's got a gun concealed on his person. They can't tell me he throws them balls with his arm." But the player who acquired the nicknames "The Big Train" (for the blinding speed of his fastball) and "Barney" (after race car driver Barney Oldfield, for his flamboyant motoring habits) was, according to Charles Carey on SABR.org, "admired all over America not only for his pitching exploits and his fierce competitiveness, but also for the modesty, humility and dignity with which he conducted himself, never arguing with umpires, berating his teammates for their errors, brushing back hitters or using 'foreign substances' on the baseball. At a time when many ballplayers were ruffians and drunkards, Walter Johnson was never in a brawl and didn't patronize saloons . . . By the time he hung up his spikes, he'd recorded statistics which seem beyond belief—417 wins and 279 losses, 3,509 strikeouts, 110 shutouts, 12 20-win seasons, 11 seasons with an ERA below 2.00, and what seems almost incomprehensible a century later, 531 complete games in 666 starts. The *Washington Post* reporter Shirley Povich once said, 'Walter Johnson, more than any other ballplayer, probably more than any other athlete, professional or amateur, became a symbol of gentlemanly conduct in the heat of battle.'"

He played his first season in the minors for a team in Weiser, in the Southern Idaho semi-pro league. He was just nineteen but already known as "The Weiser Wonder." Word of his prowess spread around the country, and in 1907 the Washington Senators offered him a contract. He was so reluctant to accept that he demanded a train ticket to return home to California in case he didn't make good. A large crowd came to the depot to see him off. As Johnson said goodbye to his pals, there were tears in his eyes. "You know how you are at nineteen," he explained later. "You want to see things."

So, this game-used ball is from the estate of another great ballplayer, the Hall of Famer outfielder Al Simmons, and carries a lengthy inscription in black steel tip fountain pen: "Last ball that won 15-inning Game 1-0. Ed Rommel vs Walter Johnson April 30, 1926, Opening Day of the Season." As per the *Baseball Almanac* website, "On Opening Day of his twentieth Major League season, Walter 'The Big Train' Johnson was still bringing it like a locomotive, pitching all fifteen in the Washington Senators' 1-0 extra-inning victory over the Philadelphia Athletics at Griffith Stadium." He pitched the entire *fifteen* innings! That is just unheard of in today's game. The last time I remember a performance even close to that was when Jack Morris pitched to a ten-inning 1-0 victory for the Minnesota Twins over the Atlanta Braves in the 1991 World Series. This ball is a testament to the time when as a starter you threw till you couldn't throw any more.

I just love these old beat-up game balls. They're just so evocative. Basically, you're holding the sweat, the grit, the DNA of the great man himself. You're transported right back to 1926 and all the scuffling that went on.

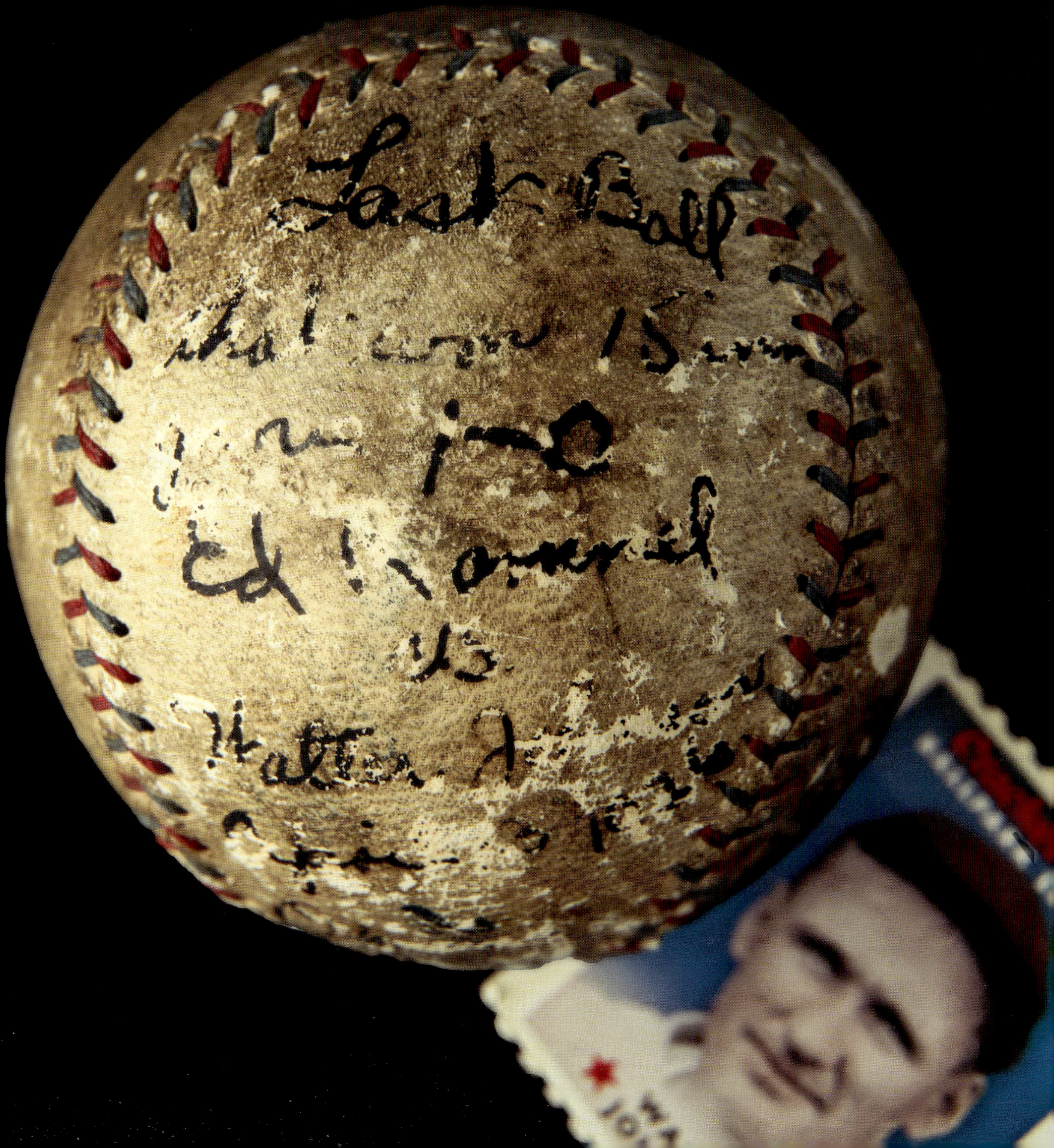
Last Ball

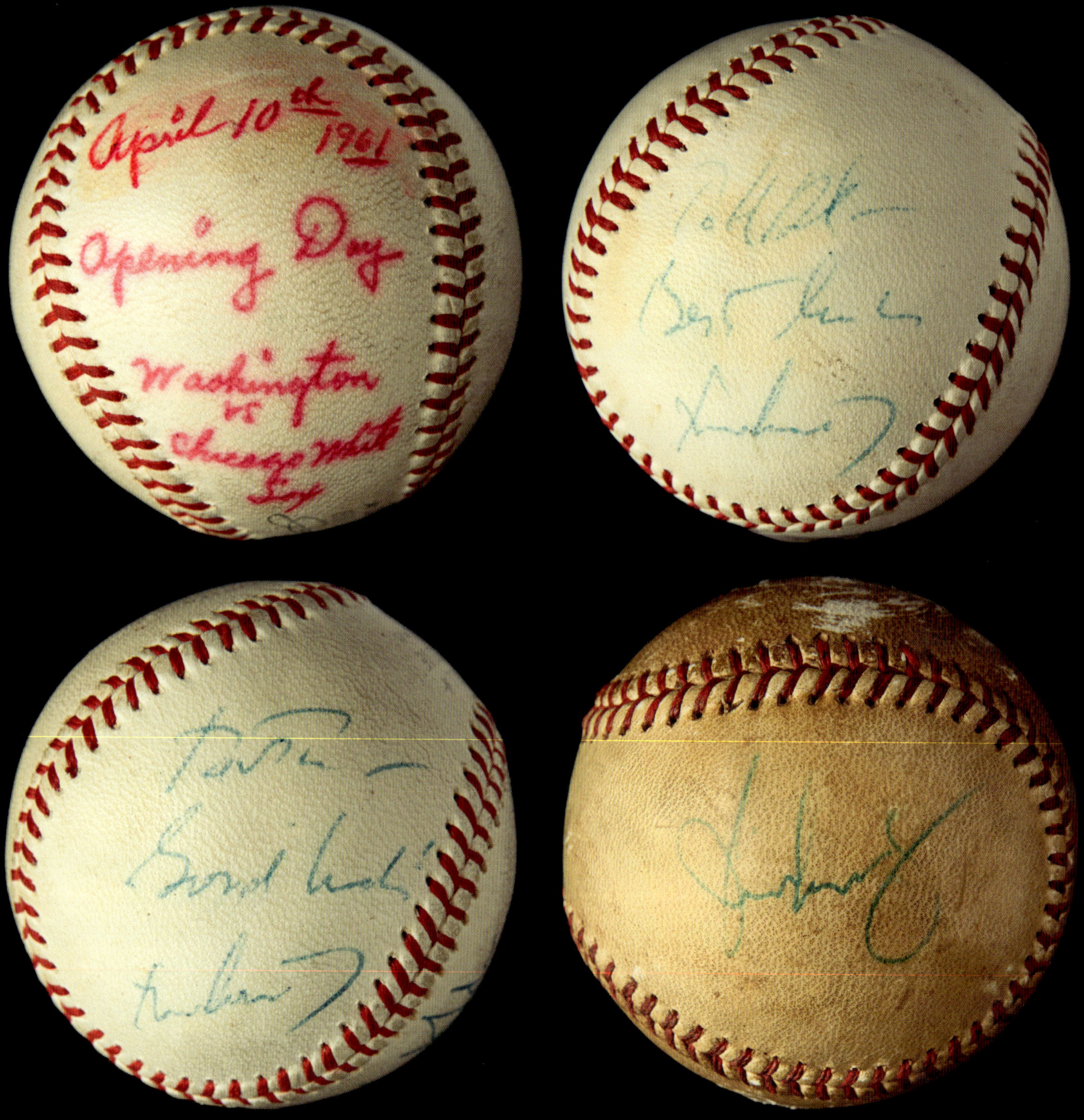
April 10th 1961
Opening Day
Washington
vs
Chicago White Sox

JOHN F. KENNEDY

AS A BOY raised in Toronto, so close to the U.S. border, I was hugely affected by American television. In many ways we all watched the world unfold through America's lens. I clearly remember John F. Kennedy's assassination and, two days later on Sunday morning in our living room, seeing Jack Ruby shoot Lee Harvey Oswald—live on TV! The events of that time are so burned into my memory that when I came across a Christie's catalogue with the ball you see here with *April 10th, 1961*, written in pink and *Good luck!* in green, I flipped out! To us Canadians, JFK was a hero, larger than life, the ultimate good guy cut down in his youth. It was a naive perspective, but a child's one in a more innocent time, when we weren't really shown the flaws of our leaders the way we are today. (Remember that movie about his torpedo boat, *PT 109*, showcasing him as a war hero?) So, when I saw that I could actually purchase a ball that he signed after throwing it out at the start of the 1961 Major League season, that was just amazing. To me there was nothing more "Americana" than a ball that represented the USA's National Pastime, signed by an actual President. Selfish as it may sound, it was a way of owning a piece of American history—as if you can "own" history! It set me down a road of obsession with first-pitch baseballs by Presidents.

The original letter accompanying that ball (which also has Lyndon Johnson's autograph) says, "This ball was caught by me, [White Sox outfielder] Jim Rivera, on opening day 1961 between the Washington senators and the Chicago White Sox. I had met President John Kennedy and Lyndon Johnson, then Vice President."

Decades later I was leafing through another catalogue and saw advertised a first-pitch ball from opening day, 1961, Washington vs Chicago White Sox, signed by John F. Kennedy, and I was like, *That's impossible, I* own *that ball!* Then I did some research and discovered that, being a true Democrat, he threw out not just one opening ball, but in a sense of fairness an opening pitch to both teams. (In point of fact, the tradition in those days was a double toss, one to each team.) Kennedy threw that one out to the Senators. On the receiving end was southpaw pitcher Harold Woodeshick, who trotted the ball back to the newly minted Commander-in-Chief for an autograph and *To Harold Best wishes!*

Kennedy attended all three of the Senators' opening days between 1961 and 1963. The third ball here was not a first pitch, but from opening day, 1962, thrown to the Senators' then coach and manager Mickey Vernon. The ball was in the family's possession until Vernon's daughter Gay put it up for sale and I bought it. It's one of a scant few signed by President Kennedy with direct provenance.

Finally we have another first-pitch ball, this one from April 8th, 1963 (the Senators' first season in D.C.) which the backstop Don Leppert caught in a free-for-all. According to the umpire Al Salerno, "After the opening ceremonies, President John F. Kennedy threw in the first ball, which Don Leppert caught. I asked Don for the ball and he threw it to me while I was standing in the runway. A short time later, when the President was leaving, he most graciously signed the ball for me."

JFK signing the opening ball in 1961.

72 Stories — 85 — Geddy Lee

SANDY KOUFAX

ONLY A HANDFUL of Jewish players ever became baseball poster boys, but we kids in the Fifties and Sixties knew all their names. Top of the list was Sandy Koufax, one of the greatest pitchers who ever lived and the idol of every Jewish boychick in North America. When he famously refused to pitch in Game 1 of the 1965 World Series because it fell on Yom Kippur, he became the *ultimate* Jewish athlete—though I have to say for us that was both good and bad: he fucked it for us because if we wanted to go out and play on the Sabbath or some special holy day, the first thing we'd hear from our parents would be, "*Sandy Koufax* vouldn't *pitch* on Yom Kippur and *you* vant to go to de *movies*?" But I never held it against him. In fact, one of the biggest thrills of my life was meeting him at the Dodgertown spring training facility in Vero Beach, California. I was so starstruck. I was in the presence of a god!

"I'm praying for rain," he said in the days before that famous game. "It has to rain. It would solve the whole matter." (His boss, Walter O'Malley, took it one level higher, quipping that he'd "ask the Pope what he can do about rain on that day.") But really, he didn't take the matter of faith over sports lightly. In 1959, he'd requested to skip his start on the first night of Passover, and in 1961 and 1963 skipped his turns in the rotation on Rosh Hashanah, the Jewish New Year.

His decision was not without precedent, but I'd say it was the purest. In 1954, for instance, Al Rosen of the Indians said he would not play in Game 5 of the World Series, which fell on Yom Kippur, but a Giants sweep of the Indians made that a moot point! Hank Greenberg, also a Member of the Tribe, was actually the first player to wrestle with the conundrum. In 1934, during the heat of a pennant race, he did agree to play on the more celebratory Rosh Hashanah (and hit two home runs!) but drew the line at Yom Kippur, and when he walked into Synagogue on the Day of Atonement, he received a standing ovation from the congregation. (In a poem entitled *Came on Yom Kippur*, the People's Poet Edgar Guest voiced Irish Catholics' admiration for Greenberg's adherence to the faith: "Said Murphy to Mulrooney 'We shall lose the game today!/ We shall miss him in the infield and shall miss him at the bat,/ But he's true to his religion – and I honor him for that!'")

Koufax threw four no-hitters in his brief but remarkable career. After his fourth and final no-no, the legendary perfect game of September 6th, 1965 (selected in a 1995 poll of members of the Society for American Baseball Research as the greatest ever pitched), he gifted this game ball to a member of the Dodgers ground crew.

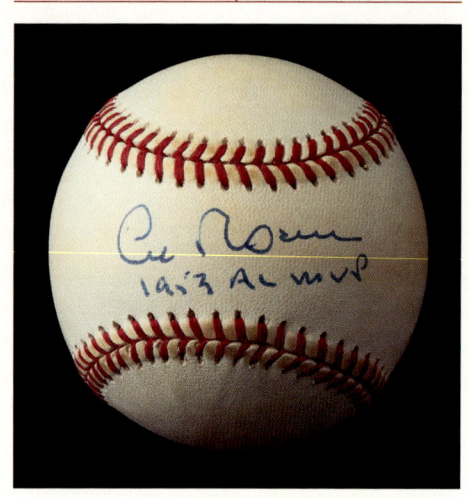

OPPOSITE:

9 – 9 1965 / CAUGHT / "NO-HIT" /
GAME VS CHICAGO CUBS / "SANDY" KOUFAX PITCHING
/ TO GUS / BEST WISHES / SANDY KOUFAX

*[signed in pencil; also signed, barely legibly,
by catcher Jeff Torborg]*

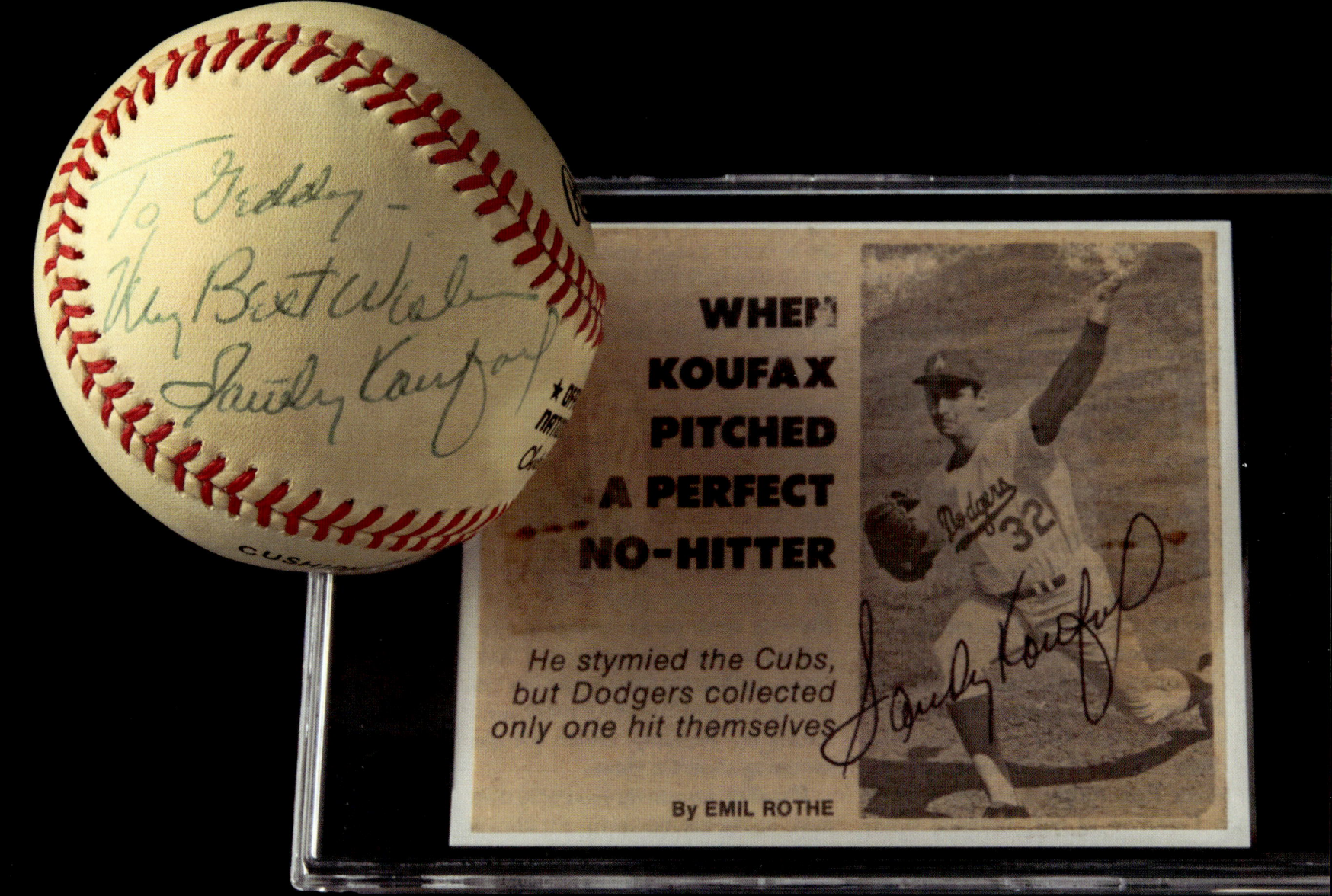

To Geddy –
My Best Wishes
Sandy Koufax

WHEN KOUFAX PITCHED A PERFECT NO-HITTER

He stymied the Cubs, but Dodgers collected only one hit themselves

By EMIL ROTHE

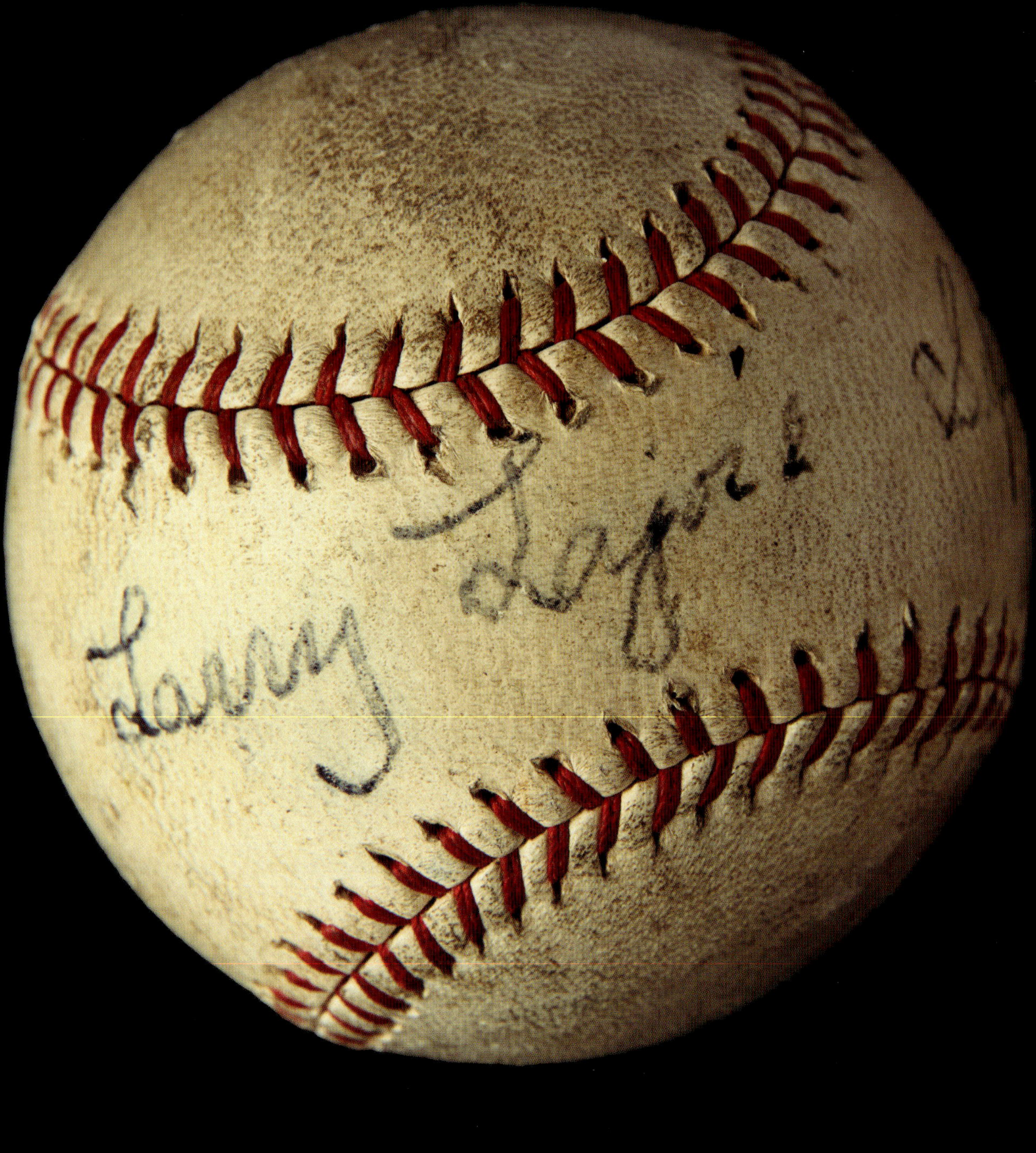
Larry Lajoie

NAP LAJOIE

I LOOKED FOR YEARS to find a good single-signed Napoleon "Larry" Lajoie baseball . . . and then spent time learning how to properly pronounce his name. Some Americans say, "La *Joy*," while others insist on "La *Jooway*." Napoleon himself is supposed to have preferred the French pronunciation—"La *Jwah*," which is how we Canadians like it too. And in fact, the Québecois Lajoie clan traced its origins to Auxerre, France, before Nap's family emigrated to the United States. So, although he was in fact born in 1874 in Woonsocket, Rhode Island, I claim him for Canada!

"The Frenchman" made his debut with the Philadelphia Fliers in 1896, quickly demonstrating an aptitude for all positions on the field. As Stephen Constantelos and David Jones write on SABR.org, he "combined graceful, effortless fielding with powerful, fearsome hitting to become one of the greatest all-around players of the Deadball Era, and one of the best second basemen of all time. At 6′1″ and 200 pounds, he possessed an unusually large physique for his time, yet when manning the keystone sack, he was wonderfully quick on his feet, threw like chain lightning, and went over the ground like a deer. 'Lajoie glides toward the ball,' noted the *New York Press*, 'gathers it in nonchalantly, as if picking fruit.'"

Connie Mack said, "He plays so naturally and so easily. It looks like lack of effort. But his reach is so long and he's fast as lightning to throw to second base. He is ideal. All the catchers who played with him say he's the easiest man to throw to in the game today. High, low, wide, he is sure of everything." As much as we "Rotisserie" fools often rank hitting over fielding (we love a great hitter at every position even if he's a bit crappy with the glove), it's the defensive wizards that make the game a joy to watch. But Nap was ever dangerous at the plate, capable of hitting to all fields *and* an expert bunter to boot.

On May 23rd, 1901, he became just the second player to be intentionally walked with the bases loaded, an act that has occurred a mere eight times in the game's long history. (The first? Abner Dalrymple in 1888, a fact only discovered in 2007.) Nap's lifetime batting average was .339; in 1901, he won the Triple Crown, led second baseman, led the league, led all second basemen in the league in fielding average, and batted .426, an American League mark that has yet to be topped. He was elected to the Hall of Fame in 1937.

He was also famous for run-ins with umpires. He was suspended for throwing chewing tobacco into umpire Frank Wyatt's eye after one ejection, and after refusing to leave the bench, had to be escorted from the park by police. In 1903, he became so infuriated by an umpire's decision to use a blackened ball, that he picked up the sphere and threw it over the grandstand, resulting in the forfeit of the game. (Remember, they didn't have a million balls like they do now; they'd use the same one until it was ratty and tattered and blackened.)

A fascinating footnote: in 1905 Nap's leg nearly had to be amputated after the blue dye in his socks poisoned a spike wound. The incident led to a new rule requiring teams to use sanitary white socks—thus began the tradition of wearing knee-high sanitaries!

And finally, to bolster my claim of "Nap for Canada," in 1917 Lajoie became playing manager of the AAA Toronto Maple Leafs, and that year they won the pennant!

KENESAW MOUNTAIN LANDIS

IT'S NOT JUST player signatures I've collected, but ephemera from significant administrators of baseball's early history too, among them A.B. Chandler, Bart Giamatti and Kenesaw Mountain Landis. This ball, according to its letter of authenticity, was signed in 1940 by Landis, organised baseball's first Commissioner, "best remembered for banishing the Chicago Black Sox conspiracists. His signature on a solo-signed baseball is rare, and this full-name variation is particularly scarce." (The letter beside the photo is addressed to Chandler, who would succeed Landis in 1945.)

Ohio-born Landis was only 5'6" high and weighed just 130lbs, but was an intimidating presence. Players and owners alike quaked when they were called to his Chicago office. A magazine profile at the time said of him, "Vivid in appearance, his shaggy white hair and trademark as inescapable as the snow on the top of Mount Everest, he had everything it takes to catch the public eye and keep it. Not since Abraham Lincoln had a person in public life possessed features so memorably, so indisputably honest. A picture of rigid dignity."

He had one hell of a stern countenance. Dan Busby of the SABR site says, "Some said that baseball owners found Judge Kenesaw Mountain Landis on the federal bench, but Leo Durocher got it right when he said, 'They got him right out of Dickens.' Ruth put the fans back in the park, but Landis made sure what they witnessed was honest. The Sultan and Czar worked different sides of the street but between them, they saved the game."

But he wasn't just a pretty face. Baseball was plagued by gambling and corruption, and Landis was brought in to do something about it.

Fixing baseball had been associated with baseball since the start. As Eliot Asinof wrote in *Eight Men Out*, "A ball game afforded a pleasant, even exciting afternoon in the sunlight, an event to which a gentleman could take his lady—and bet." Baseball historian Lee Allen said: "The situation was especially bad in Brooklyn where the Atlantic club fostered so much betting that one section of the grounds was known as the Gold Board, with activity that rivalled that of the stock exchange." The time of the 1920 World Series, when Landis was first elected commissioner, was one of the stormiest periods ever recorded in the history of Major League Baseball.

Controversies to date had been addressed by the two leagues' heads at the time, John Heydler and Ban Johnson, but the Black Sox Scandal made clear that one authority was needed to restore public confidence in the game. Eight players involved were indicted by a Chicago grand jury, but the following year were cleared in court; even so, Landis, who by then had been unanimously elected as Commissioner, banned them for life, declaring, "No player who throws a ball game, no player who undertakes or promises to throw a game, no player who sits in conference with a bunch of crooked players and gamblers where the ways and means of throwing baseball games are planned and discussed and does not promptly tell his club about it, will ever play professional baseball."

It was a tough stance he took (it broke poor Joe Jackson) but you can't argue with the results. He was intent on making the game squeaky clean, and it's never really changed since. Just ask Pete Rose.

Dear AB / Whenner / You gonna / Write me that letter? / Ide kinda likit / This year / Yrs / KW Landis

72 Stories **90** *Geddy Lee*

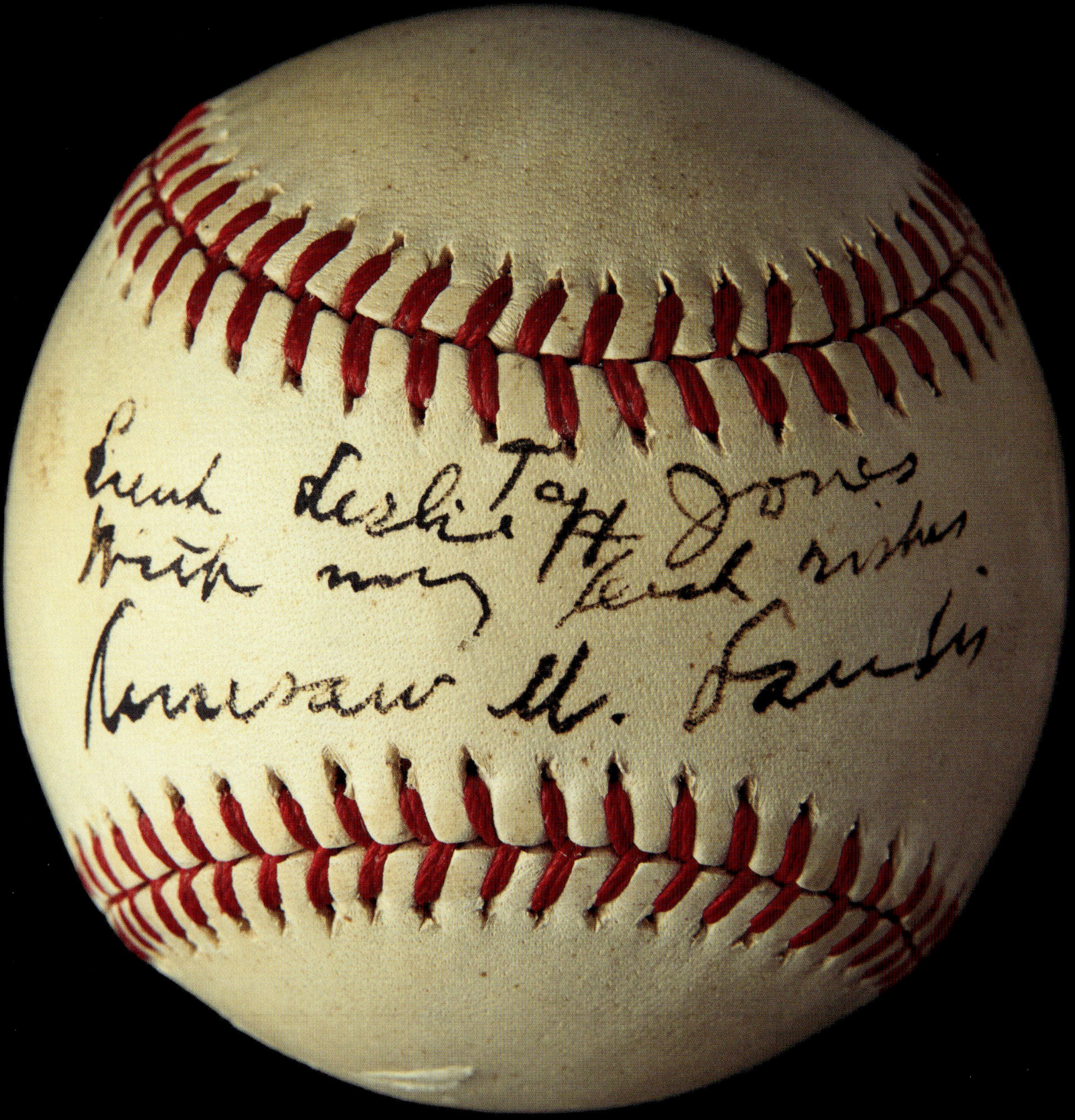
Friend Leslie "Topp" Jones
With my best wishes
Kenesaw M. Landis

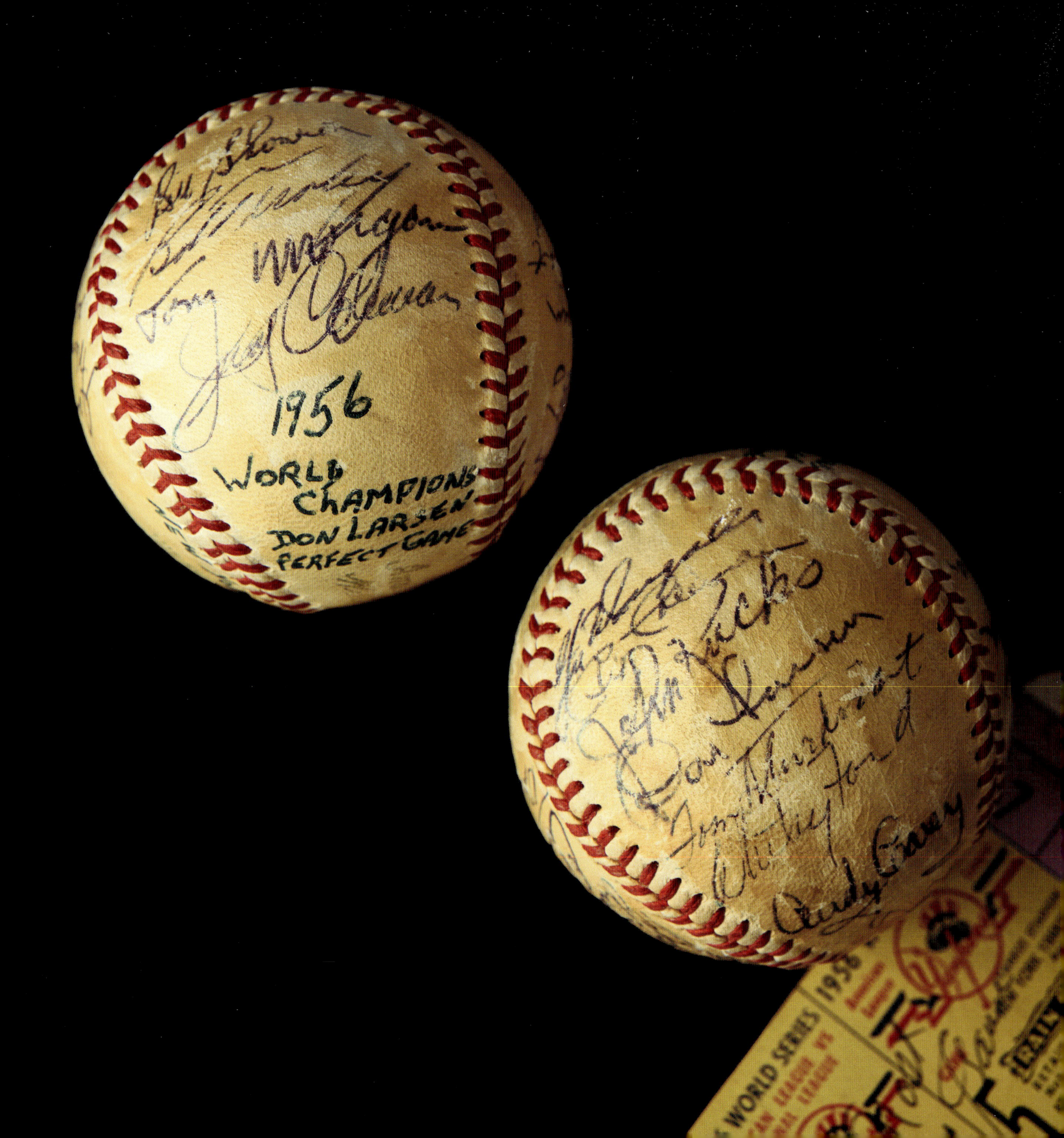
1956
WORLD
CHAMPIONS
DON LARSEN
PERFECT GAME
WORLD SERIES

DON LARSEN

"To whom it may concern: This baseball, autographed by myself and the rest of the 1956 New York Yankee team and coaching staff, which is owned by Frank Gorman, is a game ball from my perfect game victory over the Brooklyn Dodgers. It was signed by the team and myself in the clubhouse following the game and given to Mr. Gorman's grandfather for him, along with the team picture, which I also autographed."

This is a very, very significant baseball, a reminder of a phenomenally famous moment, because of the fact that there have been so few perfect games in the history of the game, let alone perfect games in a World Series. As described by Charles F. Faber on the SABR site, "It was a perfect day for a perfect game under a clear blue skies. 64,519 fans trooped into historic Yankee Stadium to witness a World Series contest between the two dominant teams of the era. The world champion Dodgers were facing a club that had won more World Series titles than any two clubs combined. Facing each other on the mound that day were two pitchers with vastly different career records. Brooklyn started Sal Maglie, who had 108 major league victories and only 49 losses for a sparkling .688 winning percentage. New York countered with Don Larsen, who had a record of 30-40, .429. [A *losing* percentage, note.] In 1956, Larsen had started Game Two for the Yankees and was knocked out of the box in the second inning. It is only natural that some of his teammates were *flabbergasted* that manager Casey Stengel elected to go with Larsen in Game Five."

The night before the pivotal game, even though Larsen didn't actually expect to pitch again in the Series, he told the sportswriter Arthur Richman, "I'm gonna beat those guys tomorrow. And I'm just liable to pitch a no-hitter." The next morning, he learned he was the starting pitcher....

Throwing mostly fastballs with some sliders and a few curves, he shut the Dodgers right out, walking not a single batter. "I never had such good control in all my life as I had in that game," he later said, "That was the secret to my success. I was throwing the ball right on the black of the plate." You can picture it: with him literally on the border all night, time after time those Dodger hitters would have had just a fraction of a second to decide if the pitch was going to be a ball or not, and time after time they fanned out.

You might say that the Dodgers' broadcaster Vin Scully was also right on the black when he said, "Ladies and gentlemen, it's the greatest game ever pitched in baseball history." And Larsen himself said, "When it was over, I was so happy, I felt like crying. I wanted to win this one for Casey. After what I did in Brooklyn, he could have forgotten about me. And who would blame him? But he gave me another chance. And I'm grateful." No hits, no walks: a perfect game, one of only three no-hitters in MLB postseason history, and the only perfect-game ball ever to be thrown in a World Series game. This is the ball, how cool is that? *And* it comes with a ticket from that game.

BILL LEE

IN THE OFTEN conservative world of professional baseball, Bill Lee was a wildly eccentric character. As Jim Prime writes on the Society for American Baseball Research website, "Lee was one of those rare ballplayers whose off-field persona overshadowed his significant on-field performance. In baseball parlance, Lee is known as a 'flake,' a term that includes anyone who doesn't give pat answers to pat questions or dares to admit to reading books without pictures. He was an original in a sport that frowns on any show of originality. In fairness, Lee would have been an eccentric in almost any field he chose to pursue. But in baseball, he was considered positively certifiable. [This] earned him the nickname 'Spaceman,' a title he never fully embraced, arguing that his first priority was always Mother Earth. Nevertheless, Lee's record speaks for itself and places in the company of some of the best pitchers in Red Sox history."

Bill's personality gave birth to an abundance of myths, including one where after a game the press were gathered around him in the locker room and a reporter asked, "Bill, how do you handle a tough loss?" And he said, "Well, I just roll myself a big fat joint and smoke it." Now, this was a time when you didn't say that kind of thing in public, *especially* if you were a baseball player. I don't know if that story's true, but I sure hope it is!

Anyway, Lee quit the Major Leagues on May 7th, 1982. In a fit of anger at his good friend, second baseman Rodney Scott, being released by the Expos (and a series of arguments with Montreal management prior to that), he took off his jersey, tore it in half, marched out of Olympic Stadium straight to the bar across the street, where he proceeded to drink some quantity of beer. This is the very jersey, and here's how I came to own it....

On tour with Rush in the 1980s, I was checking into a hotel in Pittsburgh when the friendly concierge came up to me and said, "Hey, you just missed the Colorado Rockies. Larry Walker checks into hotels under *your* name." (Funny, that. I used to use pseudonyms too, but the other way around. For the longest time I was Hank Greenberg.) Larry and I became friends not long after, and one time he called me and said, "I was just talking with Jim Fanning [the manager of the Expos the year Lee quit]. After that argument, he picked up Bill's jersey and he's kept it all these years. Jim's son is a Rush fan, they've heard about your collection, and they would love to offer it to you."

And I said, I'm abso-fucking-*lutely*. What an appropriately odd, quite fabulous bit of Expos history. After all, they were Canada's team, our first entry into the Major Leagues which we all loved dearly and then lost. Thinking about the Expos takes me back to the early Eighties when, I used to listen to Expos games on the radio between recording sessions at Le Studio in Quebec, a marvellous escape from the intensity of making those albums.

I've never collected things strictly for investment purposes. Although it's nice to think that in time some of these items will go up in value, it's not enough of a reason to buy a piece. A collector is driven by other things, and with baseball it's the fascination and respect for the achievements of the player that's makes it all irresistible. Even though I paid for this jersey (just a nominal fee), I consider it a gift, handed down from Jim Fanning via Larry Walker to me. It's not a thing you can put monetary value on, and I could never part with it.

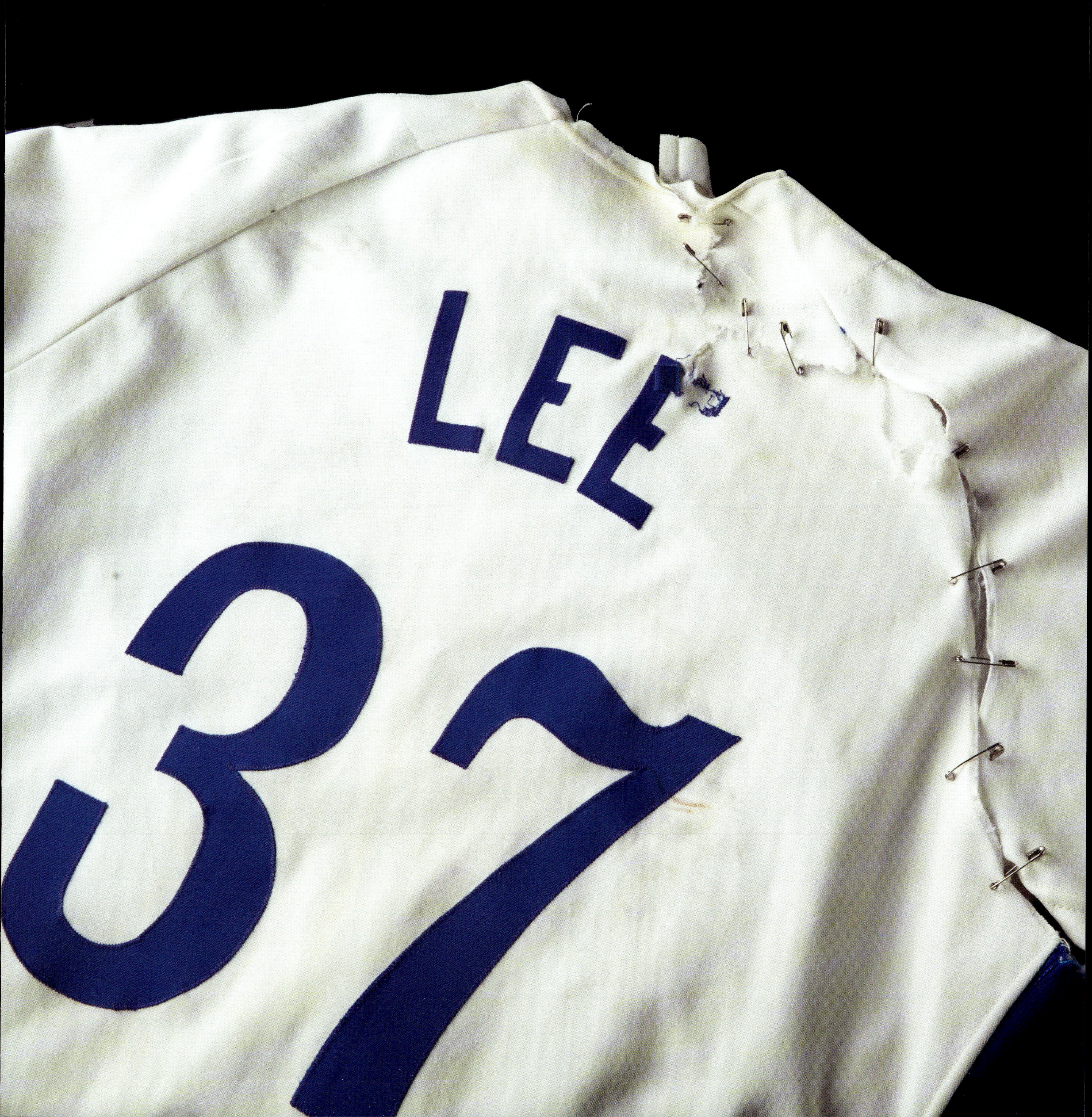
LEE
37

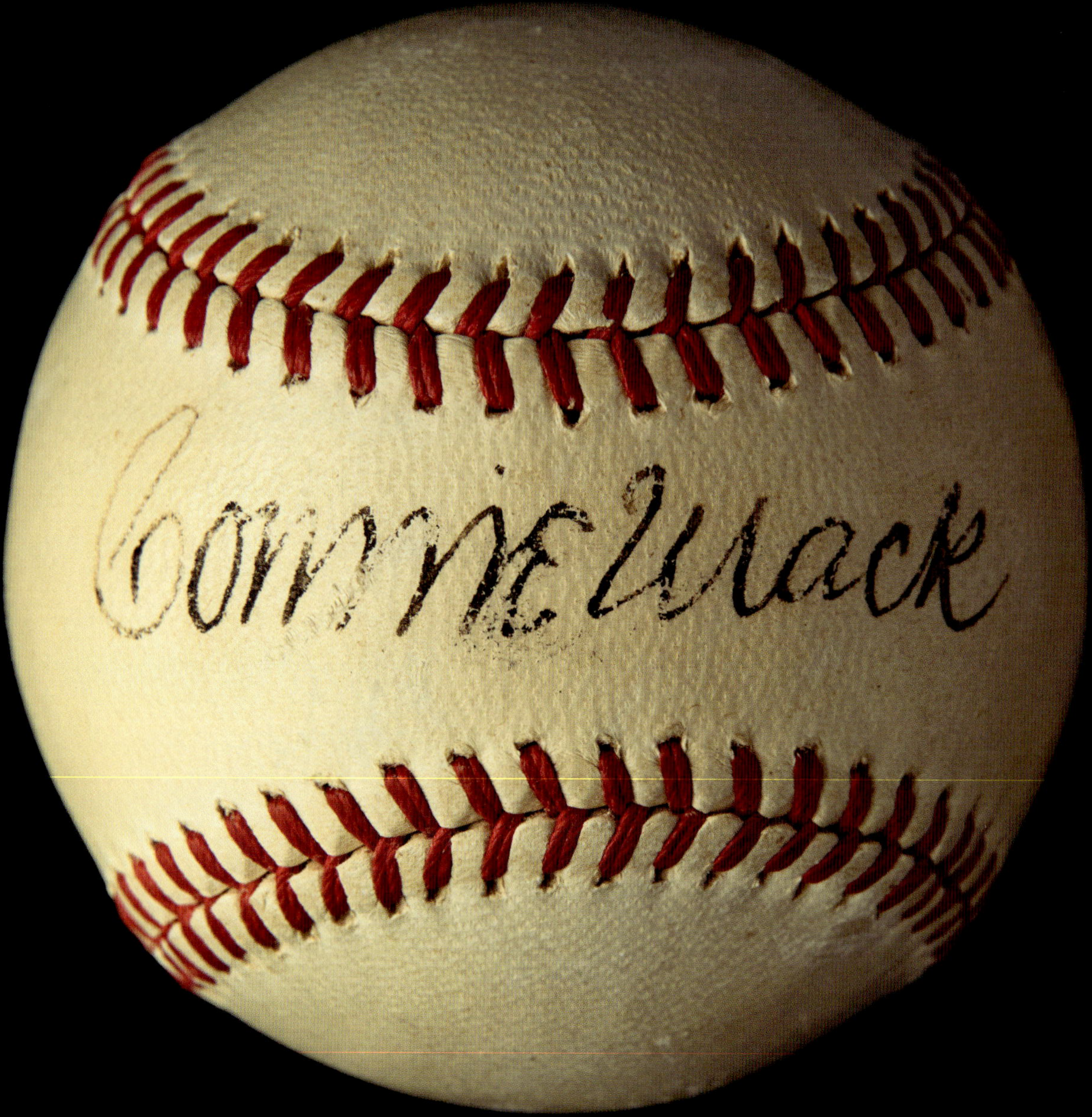
Connie Mack

CONNIE MACK

I DON'T THINK ANY baseball collector obsessed with the game's history should be satisfied without a Connie Mack signature. An old and authentic one like this is always worth the extra effort to seek out.

Cornelius McGillicuddy was the longest tenured manager in Major League history. Known as "The Tall Tactician," he was (according to Doug Skipper on SABR.org), "baseball's grand old gentleman for more than a generation. Statuesque, stately, and slim, he clutched a rolled-up scorecard as he sat or stood ramrod straight in the dugout, attired in a business suit rather than a uniform, a derby or bowler in place of a baseball cap. He carried himself with quiet dignity, and commanded the respect of friend and foe."

Even before I became fanatical about the game, I couldn't help but notice how Connie stood apart from his players in his high starched collar, the basic male attire at the turn of the century, long after it had become unfashionable. I liked that, and have always thought it's kind of unseemly for aging—or shall we say, "less than fit"—managers to be dressed in what really amounts to a pair of pyjamas. As far as I know, it's the only major sport where managers dress like their players. It's really a holdover from the old player-manager days, but still, I think the modern game could take a sartorial tip or two from Mr. Cornelius McGillicuddy.

He had a Hall of Fame career spanning sixty-five Major League seasons as player, manager, team executive and eventually owner. His career stats boast 3,731 wins—more than 1,000 over any other Major League manager. He was the first manager to win three World Series titles and the first to win consecutive titles twice. But it wasn't all champagne, as he lost more games than he won; a Major League record: 3,948. I guess that's what comes of being a manager for fifty years! He serves as a reminder of how every team has its peaks and valleys.

He spent most of his on-field career as a catcher with a reputation as a smart and cunning, if not particularly distinguished, player. He was one of the first to position himself directly behind home plate instead of in front of the backstop, and was adept at "tipping" bats—brushing them with his mitt "accidentally"; he'd mimic the sound of a foul tip; in one game, he intentionally dropped a popup and turned it into a triple play; "Mack never was mean," Wilbur Robinson once said, "but if you had any soft spot, Connie would find it. He could do and say things that got more under your skin than the cuss words used by other catchers."

As a manager, on the other hand, having seen many players destroy themselves and their teams through heavy drinking, he valued intelligence and "baseball smarts," and always looked for educated players, players with quiet and disciplined personal lives. (He traded away Shoeless Joe Jackson despite his talent because of his bad attitude and unintelligent play.) If you stopped to discuss the players or "Mackmen" who played for him, you'd be here all day; Rube Waddell, Eddie Plank, Christy Mathewson....

He was apparently one of the kindest, most soft-spoken of fellows, always insisting that he could get better results that way. There's a Major League Manager of the Year Award, which I don't think sounds very creative or distinguished. I would much prefer it be called the Connie Mack Award. He deserves that accolade.

MICKEY MANTLE

As a batter Mickey Mantle had immense power from both sides of the plate, hitting some of the longest home runs in baseball history. He had blazing speed and excelled in centre field. But his career was plagued by injuries. In his first year, he was groomed to be Joe DiMaggio's successor, but because Joe was still planted at centre, Mickey was pushed to the right. In the fifth inning of the second game of the 1951 World Series, when a fly ball was popped into the gap between the two players, Mantle instinctively went for it, but at the last second DiMaggio called him off. Mantle put on the brakes and caught his cleats in the outfield's underground sprinkler apparatus, spraining his knee. That put him out for the rest of the season, and though he went on to become one of the best players of all time, they say that had he never injured that knee, who knows how great he really *could* have been.

But the game I really want to talk about is Game 2 of the 1960 World Series, when Mantle hit two home runs in a Yankees 16-3 victory at Forbes Field.

First I acquired a bat. It came with a letter written to Mickey Mantle in October of 1991 by Tanya Terry, the wife of Mantle's good friend and pitcher for the New York Yankees, Ralph Terry, asking Mantle for a souvenir for someone they knew. Mantle gave them the bat. Anyway, the important thing is that she then printed up cards to verify that this was a bat he used in that World Series. They say, "I, Mickey Mantle certify that the bat in possession of J___ is authentic and is the bat used by Mickey Mantle in the 1960 World Series in Pittsburgh, hitting two home runs over the left field fence. [signed] Mickey Mantle, New York Yankees." Also, Ralph Terry verifies and signs a similar card. So it's all quite cute, very homespun, before the days of all the professional authenticators. These are the actual players involved in the gifting of this important bat.

Separately, I also had purchased a baseball hit by Mantle during the same game, but in the stupidity of my brain, I never made a connection between the two.

So, I'm looking through all this stuff that came with the ball that I bought at a Robert Edwards auction, including a newspaper article that shows the kid who caught the ball and a letter from a guy who, while doing machinery installation work in Pittsburgh, attended two World Series games that summer. For some reason he had to leave the second game at the start of the seventh inning, and he was walking around the field to his car just as Mantle stepped up to the plate. The crowd let out a huge roar—Mantle had hit a home run! As the letter goes: "A young boy retrieved the ball and as we passed him I held out a five-dollar bill and asked which he would rather have, the bill or the ball? A five-dollar bill to a boy of that age in '60 was a fortune, and he gladly accepted it...."

And so, both bat and ball sat in my collection for years, until one day I go, " Holy shit, did the great Mickey Mantle hit this ball for an historic W.S. home run with *this* very bat?" I don't think that's likely, but it makes a great story nonetheless, and both items do share the same Mickey Mantle 1960 World Series D.N.A. As baseball announcer Mel Allen would have said, "How about that?"

125
MADE IN U.S.A.
GENUINE
Mickey Mantle
LOUISVILLE SLUGGER
HOME RUN
BY MICKEY MANTLE
SECOND GAME WORLD
SERIES 1960 7TH
PITS PIRATES 3
NY YANKS 16

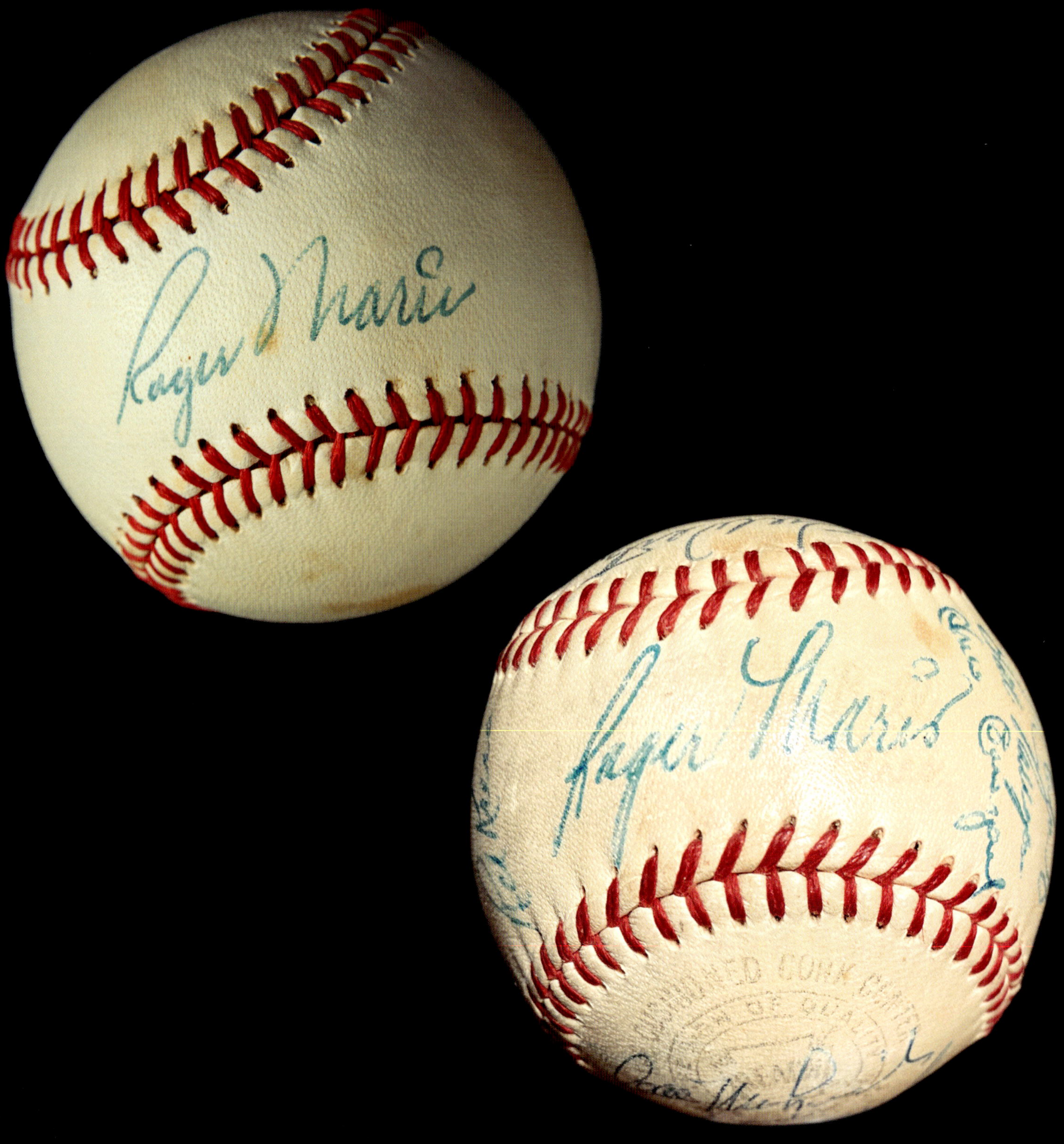
Roger Maris
Roger Maris

ROGER MARIS

WHEN I THINK of Roger Maris, I think back again to the Saturday afternoons of my childhood spent watching the Yankees play the Detroit Tigers on NBC's *Major League Game of the Week*. 1961, when I was eight years old, was a particularly exciting year, with Mickey Mantle and Roger Maris both challenging Babe Ruth's 34-year-old single-season record of 60 home runs. I remember collecting baseball cards, and how if you got one of "the M&M Boys," you were the coolest, but I was oblivious to what Maris was actually going through; it was only years later that I learned what a stressful pursuit it was for the poor man.

For a while, he and Mantle were one-on-one as they battled for the record, but when Mantle got hurt and taken out of the lineup, Maris was entirely unprepared for the media frenzy that engulfed him as he took centre stage. He wanted to be a ballplayer and not a celebrity, and in that way he reminds me of Neil Peart; he was a shy, quiet dude, a plain-spoken Midwesterner who didn't care for the spotlight, suddenly mobbed on the road, hounded everywhere, pestered by reporters, subjected to death threats from people who didn't want him to break the record, unable to even attend church in peace. He tried to hide from it all in the training room, but became anxious and short-tempered, had trouble sleeping and started losing his hair in clumps. Then, when he *did* break the record, he never really got his due because, as an asterisk in the record books always reminds us, the '61 season had 162 games, whereas Ruth's had only 154. Yet Maris's plate appearances only differed from The Babe's by a mere seven—a 1% differential. But Ford Frick's "distinctive mark"—his effin' asterisk—remains an unfair blight on his tremendous accomplishment. Oh, the minutiae of statistics!

His accomplishment was also somewhat overshadowed by a consequence of the Major League's expansion that year: the arrival of players who would likely not otherwise have made the cut, i.e., more meatballs for home run hitters to feast on. As Bill Pruden puts it on the SABR website, "It was soon apparent that the 1961 season was going to be remembered for an unprecedented explosion of hitting power, with New York at the centre of the fireworks." So, to me he's a heroic yet somewhat tragic figure. He reached heights that most players can only dream of, but was met at every turn with some sort of "Yeah, but....," which I think is pretty unfair. It's not that he wasn't fêted for his accomplishments—in '61 he won both his second MVP award and the Hickok Belt for most outstanding Professional Athlete of the Year—but after a stellar if relatively short career, he never made the Hall of Fame. I wonder if he really ever enjoyed the record he set.

OPPOSITE:

A 1957 Cleveland Indians team-signed baseball, with rookie Roger Maris signing on the sweet spot.

CHRISTY MATHEWSON

FROM THE *NEW* York Post: "Many years after he would accidentally inhale a poisonous dose of mustard gas during World War I and die too young, Christy Mathewson was remembered this way by Connie Mack, the legendary manager of the Philadelphia Athletics: "Mathewson was the greatest pitcher who ever lived. He had knowledge, judgment, perfect control and form. It was wonderful to watch him pitch...when he wasn't pitching against you."

According to Eddie Frierson on SABR.org (though I'm sure the family of Mordecai "Three-Finger" Brown would have something to say about this), "In the time when Giants walked the earth and roamed the Polo Grounds, none was more honored than Christy Mathewson. Delivering all four of his pitches, including his famous 'fadeaway' (now called a screwball), with impeccable control and an easy motion, the right-handed Mathewson was the greatest pitcher of the Deadball Era's first decade. In 1909 he went 25-6 with a career-best 1.14 ERA [that's *minuscule*—barely over a run for nine innings], helping the Giants win three consecutive NL pennants from 1911 to 1913, and leading the NL in ERA in both 1911 and 1913. He compiled a 2.13 ERA over seventeen seasons and set modern National League records for wins in a season."

Mathewson was a handsome, dapper, devout, college educated man who raised up the rowdy world of baseball to the league of gentlemen. For many he was the model of the idealized athlete, an inspiration to many authors over the years and even the subject of an off-Broadway play. In 1910 he wrote a lengthy treatise for the Colombian Magazine called *Base Ball: The National Game*, a rare copy of which I own, in which he made a critical assessment of the teams of the season, and featured photos of key players (including himself) sporting those old mitts that were basically a pile of cushion wrapped in calfskin, and a roundup of their coaches and fans: "Pittsburgh's rooters are freer with applause than Chicago's. Boston's fans are apathetic wonders. They sit there with a dazed 'I wonder what's going to happen' expression. Cincinnati fans are unreasonable. They cannot see why their team should lose a game. New York fans are very fair, broad-minded and appreciative...." (*Plus ça change?*)

After his playing retirement, "Matty" went on to manage the Cincinnati Reds, and at a time when greasing the palms of players was not uncommon, called out his own first baseman Hal Chase on some suspicious-looking misplays and a $50 payment to pitcher Jimmy Ring. This was right before the infamous 1919 World Series, which he covered for the *New York Times*, subsequently cementing his probity by reporting to the National Commission that he had seen Chase acting as a go-between for several White Sox players and a gambling syndicate.

This is an official game-used ball, the kind manufactured between 1919 and 1924, the somewhat rubbed-out words spelling "Spalding No.1 Cork Center Official National League." Due to its scarcity and, of course, his status, Mathewson's autograph is one of the most desirable around (he had elegant handwriting too!). In fact, most of the known Mathewson signatures are found on documents such as checks and contracts; after his death in 1925 by tuberculosis (the mustard gas connection is now in doubt), Mathewson's wife would sometimes send signed checks in response to those seeking old examples of his autograph through the mail.

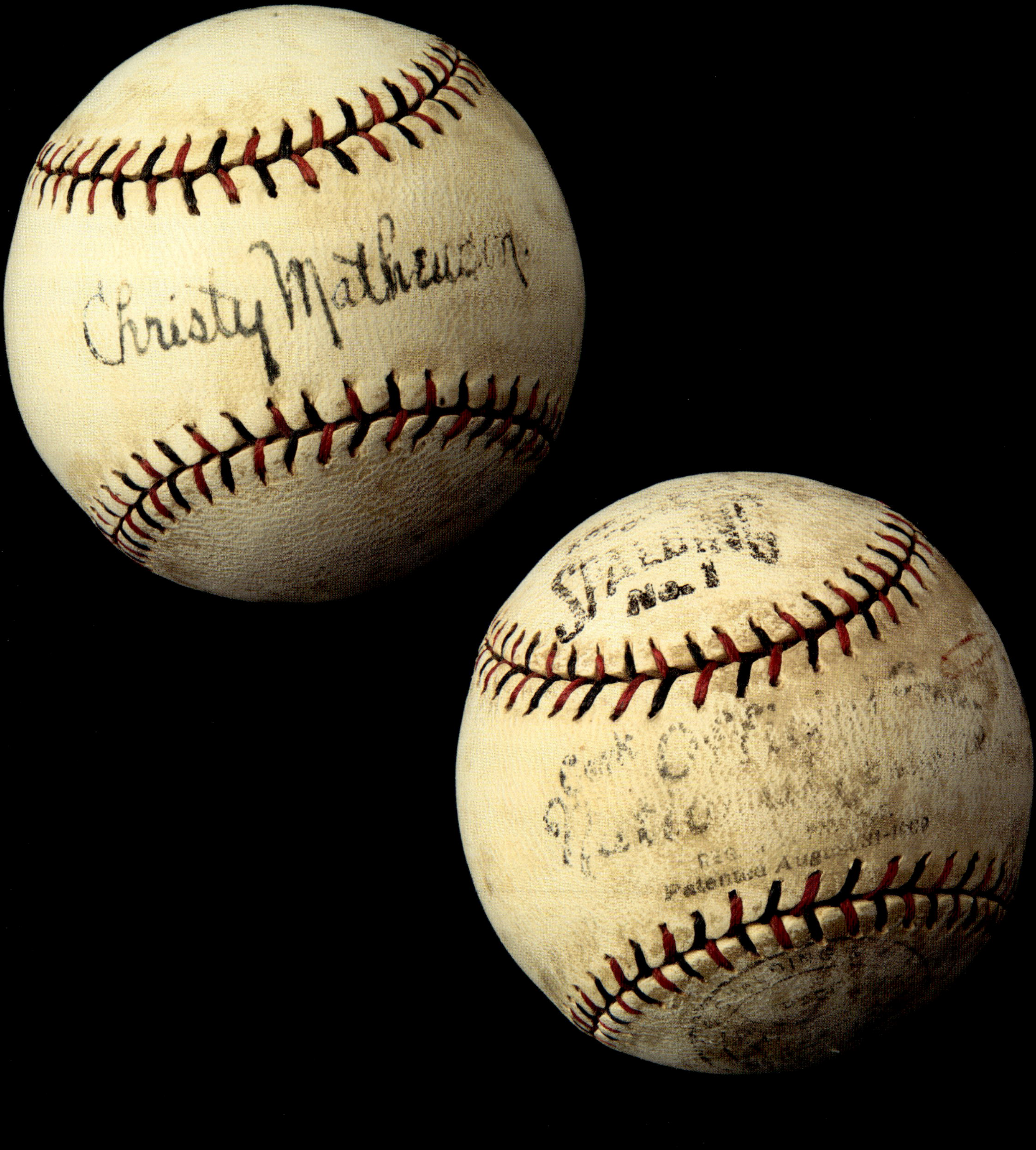
Christy Mathewson

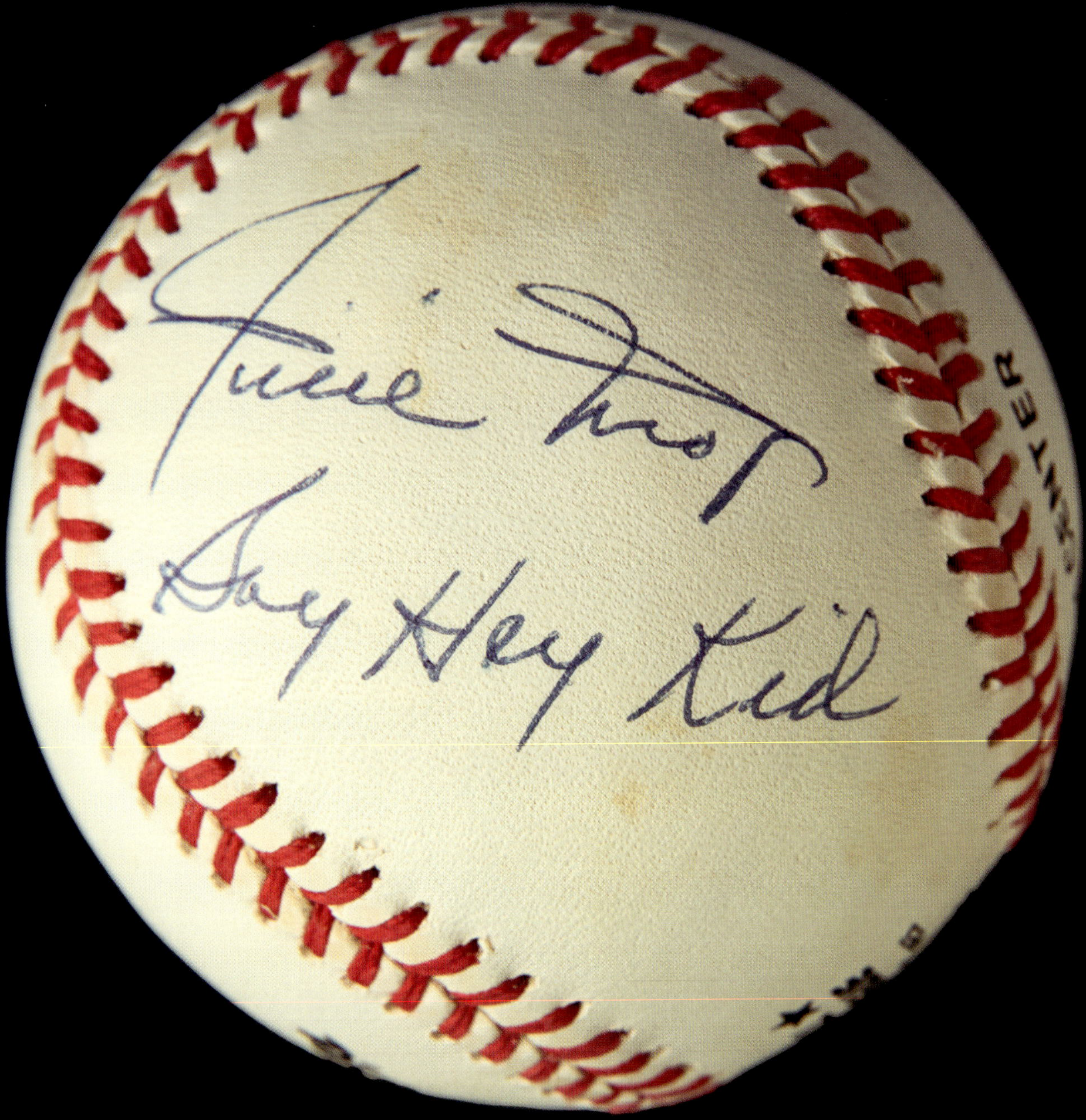
Willie Mays
Say Hey Kid

WILLIE MAYS

WILLIE MAYS' AUTOGRAPH is not rare, because he's so contemporary and was such an affable guy—he signed for everybody—but I love that he signed this one "Say Hey Kid." According to some, he earned his nickname from his habit of uttering, "Say who?," "Say what?," "Say where?" and "Say hey!" but for the record, that's likely an embellishment (he did apparently say "Hey!" with regularity, as well as pitch in some vocals on The Treniers' 1954 "Say Hey," but that's about it). But an account of his playing career requires no embellishment at all. He was, quite simply, one of the best outfielders of all time.

His over-the-shoulder catch off of Vic Wertz's bat in the 1954 World Series—since known simply as "The Catch"—is surely the most famous defensive play in baseball history, but it was just one of a record-setting 7,095 he made in his career, many of them with his glove resting nonchalantly at his hip instead of in front of his face like every other outfielder. Sportswriters have opined as to whether his technique made him a better fielder or simply made him more exciting to watch. His patented "basket catch" had its origins in his time with the Chattanooga Choo-Choos, the farm team for the Birmingham Black Barons in the Negro Leagues, and like Satchel Paige he considered himself something of an entertainer, deliberately slipping to the ground for catches to make them look tougher than they really were, and wearing his cap one size too big so it would fly off when he was running the bases. "My job," he said, "was to give the fans something to talk about each game."

I don't know if many people realize that he was a Negro League player, albeit just briefly in the late 1940s, since the MLB was already integrated then, and he was signed to the Major Leagues pretty quickly. Leo Durocher says in his book *Nice Guys Finish Last* that the Giants' scout Eddie Montague discovered him, reporting back, "They got a kid playing centre field practically barefooted that's the best ballplayer I ever looked at. You better send somebody down there with a barrelful of money and grab this kid."

"If somebody came up and hit .450, stole 100 bases, and performed a miracle in the field every day," Durocher also wrote, "I'd still look you right in the eye and tell you that Willie was better. He could do the five things you have to do to be a superstar: hit, hit with power, run, throw and field. And he had the other magic ingredient that turns a superstar into a super Superstar. Charisma. He lit up a room when he came in. He was a joy to be around."

Mays played six years in New York and fourteen more in Frisco—a very long time with one single team—before being traded to the Mets in 1972, taking him back to his New York roots. In his first game at Shea Stadium, he put the team ahead against the Giants with a fifth-inning home run, receiving ecstatic applause from the fans, but by then his skills were already diminishing, and he only played one more season. No matter. In his prime he was an incredible player: 660 career home runs, a .301 batting average (only he, Hank Aaron and Eddie Murray have 500 homers and 3,000 hits), his OPS 0.940: numbers completely deserving of his induction into the Hall of Fame in 1979, yet some baseball writers failed to vote for him, inducing outrage from *New York Daily News* sportswriter Dick Young who wrote, "If Jesus Christ were to show up with his old baseball glove, some guys wouldn't vote for him. He dropped the cross three times, didn't he?"

JOHN MCGRAW

HERE'S ANOTHER LARGER than life character from baseball's early days. According to Don Jensen at SABR.org, "John McGraw was perhaps the National League's most influential figure in the Deadball era." From 1902 to 1932, he led the New York Giants to ten National League pennants, three World Series championships, and twenty-one first or second place finishes.

Like his contemporary Connie Mack, McGraw came from an Irish immigrant family. He made his Major League debut in 1891 with the Baltimore Orioles (then in the American Association), hitting .270 in thirty-three games. He'd soon become the National League's best leadoff hitter, batting over .320 for nine straight years. However, as one reporter wrote, "McGraw uses every low and contemptible method that his erratic brain can conceive to win a play by a dirty trick." He was known to grab opposing base runners' belts and even tackle players on the field. (For sure it was a much dirtier game back then, but you have to remember that they were fighting for their livelihoods back then. These weren't wealthy or even middle-class players. Unlike Major Leaguers nowadays, if you got cut or lost too many games, you could be left unable to feed your family. Like the Mafia used to say, *Don't mess with a man's living.*)

"His fiery personality made him fascinating to contemporaries outside sports" (Jensen continues). "Gamblers, show-business people, and politicians were drawn to him. As his celebrity grew, he became involved in various, sometimes questionable off-field activities, venturing into vaudeville, appearing with such acts as 'Odiva the Goldfish Lady' and purchasing a poolroom in Manhattan with gambler Arnold Rothstein, who later became the principal financial backer of the 1919 World Series fix."

He was pugnacious (as you might expect someone with a rough-and-tumble name like McGraw to be!). As a player he was nicknamed "Muggsy"; as manager, "Little Napoleon": he monitored his teams strictly, imposing an 11:30pm curfew when on the road, watching the players' diet, fining them for hanging out with opponent players and frowning on smiles in the dugout. All in all, he was ejected from a hundred and eighteen games—a career record until the great Bobby Cox (for a short while the Blue Jays' manager) surpassed him in 2007. The Giants' coach Arlie Latham said, "McGraw eats gunpowder every morning for breakfast and washes it down with warm blood." (My god, those guys were nothing if not inventive with language! I don't think you ever hear such colourful talk in the modern game; today it's mostly safe, routine sound bites, except of course for the occasional social media faux pas.)

He was a proponent of Inside Baseball—strategy and guile, an emphasis on stealing bases, suicide squeeze, hit and run and so on; in short, *manufacturing* runs. But he also evolved; he considered small ball far more interesting than the Power Game (the formula that fifty years later the Orioles' great Earl Weaver would sum up as, "Pitching, defence . . . and three-run homers") but was flexible enough to beef his lineups up with sluggers, and though he never led the Giants to victory after 1923, he fielded some excellent teams in his final years, before his resignation in 1932. In the end, his 2,763 managerial victories were second only to Connie Mack's 3,731. Mack, ever the gentleman, said, "There has only been one manager, and his name is McGraw."

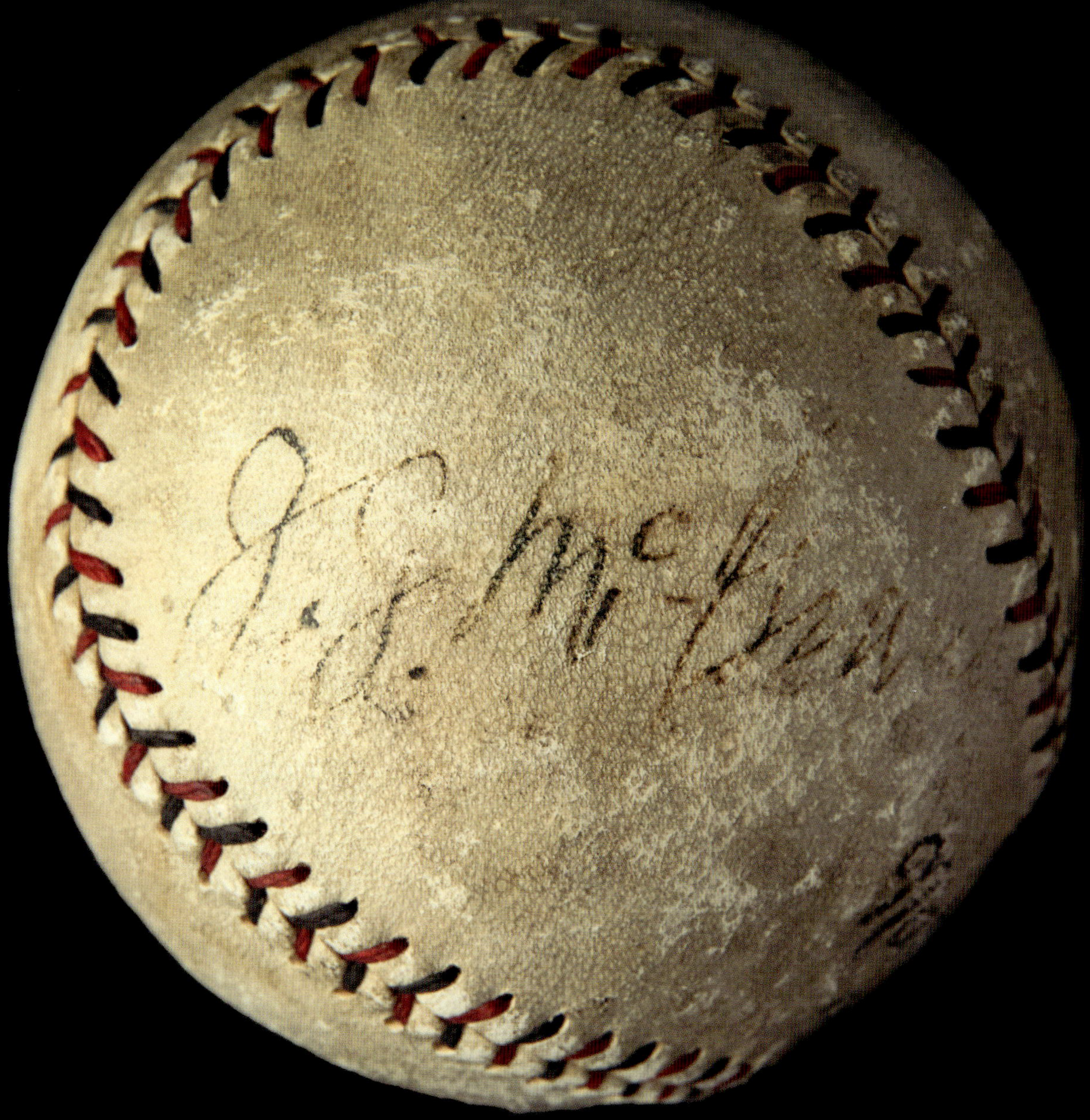

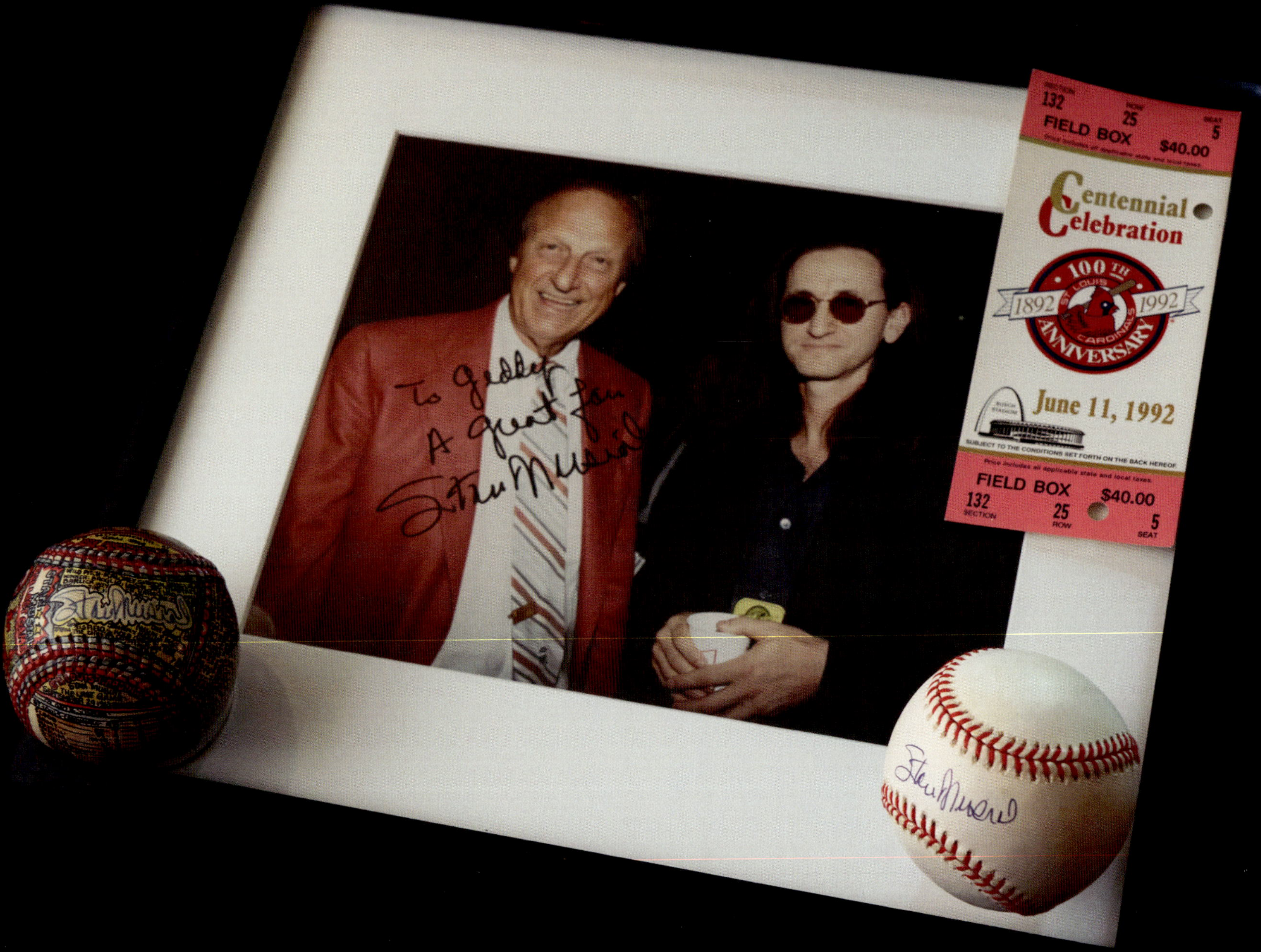
To Geddy
A great fan
Stan Musial
SECTION 132
ROW 25
SEAT 5
FIELD BOX
$40.00
Centennial
Celebration
100TH
1892
1992
ST. LOUIS CARDINALS
ANNIVERSARY
June 11, 1992
BUSCH STADIUM
SUBJECT TO THE CONDITIONS SET FORTH ON THE BACK HEREOF.
Price includes all applicable state and local taxes.
FIELD BOX
$40.00
132 SECTION
25 ROW
5 SEAT

STAN MUSIAL

COMPETING WITH MY school chums to collect baseball cards, having a Stan Musial was tip top. We didn't get many National League games on TV in Toronto—usually just a playoff game or *This Week in Baseball* with Mel Allen (*"How about that?"*), but we understood that he was equal to Mickey Mantle over in the American League. That speaks well of the man, because by the time we were playing "Leansies" and "Closies" in the schoolyard, Mantle and Maris and Koufax were legendary but still youthful while Musial had already retired. I now have a number of Musial-signed items, including a uniform (not game-played but signed); and this Sosnak-illustrated ball is one of the busiest you'll ever find, so packed with biographical information and statistics on it that there's barely any free space remaining.

He's a legend in St. Louis (one of my favourite places in America to play music and to watch baseball, by the way; whenever the Jays get knocked out of the running, I look to the National League and root for the Cardinals. The fans there are really knowledgeable, the people the friendliest on earth; if you ever find yourself stranded on a desert island with someone, cross your fingers that it's with someone from the Midwest!). His career numbers are stunning: .331 lifetime batting average, .417 on-base percentage, .559 slugging percentage, 3,630 hits, 725 doubles, 177 triples, 475 home runs, 1,949 runs and 1,951 RBIs... He's the only player to finish his career in the top twenty-five in *all* of these categories. Furthermore, he had 1,815 hits at home and 1,815 hits on the road—a feat, says Jan Finkel of SABR.org, "that must have required years of planning." No kidding! Many players' home numbers outweigh their road ones, but he was the same hitter wher*ever* he played.

Paul Warburton, writing in the *Baseball Research Journal*, describes Musial's stance vividly: "A lefty, he dug in with his left foot on the back line of the batter's box, and assumed a closed stance with his right foot about twelve inches in front of his left. He took three or four practice swings and followed up with a silly-looking hula wiggle to help him relax. He crouched, stirring his bat like a weapon in a low, slow-moving arc away from his body. As the pitcher let loose with his fling, 'The Man' would quickly cock his bat in a steady position and twist his body away from the pitcher so that he was concentrating at his adversary's delivery out of the corner of his deadly keen eyes. He would then uncoil with an explosion of power. His line drives were bullets."

I wonder if anyone before Musial was ever called Stan the Man. Was it always a nickname for *any*one named Stan? (I mean, I call my dog Stanley "Stan the Man.") Well, I know you can't trust everything online, but the Wikipedia entry for *Stan the Man (nickname)* has Musial as its earliest incidence. Another curious thing about his name is that when I was a kid I thought it had a consonant missing; I seriously reckoned it ought to be *Musical*. Then many years later, courtesy of my pal, Cardinals pitcher Bryn Smith, I received an invitation to the 100th anniversary celebration of the St. Louis Cardinal franchise, where "Smitty" introduced me to a few of the greats, including Musial himself. He not only turned out to be full of pepper, one of the funniest, spryest, most jovial chaps I've met, availing himself from time to time of a secret flask in the form of a see-through acrylic screw top on his cane, but as we were talking, he pulled a harmonica from his pocket and started playing it. Aha! So Stan Musial *was* Musical after all.

ODDBALLS

WHAT CAN I really say about this one? I mean, there are a number of balls in my collection that are kind of goofy and, you might say, of iffy historical value—balls I'm drawn to mainly because they're *funny*. Monica Lewinsky and Bill Clinton on the same baseball: that's high comedy to me, in the same way my Mickey Mantle ball that says, "Happy Hanukkah" is funny, or the one after an argument over a play, on which he wrote, "He was safe, asshole." They're unique and put a smile on my face every time I look at them. Basically, whether or not they're within the confines of serious baseball ephemera, I'm always drawn to the balls with a *story*. I love quirks like these, the jokes from without and within, even the things that really have no business coming to baseball (except that at least one doctoral thesis has been written that makes a claim for Clinton's importance to baseball: *Bill Clinton at the church of baseball: the presidency, civil religion and the national pastime in the 1990s*, by Chris Birkett, King's College London, which argues "that by instrumentalising baseball as an expression of American civil religion Clinton sought to validate his leadership at times of scandal, even while his critics summoned the same civil religious symbolism to question his moral fitness for office." So it's not *all* jokes).

Anyway, I don't know what the story of this ball is, but we *all* know the *back*story. And, by the way, I have no particular political perspective on either the Clinton/Lewinsky scandal *or* the ball, but when people look at it, I like to ask them, "Who do you think signed it first?"

It's the same with several others I have, such as the three balls signed by teammates of Babe Ruth after a particularly combative Game 3 of the 1932 World Series between the Yankees and the Cubs, when both teams and members of the audience exchanged jibes, jeers, insults and a raft of rude gestures. One of the great Babe Ruth myths, known as "the called shot," arose from this game. Supposedly, while standing at the plate, he pointed to the outfield indicating where he was going to hit a home run—and hit that ball to *that very spot*. According to Joe Williams, the *New York World-Telegram*'s provocative columnist, "In the fifth, with the Cubs riding him unmercifully from the bench, Ruth pointed to center and punched a screaming liner to a spot where no ball had been hit before." Well, the three baseballs I have, signed by his teammates at the time, dispute the story....

On one of them, outfielder Ben Chapman wrote, "Babe did not call his shot!! Period."; shortstop Frank Crosetti signed, "The Babe did not point to center field – he put one finger up meaning he had one more strike left"; and third baseman Woody English maintained, "Babe Ruth did not call his home run – pointing to the pitcher saying that's only two strikes."

I love this trio, a contribution to one of innumerable arguments, the legendary moments that make baseball so vibrant and alive. I keep them displayed together surrounding a little Hartland statue of The Babe holding his bat out and pointing to centre field. Yes, folks, baseball can be funny too!

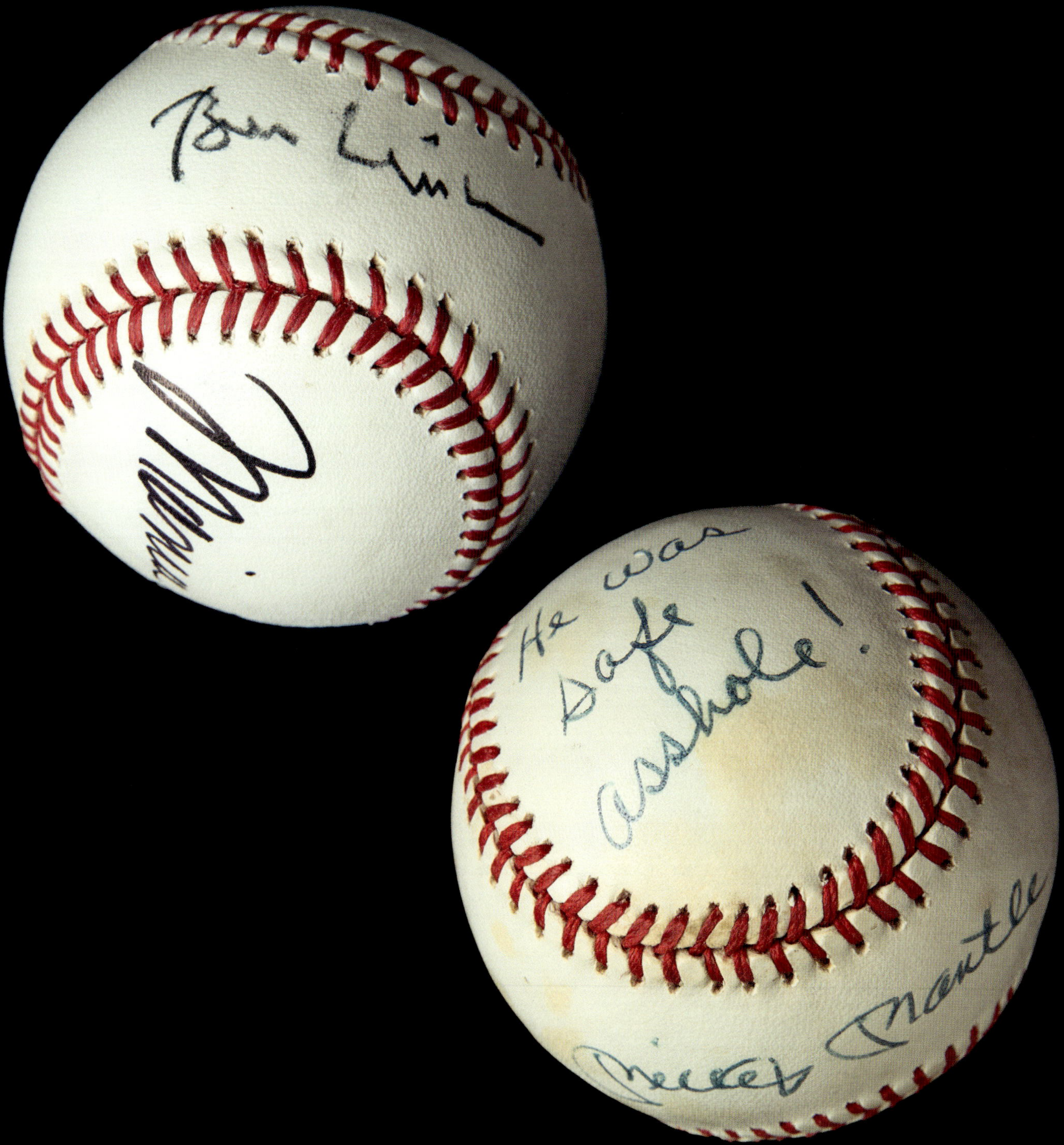

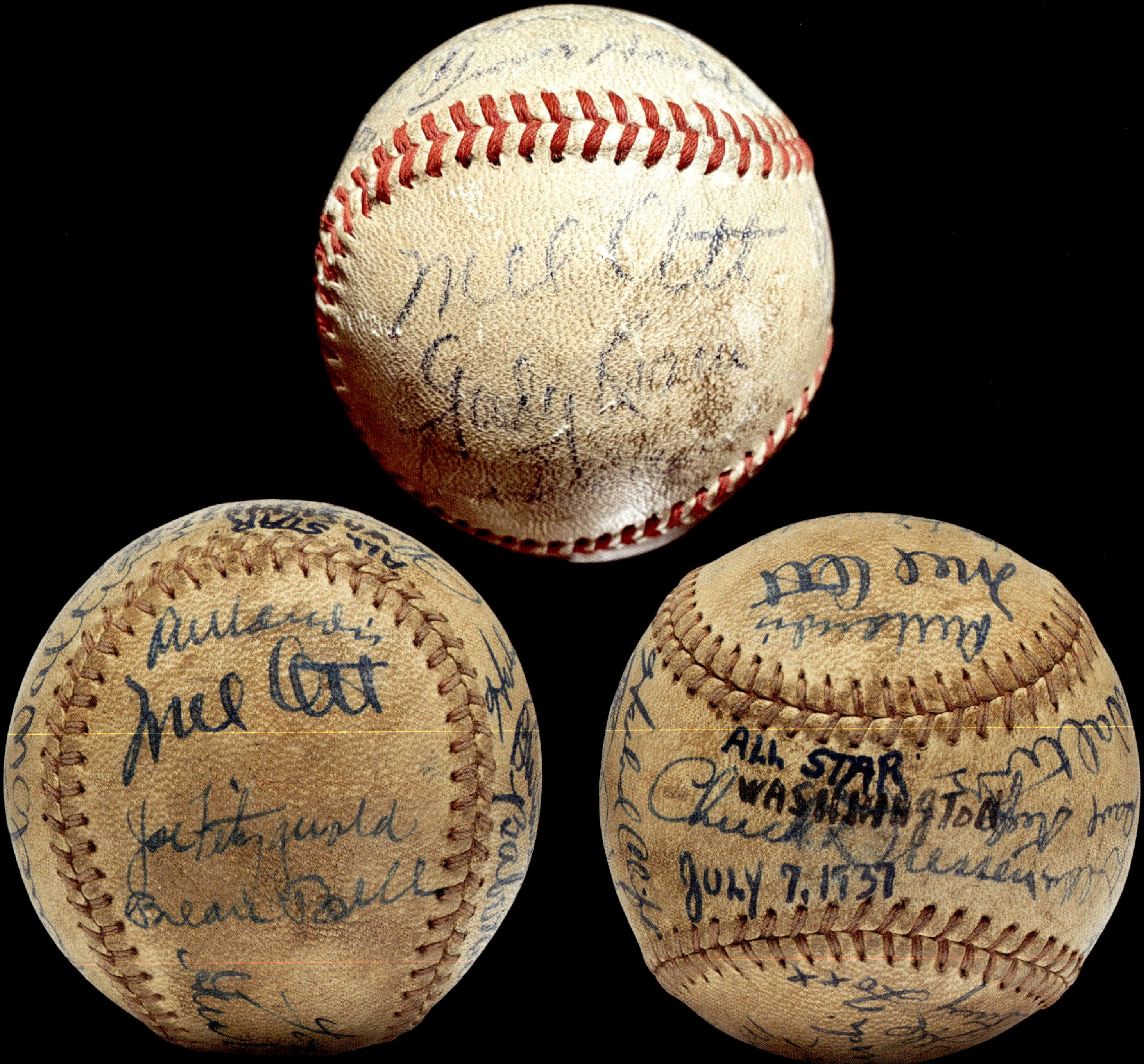
ALL STAR
WASHINGTON
JULY 7, 1937

MEL OTT

THE PEOPLE *LOVED* Mel Ott. "He was one of the most popular men ever to play the game," writes Fred Stein on SABR.org. "In 1938, when he shifted between right field and third base, a cereal company ran a contest to determine the most popular major league player at each position. Mel received the most votes for *both*. And despite the Giants' awful season in 1943, his popularity with the fans remained undiminished. *Sport Magazine* named him Sports Father of the Year. In a nationwide vote by war bond buyers in 1944, he was selected as the most popular sports hero of all time, beating out Babe Ruth, Lou Gehrig, Christy Mathewson, Joe Louis and Jack Dempsey."

That's pretty elite company for a guy who's not talked about very often anymore, but at the time he had 511 career home runs, over 200 more than any other national leaguer, and a total exceeded only by Babe Ruth and Jimmy Fox. "His life," Stein continues, "is a classic rags-to-riches story of a naive, unheralded, teenager from a small Southern town who rose to great heights in New York, the country's largest and most forbidding city at the time."

What's most interesting to me is how the New York Giants' manager John McGraw first put the seventeen year-old Ott on the Major League roster as an apprentice instead of having him cut his teeth in the minors. (It puts me in mind of Jimmie Foxx, who went pro at *six*teen.) These days, we think it remarkable when a twenty- or twenty-one-year-old phenom gets called up, but here was a teenager the owners felt was so promising that he'd best learn by sitting on the end of the bench just *watching* the game and listening to McGraw's cuss-filled sermons on the mound.

1929 was his breakthrough season. He had career highs in doubles, home runs, RBIs, runs scored and slugging percentage. His 42 homers and 151 RBIs are the most ever for players twenty or younger when the season began. He proved to be a first-rate right fielder too, expertly playing caroms off the Polo Ground's tricky right field wall, with an impressive 26 outfield assists. (He never matched that in subsequent years, after baserunners realised how risky it was to advance on balls hit in the "rifle-armed" Ott's direction.)

When McGraw first saw Ott's batting style, he called it "the most natural swing I've seen in years." The shortstop Alvin Dark said that he "lifted his lead foot right off the ground like he was getting ready to kick out a dog." Since then, many players, like Sadaharu Oh, Harold Baines and Kirby Puckett, have adopted Ott's foot-lift thing, but back then it was highly unorthodox. Meanwhile, 63% of his 511 career home runs were achieved at home, and have historically been downplayed because the foul line at the Polo Grounds was so short, running only 257 feet. In yet another sign of the casual racism that pervaded baseball back then, sportswriters jokingly referred to Ott as the master of the "Chinese home run"—what they used to call short homers. Ott liked to respond that if it was *that* easy, all the other hitters in the league would be doing it too.

(*À propos de rien*, Ott was born in Gretna, Louisiana, which is funny to me because "Gretna" was a nonsense word we invented for the members-only Rush lexicon, meaning a Canadian dollar—which, you see, wasn't worth as much as an American dollar and, we decided, not deserving to be called one at all. We'd never heard of the actual place!)

The 1946 Giants are the original subject of the phrase "nice guys finish last," a condensation of a reference to them by Leo Durocher of the Brooklyn Dodgers. The original quote by Durocher was "The nice guys are all over there, in seventh place"—seventh, of course, being last in the National League.

SATCHEL PAIGE

ON TOUR IN the early Eighties, I had Satchel Paige's "How to Keep Young" printed out and affixed to my dressing room case amongst photos of friends and drawings from my kids, signed baseball cards, etc., and it travelled with me right through to 2015:

1. *Avoid fried meats which angry up the blood.*
2. *If you stomach disputes you, lie down and pacify it with cool thoughts.*
3. *Keep the juices flowing by jangling around gently as you move.*
4. *Go very light on the vices, such as carrying on in society. The social ramble ain't restful.*
5. *Avoid running at all times.*
6. *Don't look back. Something might be gaining on you.*

Paige claimed not to know his own age—that a goat "ate the Bible with the birth certificate in it." As Larry Tye on SABR.org tells it, "Paige's record in the big leagues of just 28-31, with a 32.9 earned run average [sounds] mediocre until you consider he was forty-two years old when he started, and fifty-nine years, two months, eight days when he ended it with the Athletics in 1965." Six years later, he was inducted into the Hall of Fame—the first old-time Negro Leaguer to make the grade. The stories about him are the stuff of legend:

- Growing up in Mobile, Alabama, he worked as a deliveryman, porter and shoe polisher. Calculating that ten cents a day would never make a living, he built a contraption from rope and a pole so he could sling several satchels all at once, quadrupling his income. One of the other baggage boys quipped, "You look like a walking satchel tree!" and the description stuck (although Larry Tye, author of *Satchel: The Life and Times of an American Legend*, writes, "His buddy Wilbur Hines tells a slightly different story, which is rather than lugging suitcases, Satchel was filching them and that he, Wilbur, dubbed him Satchel for *that* reason").
- Sometime during the war years, Satchell streamlined the spelling of his name, dropping the extra L and becoming "Satchel." Conversely, I first spelled my adopted nickname as "Gedy"; by the time I legally changed it from Gary, I had added a second "d," cuz I thought "Geddy" just looked cooler.
- He learned to pitch in reform school, after being arrested for shoplifting, later saying, "You might say I traded five years of freedom to learn how to pitch."
- Armed with a personal phrasebook as extensive as his technique, he gave his pitches such names as "Bat Dodger," "Thoughtful Stuff," "Long Tom," and "Bee-Ball" (and as he grew older), "Midnight Creeper," "Wobbly Ball" and "Whipsy-Dipsy-Do"—plus his inimitable "Hesitation Pitch," involving a mid-pitch pause to fool batters into swinging early—which his opponents complained about so much that it was made illegal.
- Like Rube Waddell, one of his favourite moves was to pull in his outfielders and then single-handedly strike out the other side.
- In a Negro League World Series game in 1942, he intentionally walked two batters so he could face the great power hitter Josh Gibson with the bases loaded; after telling Gibson where he intended to land each throw, he struck him out in three pitches.
- By his own reckoning, he threw 100 no-hitters (which, given that Nolan Ryan's Major League record is a mere seven, we must take with a grain of salt) and 2,000 wins.

This ball is inscribed, "Best wishes . . . to Don." Some people don't like it when autographs are personalised, but for me it brings the act of signing to life. And no, I don't know who "Don" was, but I still like it because if you're going to do a *fake*, you're definitely not gonna put "Best wishes to Don" on it!

Best wishes
from
Satchel Paige
To
Don

ROBBIE SURE HAD THAT FAST ONE TODAY
THE BRAVES NEVER HAD A
18
AB 3
R 0
H 1
RBI 0
BB 2
1
BB-2
AB. 4
R 0
H. 2
R.B.I. 1
EBBETS FIELD
BROOKLYN
27

ROBIN ROBERTS

ROBIN ROBERTS IS not a name that springs readily to mind, but he was really one of the greats of his era. While pitching for Philadelphia from 1952 to '55, he was the National League's top right-hand pitcher. Later, according to C. Paul Rogers III on the SABR website, he was "a crafty veteran who had a remarkable resurgence with the Baltimore Orioles. Either way, he would go out, take his turn on the mound without saying a word, and throw strikes. The standing joke was that Andy Seminick and Stan Lopata, who caught Roberts with the Phillies, always took their rocking chairs with them when Roberts was pitching, in testament to his outstanding control.

"Roberts did not try to finesse the hitters; he dared them to hit the ball. When there were men on base, he reached back and burned the corners for strikes. Roberts' slow, deliberate windup and delivery was so fluid that hitters could not wait for the pitch to come. It looked so easy; then the ball would explode over the plate, astonishing the hitters. 'He's so close, you gotta watch him like an eagle,' said umpire Jocko Conlan. Hall of Famer Red Schoendienst once remarked that Roberts' fastball 'seemed to skid across the strike zone as though it were on a sheet of ice.'"

He was a control pitcher. He didn't walk guys. When they say you've got a flame-throwing pitcher who can throw 100 miles an hour or more, usually they're a little wild; a control pitcher who can throw a number of pitches—four-seam fastball, two-seam fastball, slider changeup—knows exactly where the ball is going. Roberts was that, and also one of the last of a breed of pitchers who completed ballgames. Very few pitchers go nine innings anymore; no more than six, or even five, but in 1953 Roberts completed a remarkable twenty-eight games in a row, which is an incredible feat by any standard. He led the league in innings five times. In 1953, he pitched 346 and two-thirds innings. From 1953 to 1955, he averaged 323 innings, pitched twenty-seven complete games, while winning twenty or more games each year.

These game-used balls are mostly from 1952 and 1953. I was interested in them because I was born in 1953—and of course, one of the collectors' conceits is that we tend to be obsessed with anything related to our birthdate. I believe they were painted by his battery-mate, the Phillies' Stan Lopata. The one with the 27 on it represents an astounding twenty-seven wins that year—final outs. The one with number 1 on it was his first win in, as I said, the year of my birth. They straddle the line between symbols of greatness and true folk-art.

JACKIE ROBINSON

THESE TWO ITEMS comprise my wee homage to Jackie Robinson—as everyone knows, the first Black player to play in the Major Leagues... As Rick Swaine has it on the SABR website, "Jackie Robinson is perhaps the most historically significant baseball player ever, ranking with Babe Ruth in terms of his impact on the national pastime. Ruth changed the way baseball was played; Jackie Robinson changed the way Americans thought. When Robinson took the field for the Brooklyn Dodgers on April 15th, 1947, more than 60 years of racial segregation in Major League baseball came to an end."

Here's a hat that Jackie wore while playing for the Dodgers. It was my friend, mentor and curator of my collection, J.W. Jones at The Legacy, Kansas City's now defunct sports memorabilia store, who found it for sale. He called my wife Nancy behind my back and said, "I know Geddy's birthday is coming up. I think he would love this." So she purchased it and gave it to me as a gift. Now, here I am, turning around and selling the gift she gave me (busted!), yet with my home filled to the brim with so many fascinating things from my various collections, I've decided it's time to set some gems free for other collectors to enjoy.

The ball on the right of the cap has a story....

At the time I purchased it, it was the only known documented Jackie Robinson home run baseball. According to its letter of authenticity, "This is a ball that Jackie Robinson hit for a home run to win the game. On Sunday, May 7th, 1950, The Pittsburgh Pirates were hosts to the Brooklyn Dodgers at Forbes Field. The score was tied 2-2 at the top of the sixth. Jackie Robinson stepped onto the plate to face Pirates hurler Murray Dickson, and with an 0-1 count Robinson crushed the next pitch for a solo home run. The game winning dinger. As fate would have it, the Dodgers held on for a 3-2 victory. It was his ninth home run of the season."

The ball was hit to left field where the bullpen was located, an area then called Greenberg Gardens, after Hank Greenberg (when he retired, the area was changed to Kiner's Korner after the great hitter, Ralph Kiner). As the story goes, the Pirates' coach Lenny Levy retrieved it, kept it, annotated it, and later handed it down to his nephew Tommy, who eventually sold it... which is how it made its home in my collection for many years. So, although this ball does not bear Robinson's signature, it is nonetheless a stunning relic of historic interest.

I didn't think of this at the time we took these photos, but I should have also included my signed first edition copy of Jackie Robinson's autobiography, *My Own Story*, as well as a beautiful team-signed ball (Robinson included) from 1946, after he'd inked his Montreal Royals contract with the great Branch Rickey. Jackie made his Brooklyn Dodgers debut in 1947, soon followed by another brilliant Rickey signing: catcher Roy Campanella, who would go on to become the National League's MVP three times before his playing career was tragically cut short in 1957 by an automobile accident.

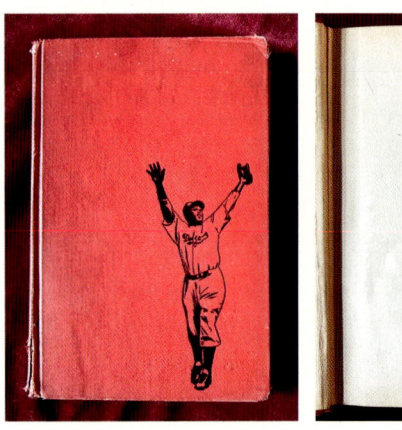

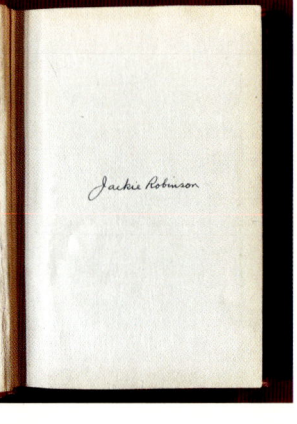

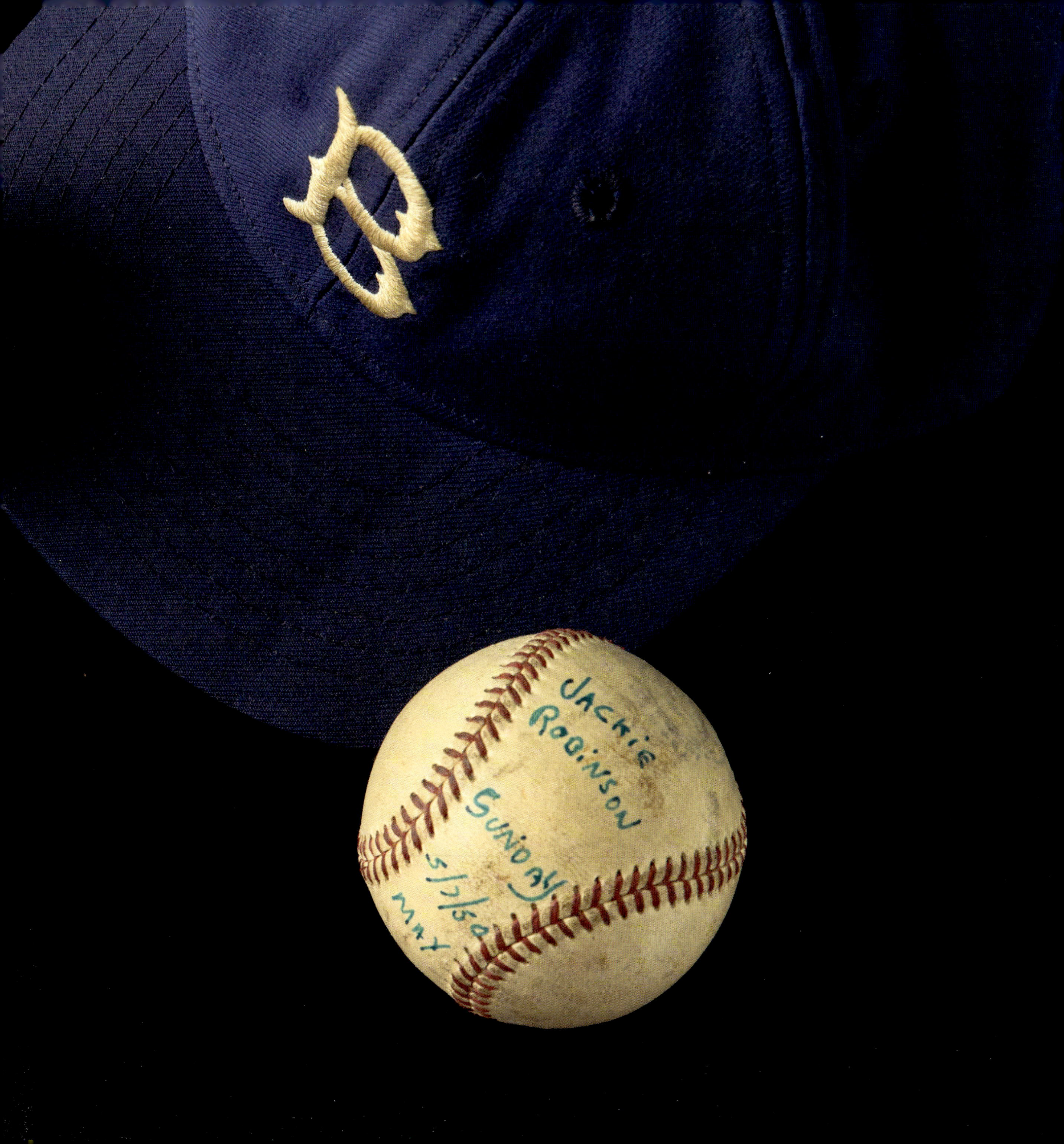
JACKIE
ROBINSON
SUNDAY
5/7/50
MAY

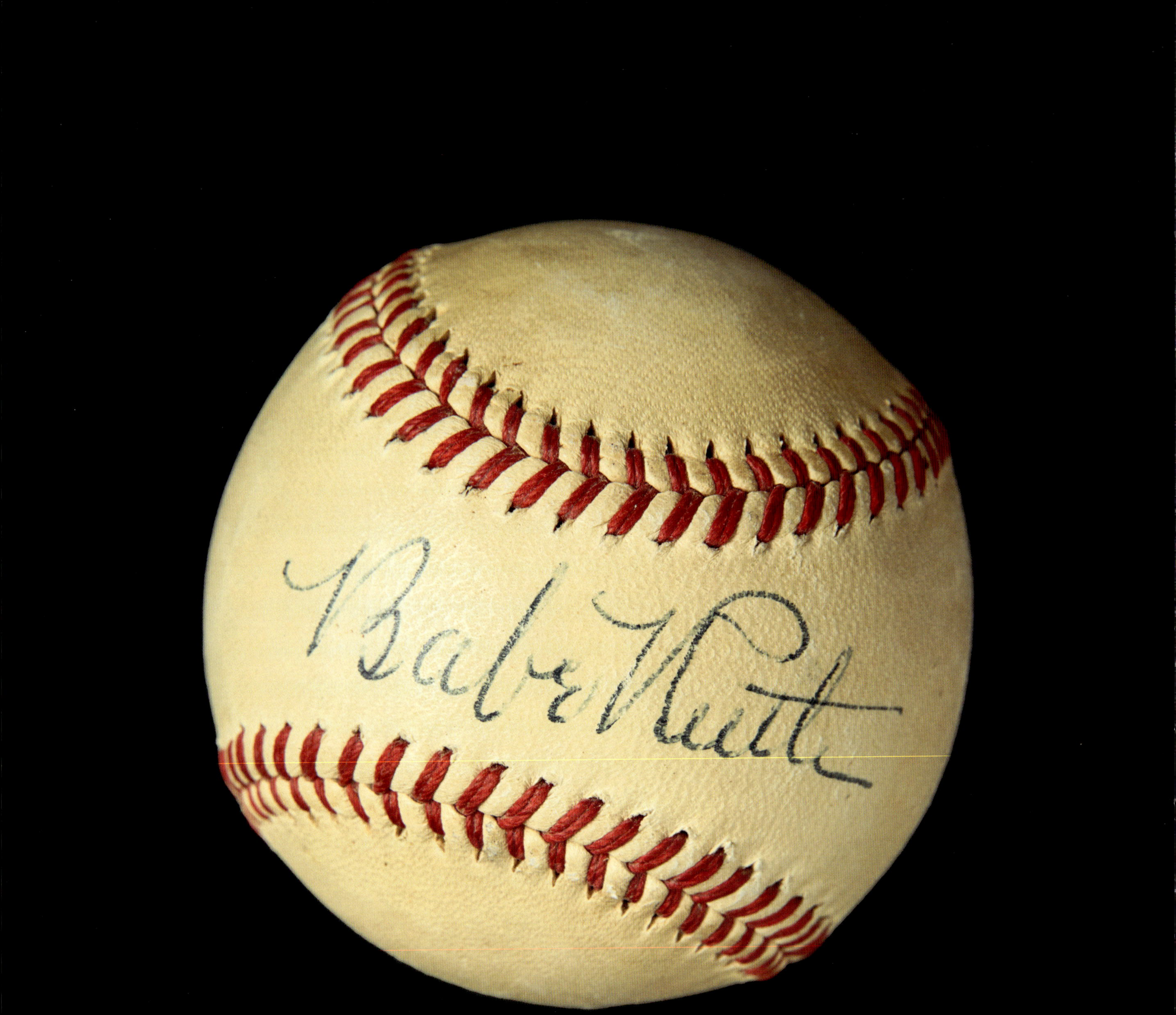
Babe Ruth

BABE RUTH

WHAT CAN ONE say about Babe Ruth that hasn't already been said?

Many of his exploits were larger than life fairy tales. Born George Herman Ruth Jr. in 1895 in Baltimore, Maryland, "Little George" is said, as Allan Wood writes on SABR.org "to have spent his days unsupervised on the waterfront streets and docks, committing petty theft and vandalism. Hanging out in his father's bar, he stole money from the till, drained the last drops from old beer glasses and developed a taste for chewing tobacco. He was only six years old."

As a player he was regarded as a bumpkin with bad social skills, but quickly distinguished himself on the diamond. His early success went straight to his head, and his arguing with umpires sparked his reputation as a tough cookie, his recalcitrant behaviour and nonstop salary demands earning him several suspensions. "Ruth is without question the greatest hitter the game has ever seen," said the owner of the Red Sox. "He is likewise one of the most selfish and inconsiderate men that ever wore a baseball uniform."

On the other hand, when he was with the Red Sox, he'd have busloads of orphans visit his farm for picnics, sending every kid away with a glove and an autographed baseball. He'd arrive at Fenway Park early to help the vendors, mostly boys in their teens, bag peanuts, talking a blue streak the whole time, telling them to be good and play baseball because there was good money in it. "He was an angel to us," said one of those kids looking back later. "He said if we worked hard enough, we could be as good as he was. We knew better than that."

I've been lucky enough to find two exceedingly rare game-used Ruth balls for my collection. One from 1927, which Babe hit for his 54th dinger of that year and that was caught in the stands. The second is an unusual keepsake, a real oddity: the first ball pitched to him in his first at-bat in his first game as a Boston Brave against the Cincinnati Reds on May 13th, 1935, signed in black fountain pen by ten members of the Reds, including Ruth and Cy Johnson.

But The Babe signed a lot of balls in his lifetime, and there are many "secretarial" signatures out there too. In 1937, winners of an essay contest on a radio show sponsored by the Sinclair Refining Company won a Spalding National League baseball with "his" autograph on it. I once paid a lot for one of those, a beautiful ball in its original box, that for years I proudly displayed in my home... before being set straight by an authenticator. Five hundred of those balls, all signed by a "ghost," were given away, so it's commonly known that they were not signed by the man himself. Except it wasn't commonly known by me! Nonetheless, there it still sits on a shelf in my office, both as an evocation of the period and a reminder of the pitfalls of autograph hunting. *Caveat emptor.*

Predictably, the first item I yearned for as a newbie collector was a Babe Ruth-signed baseball. It would take a while to find a nice one, in the meantime satisfying myself by buying baseballs and photos signed by various other players. That's when (given my obsessive-compulsive nature) the proverbial *trouble* began. I did eventually find the one that's pictured here—and as you can see it's a beauty. Oh... and genuine to boot!

NOLAN RYAN

I'VE SEEN NOLAN Ryan pitch—or I should say that I've *heard* him, because one of the most distinguishing things about him throwing a fastball was that throughout the stadium you could hear him *grunting*. You could viscerally feel the force of his throw.

I have many balls signed by him. The ones you see in this picture are from his third, fifth, sixth and *seventh* no-hitters. Think about that accomplishment. I also have a game ball from his 300th win, and one from the game in which he struck out the 5,500th batter of his career.

The one at bottom left comes from 1974; Nolan Ryan's game-used, autographed, third no-hitter, dated and inscribed with almost comic earnestness by one Paul Hirsch, "I was a ball boy for the California Angels for the 1974 season. During the game of September 28, I took this ball out of play when it became possible that Nolan Ryan would throw his A.L. record-tying third no-hitter. After the game, Ryan signed the ball for me and made the "9/28/74 NO HITTER VS TWINS" notation. My picture appears on page 42 of the 1975 *Sporting News Baseball Guide*, with 1974 Angels team photo."

Top left is the Nolan's fifth no-hitter, signed by him on September 26th, 1981, to the Astros' catcher Alan Ashby. The sixth and seventh (clockwise) both came from John Shulock, whose name we've seen on other baseballs and who I think had quite a business going. The sixth reads, ". . . I worked second base. After the game, I saved six balls used by Nolan Ryan, of which you now own one. You are now a member of a very elite group. To the best of my knowledge, there were only a dozen or so balls left in the ball bag after the game. Congratulations on your investment."

It's from a time when a few umpires engaged in a roaring trade taking balls from significant games and then selling them on the collectors' market—no one more, I suspect, than John Shulock. It's no wonder that not long after, I think in the late Nineties, the practice was curbed. From then on, all significant balls became the property of MLB, authenticated with a little numbered hologram sticker that refers you to a catalogue online.

While he was still playing, "The Ryan Express" was the oldest player in the game (Satchel Paige holds the all-time old-timer record at 59!), throwing his seventh no-hitter, against the Blue Jays, when he was 43. He was so good for so long that people kind of took him for granted, but come on: *seven* no-hitters? Who's *ever* going to pull that off again? He doesn't have the distinction of Johnny Vander Meer throwing back-to-back, but his career was just unbelievable.

Though he tied Sandy Koufax's career no-hitter record and broke his single-season strikeout record too, he never won a Cy Young Award. But if the Baseball Writers of America failed to recognise his greatness, hitters knew which pitcher they least wanted to face. When Ryan's night to pitch arrived, opposing team regulars often came down with a disease known as Ryanitis, a 24-hour ailment that mysteriously stopped them from playing. One victim of the syndrome commented, "A good night against Nolan Ryan is going 0 for 4 and you don't get hit in the head." He was *fierce*. He would throw one of his fastballs right at your head. People said, "Ryan doesn't just get you out. He embarrasses you."

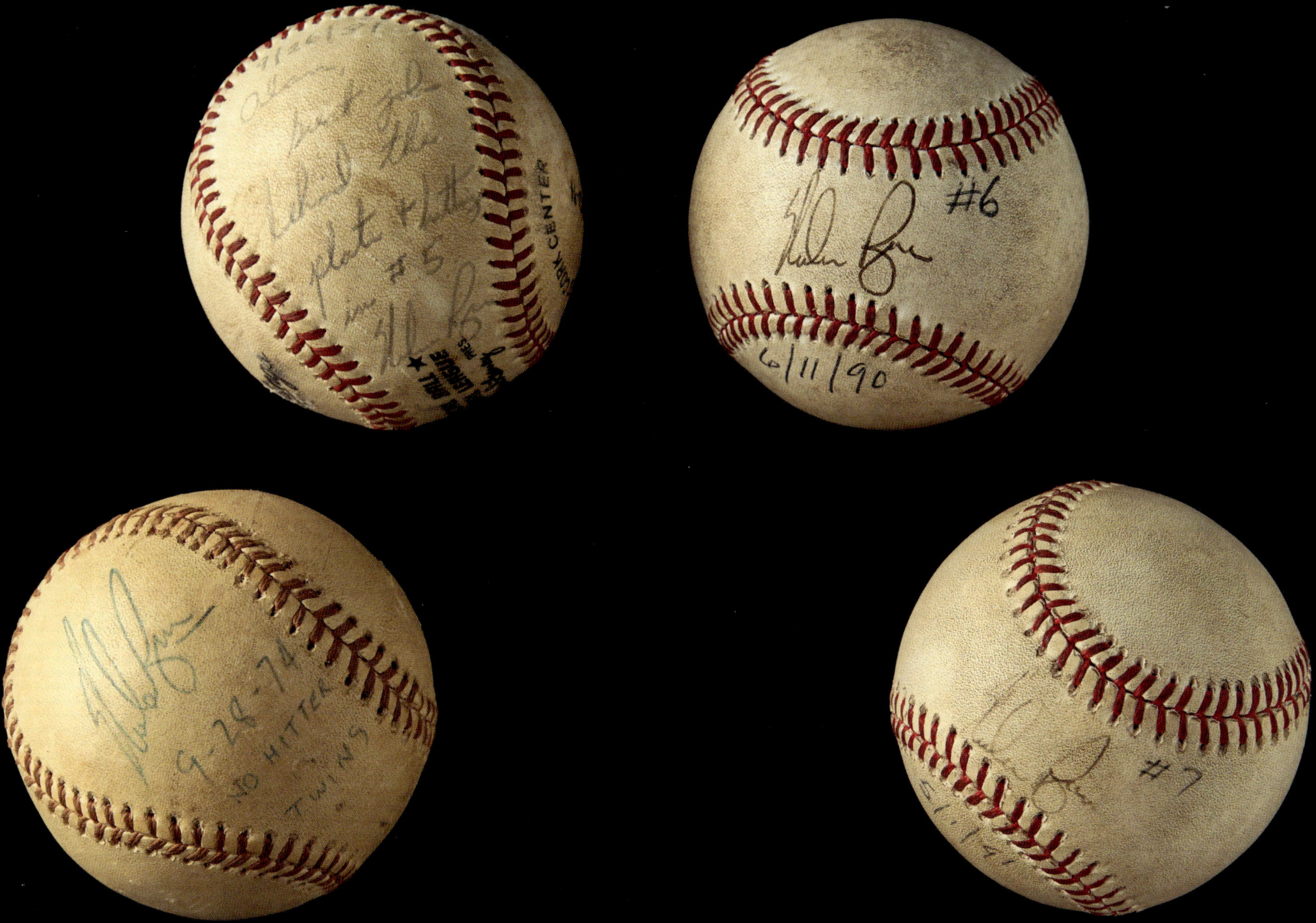

#6
6/11/90
9-28-74
NO HITTER
TWINS
#7

6/16/78

TOM SEAVER

SEAVER WAS A wee bit before my obsession with the game. I can't say I was ever a hugely knowledgeable fan of his, but I always knew that he was incredibly well respected—reminiscent in some ways of Christy Mathewson, who was also a well-liked, well-rounded, clean cut all-American dude, *and* an outstanding righthanded strikeout pitcher. One of his nicknames was "The Franchise," i.e., the team's most valuable player, without whom there'd *be* no franchise. That's high praise indeed.

In 1967, after the Braves' owner Bill Bartholomay had tried to sign Seaver but lost him on a technicality, and then his team lost 0-4 against the Mets, he said, "I get sick every time I watch him pitch." Playing for the "Miracle Mets," Seaver was also called "Tom Terrific," becoming the first Met in history to win the Rookie of the Year Award. In 1992 he was elected to the Hall of Fame by 98.84% of the Baseball Writers' Association of America vote. Now, that's *really* high. It shows the level of admiration and respect that he commanded. As the SABR website puts it, "No member of the team was as intricately associated with their meteoric rise from the cellar dwellers to world champions."

One of Seaver's most striking characteristics was the way he was never satisfied. In Atlanta on May 21st, 1968, for instance, when he shut out the Braves, he improved his record to 6-2 and the Mets evened theirs at 18-18, to him it was no milestone. SABR again (Maxwell Kates writing): "He defined the .500 mark as 'neither here nor there' and said that his teammates' embrace of mediocrity 'isn't going to get us very close to a pennant.'" That's the kind of role he played on that team—a leader, a motivator, crucial for the Mets to win. Ralph Kiner, the well-respected broadcaster (and big home run hitter before that), wrote in his memoir *Baseball Forever*, "Tom Seaver was the driving force behind the players, always pushing the team to be better than they were, never letting them settle."

By June 16th, 1978, the date on this ball, Seaver was already a sort of god of the game. He'd won three Cy Young Awards, five strikeout titles and a World Series championship. In this game, blanking the St. Louis Cardinals 4-0 (with only three Cardinal batters reaching base, all on walks), he got his first and only no-hitter. It was the 211th win of his career, but he wasn't done by any stretch, as he'd go on to clinch a hundred more.

"This is to verify," he wrote in the letter that accompanies the ball, "that this was an actual game-used ball used in my no-hitter." That's the sort of succinctness that typified him, as is the way he marked the ball: the date and a zero, that's it. There's a kind of eloquence to the way that zero represents, if not exactly the rectangular strike zone, the bullseye of a pitcher's focus. It's a great-looking ball, a historic ball, representative of an incredible career.

BERT SHEPARD

ON SABR.ORG, TERRY Bohn writes, "Baseball lore is filled with stories of players who distinguished themselves on the diamond despite physical limitations. Examples include Dummy Hoy, Three-Finger Brown, One-Armed Pete Gray, Monty Stratton and more recently, pitcher Jim Abbott. But Washington Senators left-handed pitcher Bert Shepard remains the only player to have ever played in the major leagues on an artificial leg." I would add to that: these are all stories of extreme valor; these are all people who don't know the meaning of "physical limitations"—or, indeed, the word no.

This book is entitled 72 Stories, and what better story is there than Bert Shepard's? But check out this ball's original auction house description: "Bert Shepard, Washington Senators. Pitched one game in 1945 after losing leg in WWII. A single-signed and inscribed baseball." That's all they had to say??? I mean, that's wholly insufficient.

There I was in 2014, in serious collector's heat, thumbing through a catalogue and looking at the sumptuous photographs (very few auction houses print them now, of course, and although I know they consumed forests' worth of trees, I do miss them), and was in shock when I read that skimpy description. I was like, *Huh?* Yes, the basic story is written on the ball, but I thought he deserved more. (If you're interested too, I recommend you read Jayson Jenks' vivid and detailed account in *The Athletic* online, "The extraordinary story of Bert Shepard, Prisoner of War Turned One-legged Pitcher.")

What a patriot the guy was. We see all these fake patriots in the news all the time, these misguided cult members who *think* they're patriots, but Bert Shepard was the real McCoy. Before the war, he'd only pitched in the minors, struggling with his control (in 1940 with the Wisconsin Rapids he walked 48 batters in 43 innings—*ouch*), but after his Lockheed fighter was strafed over Germany and crashed, and he survived pitchfork-wielding farmers, lost a leg, spent eight months in a POW camp, and finally came home as part of a prisoner exchange, the only thing he wanted was to continue his career in baseball—which he did.

Robert Patterson, the Under-Secretary of War, having met and presented him personally with a Commendation Medal for service, valor and courage, pulled some strings with the Washington Senators, and Shepard made the team on his brand-new, artificial, Errey-built leg. Of course, there was never a serious intention to field him, but the team's owner Clark Griffith was impressed by his tenacity and pluck, and then, on August 4th, 1945, the Senators found themselves in the fourth inning down 14-2 to the Red Sox. With, basically, nothing left to lose, Shepard was brought on. He struck out the first batter he faced, and gave up only one run on three hits the rest of the game. "I came in with the bases loaded," he told the *International Herald Tribune* in 1993, "and struck out George Catfish Markovich to get us out of it. It was much more pressure on me than it seemed. If I would have failed, the manager says, 'I knew I shouldn't have put him in there with that leg.' But the leg was not a problem. I didn't want anyone saying that it was."

That auspicious start notwithstanding, his Major League career only lasted the one game; the next time he appeared on the field was in a ceremony to receive the Distinguished Flying Cross, General Omar Bradley pinning the medal on his baseball uniform. He persevered back in the minors for ten more years, hoping to improve his game, but ultimately took up golf ... and won the U.S. amputee golf championship. Twice!

I
LOST MY
RT. LEG WHEN
SHOT DOWN
OVER GERMANY
IN WW II.
I GOT A NEW
LEG AND
PITCHED
FOR THE
WASH.
SEN-
ATORS
VS
THE
BOSTON
RED SOX
ON AUG. 14.
1945 + GAVE
UP 1 RUN +
3 HITS IN 5 1/3
INNINGS.
Bert
Shepard
IM PROUD + HAPPY I HAD THE OPPERTUNITY
TO FLY THE P-38 + SERVE MY COUNTRY.
Sincerly Bert Shepard
Rawlings

GEDDY "THE SPACEMAN" LEE

SMITTY *and* THE CRO

HERE'S A COMPENDIUM of memories and an homage to my friends that I could call *My Effin' Life in Baseball*.

In the early eighties, while Rush was recording *Signals* at Le Studio in Quebec, the local impresario Donald K. Donald called me to say, "Warren Cromartie's a drummer and a big Rush fan. He'd love to see you guys working." So we gave him the grand tour, he asked a million questions, I asked a million questions, and we sat him in the control room and played him "Tom Sawyer" from the original digital master, full blast, which basically blew him away. Cro and I became very good friends, still are to this day. After he became a free agent and was unhappy with the offers he was getting from American teams, he went to play for the Yomiuri Giants. In 1990 I went to Tokyo to watch him play in the Japan Series, and his manager at the time, Sadaharu Oh, Japan's home run champ, a legit legend in that country, signed a ball for me.

The "1,000" ball was Cro's one-thousandth Major League hit, which he gave me out of friendship. His nickname for me was Uncle—I guess because I was the Jewish uncle he always wanted! The ball on which he wrote, "Hey, Uncle, bring this with you the next time we meet," is a Speedgun baseball, which measures the speed of your throw; he gave me that one because backstage before Rush shows I used to pass the time throwing pitches to one my roadies. The ball at far left is the first pitch Cro threw out when he was inducted into the Expos Hall of Fame in 1996 and was honored at the Olympic Stadium. Rather than keep it himself, he gave it to me, which I think is a huge honor. That's how dear our friendship is.

Through my association with Cro I met a rookie pitcher named Bryn Smith, who got me the ticket you see from July 29th, 1983, which is my birthday. Smitty wasn't a pitcher with an overpowering fastball, but he had this incredible changeup. He was an old-school pitcher's pitcher. He made his *living* on that pitch. That game was his first opportunity to start (against Neil Allen for the St. Louis Cardinals, if memory serves), so after a hitter smashed a line drive off his knee, there was no way he was coming off the field for an X-ray. Not only did he win, but ended up pitching a complete game and was made a regular member of the Expos' starting rotation. From that day forward he always wore a Rush T-shirt with the sleeves cut off under his uniform, and made his catcher Mike Fitzgerald wear one too if he was catching him that day. And if he was going through a slump he'd call me up and say, "Ged, I need new T-shirts. The luck has washed out of these ones." Baseball players are incredibly superstitious, you know.

Smitty also gave me the ball that says, "This one was for the boys." He'd come to see Rush play in Texas or somewhere and we'd partied all night long. The next day he dragged his ass into the stadium... and pitched a 2-0 shutout game! This ball was the last out from that game.

Dale Heslip, Rush's set designer and tour film director, pasted my head onto a photo of Smitty's body. It proudly hangs in my office at home, right next to the uniform of that player with the same last name, the *original* "Spaceman": Bill Lee.

GEORGE SOSNAK

THE *SPORTS COLLECTORS DIGEST* describes George Sosnak as a man "with a passion for baseball but not the athletic ability to make it fly professionally. He was a soldier, construction crew man, donut maker, recreation park supervisor, and even had a cartoon hour for children on TV but was forced to give it up as his painting began to take up more of his time. Despite his lack of athletic skill, he became an umpire, starting in the military in Germany after World War II, and rose through the ranks before settling in with the Pioneer League and later the Three-I League, but his dreams of becoming a Major League umpire never came true."

This self-taught "accidental artist" started out when he was umpiring a game in 1956, and a fan asked him if he could paint her favourite player on a ball. Sosnak obliged (he apparently *always* obliged). Every one he'd paint was an homage to baseball players or politicians, bad boys, fans and Presidents in some way connected to baseball; among the forty-odd Sosnak balls I own (Cy Young, Bob Feller, Mickey Lolich, Billy Martin, Roberto Clemente, Babe Ruth....), one on my faves features a woman named Dickie Stanky in various golf poses—it was commissioned by her husband, journeyman middle infielder, Eddie Stanky, in celebration of her numerous golfing achievements. Early on, Sosnak's works were simplistic, with maybe just a team's logo on it, but then he started completely filling up the panels. Every single detail from the box score of a particular game would go on the ball, as well as paintings of the scene—of the player in question, maybe the fans, even the stadium. In my view they're superbly detailed, tremendous examples of American folk art, and for the same reason he's slowly become revered by collectors as feverish as me.

The story behind the Kennedy ball is that he sent it to the White House, explaining who he was and asking JFK if he would mind signing on the sweet spot so he could paint around the signature. On October 1st, 1962, Kennedy's personal secretary Evelyn Lincoln returned a letter saying, "Dear Mr. Sosnak, the President was very glad to autograph your baseball. P.S. I'm also returning your dollar bill." (Sosnak had included it to cover the postage!) Incidentally, the "WINNIE" written in Sosnak's hand was his soon-to-be wife.

The Gibson ball celebrates him winning the Cy Young Award in 1970. Every centimetre is filled with his career statistics. It's staggering to hold it in your hand. I had the good fortune to meet Bob Gibson at a St. Louis Cardinals anniversary dinner, which was a thrill because he was one of the great pitchers of my youth. He was a fierce competitor with a vicious, intimidating stare on the mound. In 1968 he posted a season ERA of 1.12, which is as minuscule as it gets (and in those days, pitchers threw way more innings than they do now). He threw *thirteen* shutouts that year, the third longest scoreless streak in Major League history, finishing the season with twenty-eight complete games. That's just unheard of today.

One unfortunate thing is that Sosnak would occasionally trace over signatures, effectively harming their value—but he did so naively; underscoring the fact that for him the pursuit was never about money. There are stories of him setting up booths at baseball card conventions, where he'd paint anybody any ball for a hundred bucks! Despite all that, auction prices of Sosnaks continue to rise. Most importantly, what you're left with is the impression of a very sweet man who desperately wanted to be connected to baseball—and managed it in a gloriously roundabout way.

The man himself.

CY-YOUNG AWARD WINNER, TO BOB GIBSON, 1970: ALSO WON THE AWARD IN 1968.
BOB GIBSON, ST. LOUIS CARDINALS, RIGHTHANDED PITCHER
PITCHER OF THE YEAR. CY YOUNG AWARD

TO WINNIE
BEST WISHES
SIGNED BY PRESIDENT JOHN F. KENNEDY
IN 1962
WASHINGTON-
4
OPENER
DETROIT

JOHNNY BENCH
COOPERSTOWN
1988
JOSE CANSECO
MAYS MAKES IMPOSSIBLE CATCH
Dear Lois
1983
COMISKEY

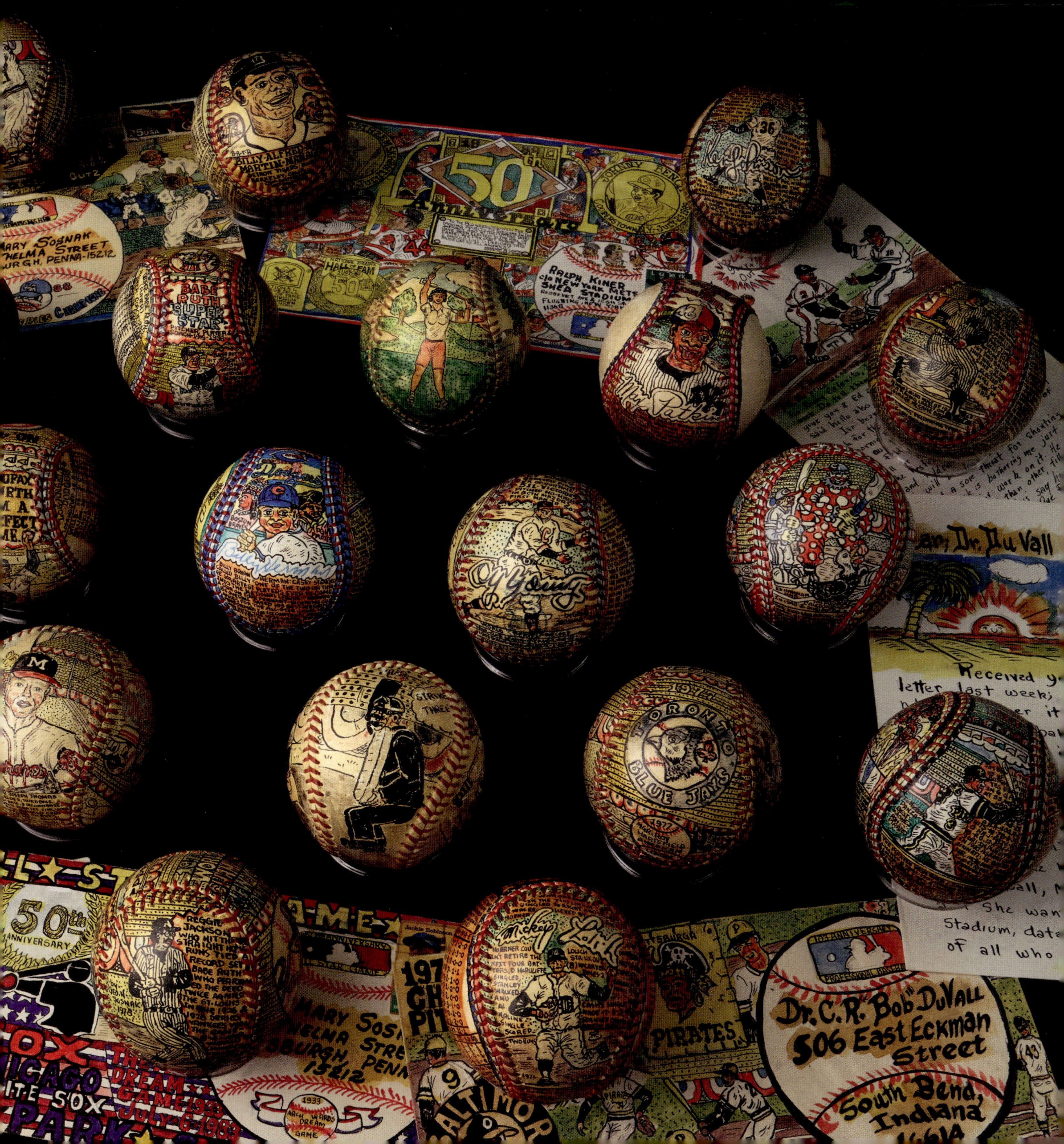

To Ralph
Best wishes
Warren Spahn
Victory 327
9/29/62

WARREN SPAHN

THIS BALL CAME to me with a nice bit of provenance from Ralph Schauer, a former UPI photographer who covered professional baseball in the Milwaukee area after the Second World War: "Spahn personally signed this for me in the locker room after this record put him ahead of John Clarkson and tied him with Eddie Plank with victories by a pitcher."

Jim Kaplan, writing for the SABR site, calls Spahn "the fifth-winningest pitcher of all time." The fifth! There's been a lot of pitchers, so what that innocent sounding sentence really means is one of the great pitchers *of all time*. "Only by remaining in the game two seasons too long did he fail to finish with an ERA under 3.00 (3.09) and a winning percentage over .600 (.597), and his totals are all the more impressive considering that he didn't record his first big-league victory until he was 25. Spahn should make everyone's list of the 10 best pitchers in baseball history." His 363 wins are the most of any left-hander, while his 35 homers are the most by a National League pitcher. He won 75 games after the age of 40, leading Stan Musial to say, "I don't think he'll ever get into the Hall of Fame because he'll never stop pitching."

In 1948, inspired by Spahn and Johnny Sain's shared pitching performance during the Boston Braves' 1948 pennant drive, the *Boston Post* sports editor Gerald V. Hern wrote a poem that's familiar to every serious baseball fan:

First, we'll use Spahn, then we'll use Sain, then an off day, followed by rain,

Back will come Spahn, followed by Sain, and followed, we hope, by two days of rain.

Regarded as the thinking man's pitcher, he once described his approach on the mound thusly: "Hitting is timing. Pitching is *upsetting* timing." He was also famous for his amazingly lofty leg lift, which he described in 1998 to the *Daily Oklahoman* as part of a deceptive style. "Hitters," he remarked, "said the ball seemed to come out of my uniform." Meanwhile, the New York sportswriter Red Smith playfully called him "goose-necked, stork-legged," and "a gawky, bat-eared old warrior with the ample nose"—a nose that I take a personal interest in. According to former Cardinals player Solly Hemus, he periodically used anti-Semitic slurs while on the mound. Some deserved karma, then, that he acquired the nickname "Hooks" not so much because of his pitching, but because after being hit in the face by a ball, his broken schnozz mended in a nice hook shape.

That being said, he served with distinction in WWII. With a Purple Heart, a Bronze Star, a battlefield commission and a Presidential Citation, he was the war's most decorated ballplayer. Returning to the game, he said. "The guys who died over there were heroes" but maintained a true hero's modesty, insisting, "After what I went through overseas, I never thought of anything I was told to do in baseball as hard work. You get over feeling like that when you spend days on end sleeping in frozen tank tracks in enemy-threatened territory. The army taught me what's important and what isn't." He kept his sense of humour, too. Because German spies would wear American uniforms, he recounted, "Anybody we didn't know, we'd ask, 'Who plays second for the Bums?' If he didn't answer 'Eddie Stanky,' he was dead."

TRIS SPEAKER

S is for Speaker
Swift center-field tender
When the ball saw him coming
It yelled, "I surrender."

—Ogden Nash in *Sport Magazine* (1949)

TRISTRAM EDGAR SPEAKER was one the legends of the Deadball era (and I mean, what an era: Lou Gehrig, Ty Cobb, Babe Ruth. . . .). Considered by many the greatest centre fielder of the time (and no slouch at the plate, either), he's one of the first names I sought out for my collection. It's a great signature, on a pristine ball, though it looks a little shaky on the T; I wonder if he signed it later in his life. . . .

"You can write him down as one of the two models of ball-playing grace," sportswriter Grantland Rice said. "The other was Napoleon Lajoie. Neither ever wasted a motion or gave you any sign of extra effort . . . They had the same elements that made a Bobby Jones or the Four Horsemen of Notre Dame—the smoothness of a summer wind." And as Don Jensen writes on SABR.org, "A man's man who hunted, fished, could bulldog a steer, and taught Will Rogers how to use a lariat, Speaker was involved in more than his share of umpire baiting and brawls with teammates and opposing players. But when executing a hook slide on the bases, tracking a fly ball at the crack of an opponent's bat, or slashing one of his patented extra-base hits, Speaker made everything he did look easy."

Born in Hubbard, Texas, in 1888, he became a left-hander after he broke his arm as a kid falling from a horse. (Wow. I broke my arm as a kid too, but it didn't make *me* a southpaw.) In 1912, he won the Chalmers Award as the league's most valuable player, led the league in doubles and home runs, and batted .383, third behind only Ty Cobb and Joe Jackson. He had a lifetime batting average of .345, sixth on the all-time list, and no one since has surpassed his career mark of 792 doubles.

In his novel *Shoeless Joe*, W.P. Kinsella writes that Joe Jackson's fielding glove was the place "where triples go to die" (whence Kevin Costner's character Ray uttering the phrase in *Field of Dreams*); that, in fact, was an accolade given to several players in baseball history, among them Willie Mays and, yes, Tris Speaker.

As a highly successful player-manager, he was one of the first skippers to fully exploit platooning, guiding Cleveland between 1919 and 1926 to a 617-520 record and a .543 average; in 1920, after they'd been demoralized by the mid-season death of shortstop Ray Chapman (who, beaned by a pitch from Carl Mays, remains the only player ever killed by a ball), he took them to the World Series. After he'd retired, the *Cleveland Plain Dealer* said, "Baseball in Cleveland and Tris Speaker have been synonymous for so long that a Speakerless team will seem contrary to natural law. What Christy Mathewson was to New York, what Cobb was to Detroit, what Walter Johnson was to Washington, Tris Speaker has been to Cleveland."

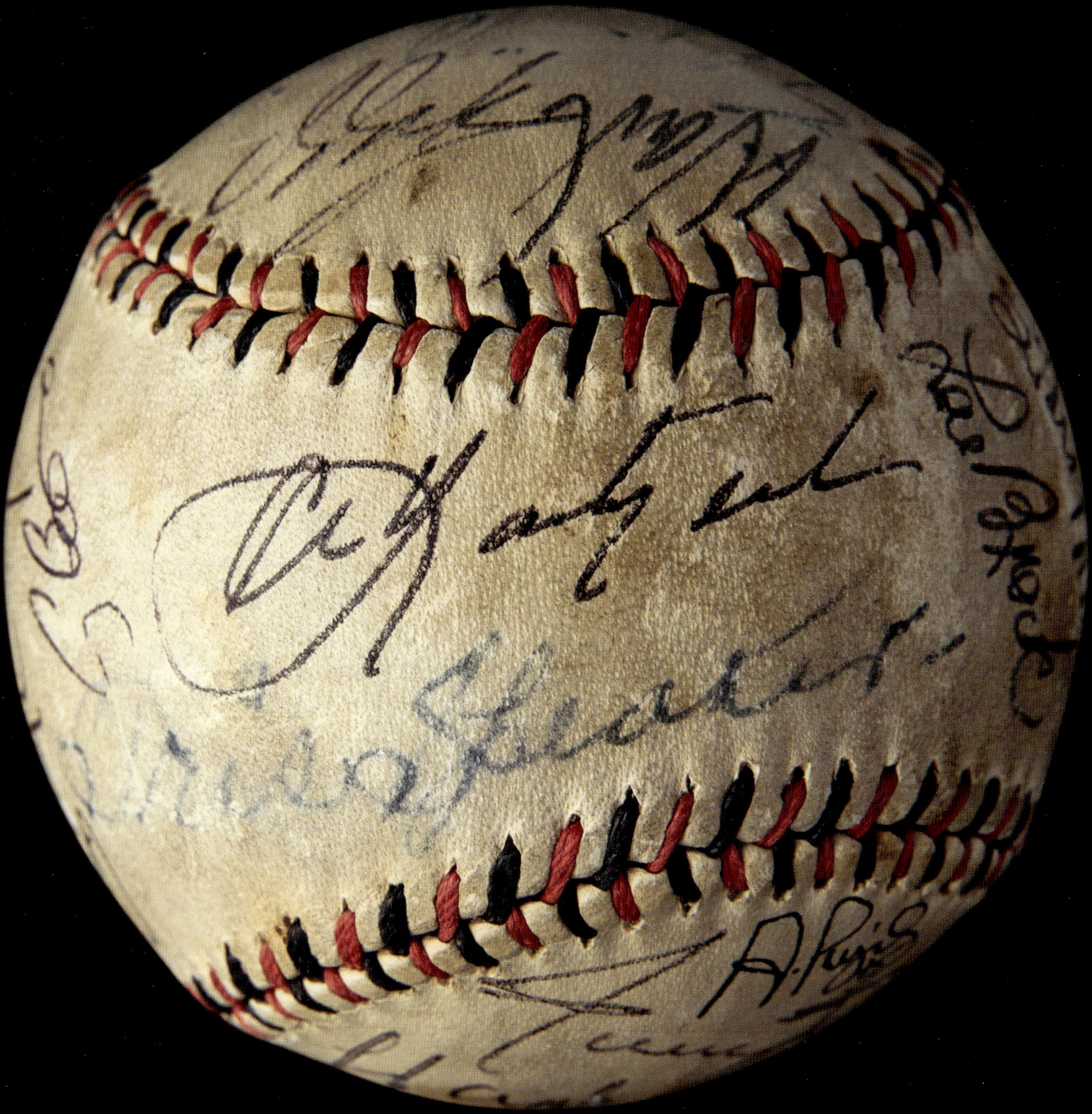

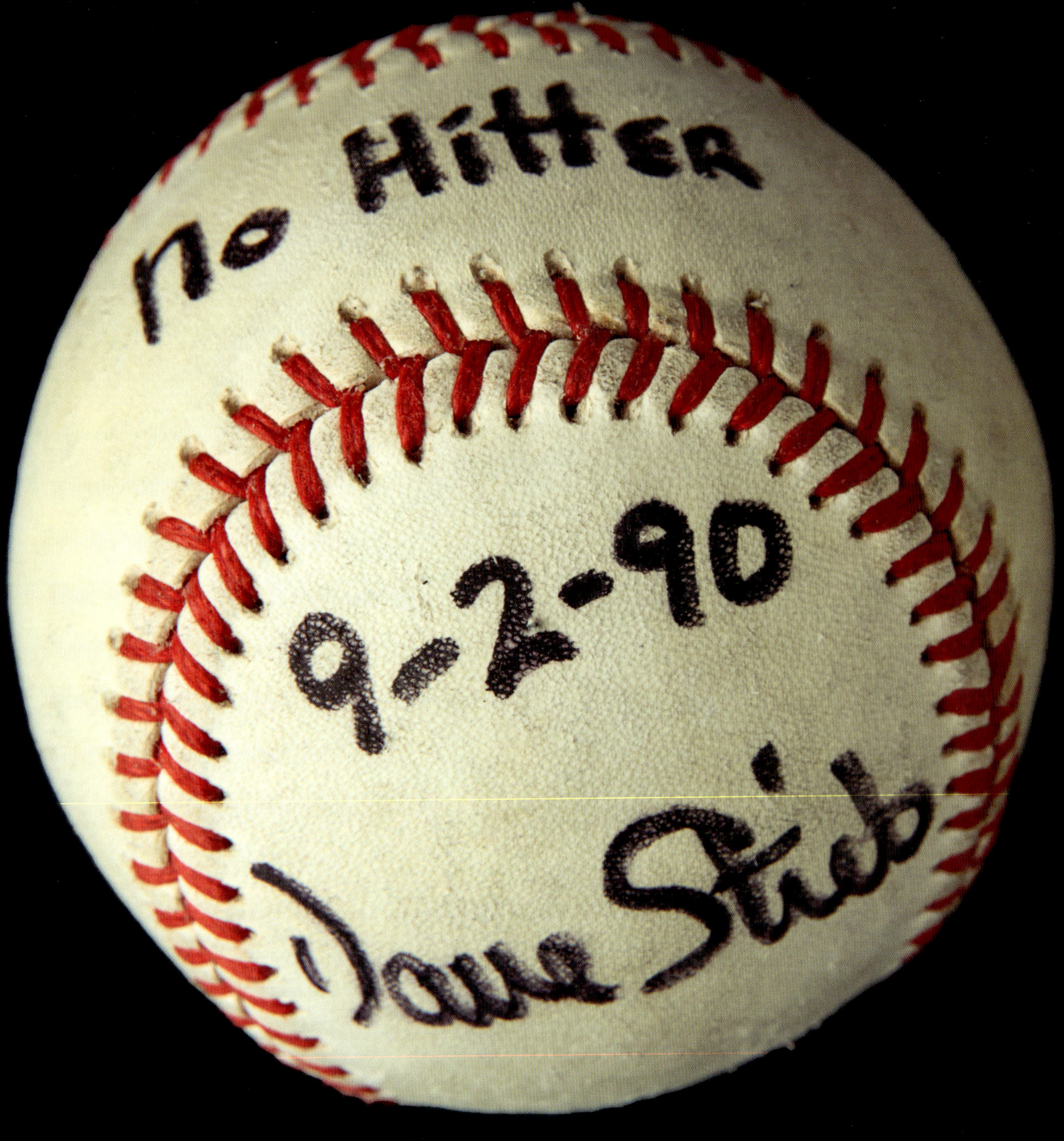
No Hitter
9-2-90
Dave Stieb

DAVE STIEB

DAVE STIEB WAS a fiercely competitive pitcher. It's generally agreed that during the 1980's he had the best slider in the game. He was a tough man on the mound, winning the second most games of any pitcher that decade. He was a seven-time All-Star, helping raise up the Blue Jays from expansion basement-dwelling status to world champions. But he may be best known for his terrible luck in attempting to close out no-hitters: four times in five years he reached the ninth inning of a no-hitter; three times in twelve months he reached the *last out* of a no-hitter; but failed to clinch it every time—until September 2nd, 1990. A quarter-century later, he remains the only no-hitter in Blue Jays history. (Roy Halladay also pitched a perfect game, but only after he'd left the Jays for the Phillies; a ball from that game also features in this book. Meanwhile, the Jays, it pains me to admit, have *been* no-hit six times!)

It's a very exclusive club. There have been only 320 no-hitters in Major League history, about three per season—an amazingly small number when you consider how old baseball is and how many games are played each year. (Even fewer players belong to the "No-No" club in the pure, original sense, meaning "no hits, no *runs*"; and as far as I know, the most singular club of all is that of guys who made their no-no's *on acid*—stand up, Doc Ellis!)

I was very fortunate during that period to be introduced to Stieb, and we became friends. When the Blue Jays played New York, I'd fly down, and we'd go out for drinks and walk around the city together. Now, on game day he'd always have his game face on. He took his job very seriously. At the same time, he loved rock and roll. One time I visited him at his home in California and jammed with him and his wife Patty on drums, which was the most relaxed and joyous I've ever seen him. We all need a way to let our hair down from time to time, and it was a major way for him to unwind. I loved seeing him reveal that other side of himself, free of his intense, competitive demeanor.

Third baseman Kelly Gruber was another rocker on that Blue Jays team of the late Eighties, early Nineties. Both he and Dave were very generous with their time. Once, during a visit to Spring Training with my brother Allan and son Jules, they wanted us to suit up and shag fly balls in the outfield, and asked manager Cito Gaston if it was cool for us to do so. I recall him saying, "OK, just make sure they don't get hurt." *Yikes.* It's a dangerous game, kids! Kelly even took Jules to one of the outer diamonds to coach him in playing 3rd base. Those are such warm and wonderful memories for me—times when I got to be a kid again—and of course, I paid them back in kind whenever they came to a Rush show.

But more than anything, to see Dave finally throw a no-hitter that day in 1990, after all his frustrations, was just a marvellous moment. I couldn't have been happier for him. This is therefore a special ball, accompanied by a ticket for that same game. They're items that I will keep forever.

Once I became fascinated with no-hitters, I gathered quite a stunning collection of no-hit balls that included the man we'll get to next... Johnny Vander Meer.

JOHNNY VANDER MEER

NOW WE'RE TALKING *real* rarities. Any fan of the game, any fan of pitching, knows about the games these balls are associated with. Johnny Vander Meer, leftie pitcher for the Cincinnati Reds, is the only person in the history of Major League Baseball to throw two no-hitters back to back. No-one else has ever done that! The first was on June 11th, 1938, against the Boston Bees (his rookie season, no less); the second only a week later (not *even* a week), on June 15th, against the Brooklyn Dodgers.

These balls came up for auction two years ago, representing the last outs of the two games. Here's the vivid description that came with them: "Nighttime itself was upstaged on June 15th, 1938, as a masterful pitching performance by the visiting Cincinnati Reds left-hander Johnny Vander Meer shone even brighter than the newly installed light towers at Ebbets Field. The famous Brooklyn ballpark became the second Major League stadium to host the night game on this date [How cool is that!], the first being Crosley Field, home of the Reds. Attendance swelled beyond capacity to 40,000 people, all drawn like moths to the glowing spectacle, which included marching bands and a series of pre-game sprinting exhibitions from four-time Olympic gold medalist Jesse Owens. But as the contest itself progressed, a thrilling new story took shape. Vander Meer was wild, walking eight guys, but his stuff was electric. Slowly, even the Dodgers fans themselves switched their allegiance, cheering every successive out as the young hurler edged closer to an unprecedented achievement. Vander Meer mowed down Woody English (batting for Luke Hamlin), Kiki Cuyler and Johnny Hudson in the eighth, fanning the first and third men. The Reds were likewise retired in order."

It was definitely the pinnacle of his career, though I don't mean to diminish his other accomplishments. "The Dutch Master," or "Double No-Hit Vander Meer" as he was also known, never made the Hall of Fame, but he was a member of the Reds when they won the 1940 World Series, was a four-time All-Star, had 29 career shutouts (ranking third on the Reds franchise list), and was one of only six National League pitchers since 1930 to lead the league in strikeouts in three straight seasons. But after such an impressive start, he had a disappointing 1939, when he fell ill during spring training and then suffered an injury when he slipped on a wet pitching mound. He'd later have trouble controlling the accuracy of his pitching, and his career was marked by inconsistent performances.

Born to deeply religious immigrant Dutch parents, he grew up in Midland Park, New Jersey, near where these two balls were displayed in the Midland Park Public Library for years before his great-niece put them up for sale. When I saw them, I *had* to have them both, and was fortunate to outbid every other poor slob who wanted them too! They really are for me the ultimate no-hit balls.

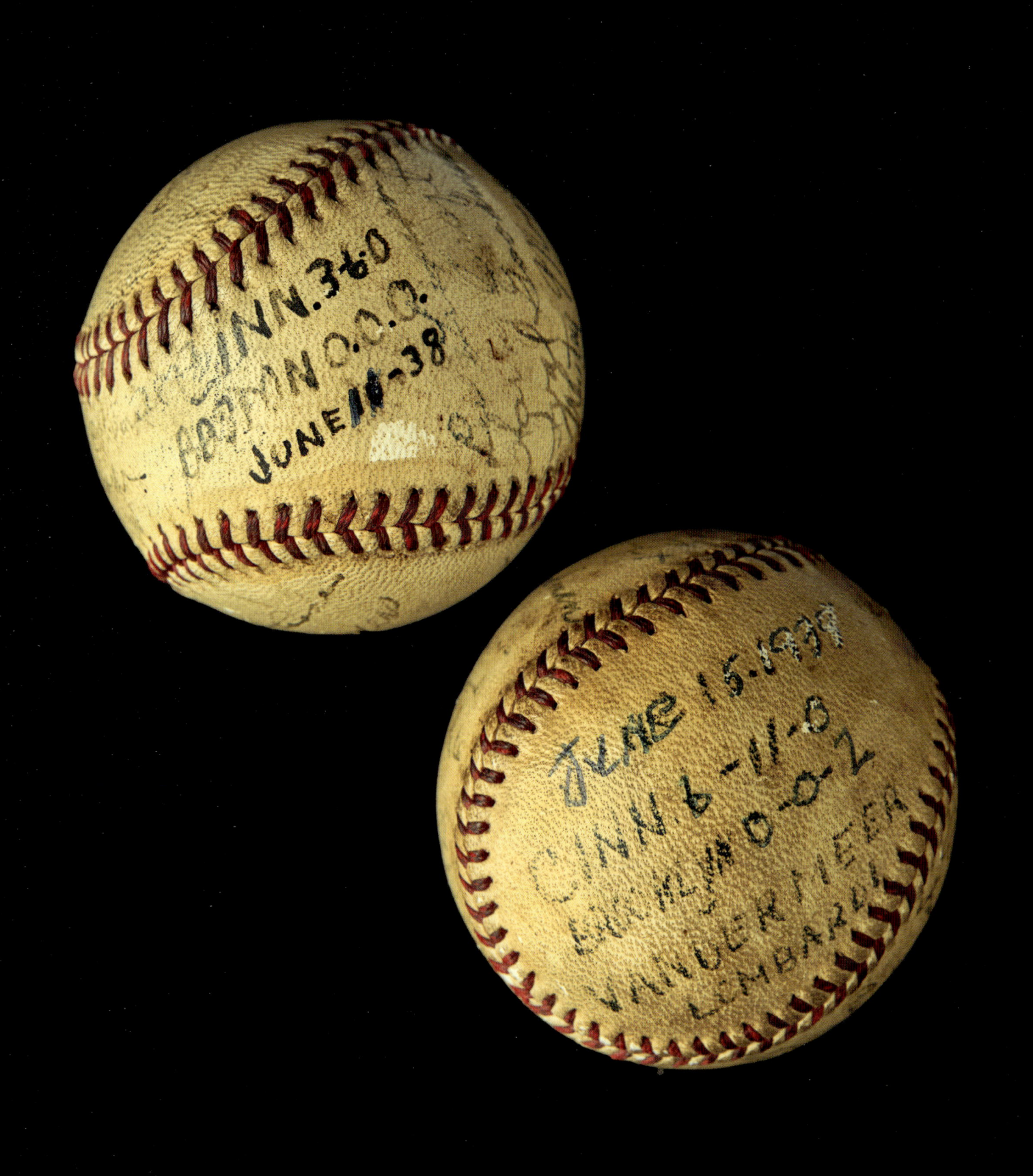

JUNE 11-38
JUNE 15. 1938
CINN. 6-11-0

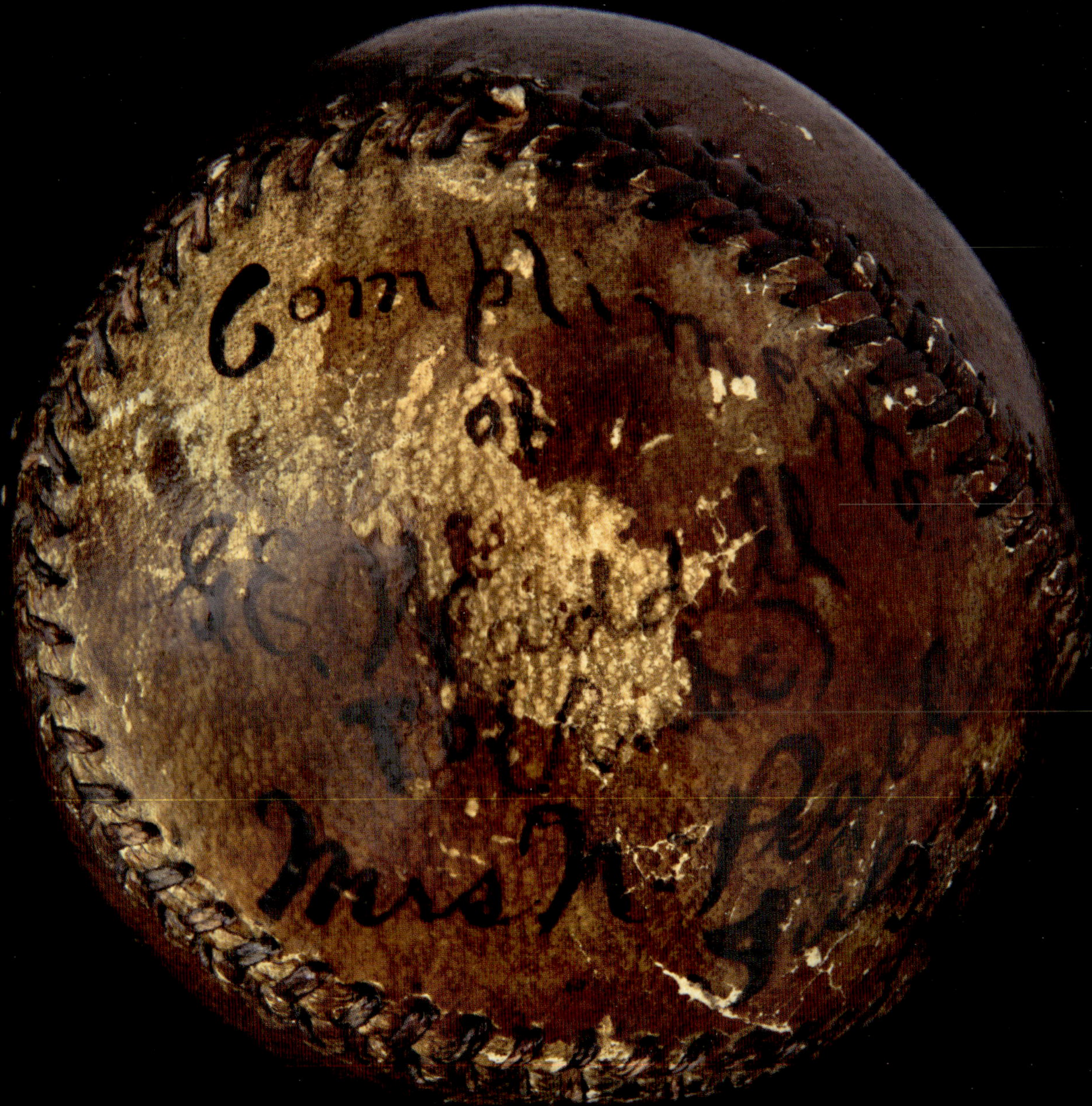
Compliments
of

RUBE WADDELL

I'VE SAID THAT I love a number of balls in my collection—which is a good sign because if you're going to be a mental collector, you'd better love what you're collecting; there's no guarantee of anything else, no real reward other than that particular love—but do I ever love this ball.

As I described in my *Big Beautiful Book of Bass*, there are collectors who only go for pristine "closet queens"—a guitar that some kid in 1961 got as a gift, say, but because they really wanted a drum set, it was slipped under their bed and lay there unopened for sixty years until it was resold. Then there are those that are beat up, so well played that they still smell from the smoky bars where for years the owner either made his living or just jammed with his pals: "relics" that tell a story. Well, I ride in both buses, so to speak. I love the perfection of "case queens," but also adore pieces that have lived a life, that embody the passion of the player. This Rube Waddell ball is a true relic, whose age and condition most definitely draw me to it, as well as the way it's so thoroughly infused with Waddell's character.

According to Dan O'Brien's biography on the SABR site (which I love to quote because it's so very well written and, you know, I couldn't do it better myself!), Waddell "entered this world on Friday the 13th and exited it on April Fool's Day. In the thirty-seven intervening years, he struck out more batters, frustrated more managers and attracted more fans than any pitcher of his era. An imposing physical specimen for his day, the six-foot 196lb Waddell possessed the intellectual and emotional maturity of a child, although a very precocious and engaging one at that. Known to occasionally miss a scheduled start because he was off fishing or playing marbles with street urchins, he might disappear for days during spring training, only to be found leading a parade down Main Street of Jacksonville, Florida, or wrestling an alligator in a nearby lagoon. Despite these and other curious distractions, his immense physical ability was undeniable. He complemented a blazing fastball with a wicked curve. His strikeout-to-walk ratio was nearly 3-1 for his career, almost 4-1 in his record-setting season of 1904...."

It goes on. He was easily distracted by opposing fans who held up puppies, which caused him to run up and play with them, and shiny objects which seemed to put him in a trance; he was so self-confident, meanwhile, that in the final inning of exhibition games he'd direct his infielders to the sidelines and strike out the side alone.

Two things now about the ball itself, signed on July 2nd, 1908, to a "Mrs N. Pearl," with a note saying, "I got mine in Chicago 5, St. Louis 1." Let me explain....

First, I'm sorry if I'm disparaging her in any way, but I'm told that there are other balls from this period, from other players, *also* signed to Mrs N. Pearl, so it's possible that she was what they referred to as a "Baseball Annie," the equivalent of a rock and roll groupie. Secondly, pitching for the St. Louis Browns against the Chicago White Sox, Rube got *shelled* in the first inning. Facing five batters, he gave up four hits, three runs and a walk, and was pulled from the game. (He pitched against the magnificent Ed Walsh, who pitched the entire game against *thirty-six* batters.) And that's what he meant by "I got mine."

HONUS WAGNER

"THERE AIN'T MUCH to being a ballplayer," said the greatest player of his time, and probably any other time, "if you're a ballplayer."

He was born in 1874 Johannes Peter Wagner. From his minor league beginnings, he hit wherever he played—between .365 and .386—showing his versatility by playing every position except catcher. But after Ed Barrow discovered him in Steubenville, Ohio, in the Inter-State League, and then introduced him to the Louisville Colonels in the National League, they weren't impressed. As Jan Finkel tells us on SABR.org, Wagner was an "awkward-looking, oddly built man, 5-feet-11, 200 pounds, with a barrel chest, massive shoulders, heavily muscled arms, huge hands, and dramatic bowlegs that robbed him of any grace and several inches of height. They took a chance, nevertheless, and were rewarded as in his first sixty-one games Wagner hit .338. He was fast, too, stealing over 700 bases, legging out almost 900 doubles and triples, and earning the nickname 'The Flying Dutchman' as he ran 'whirling like a berserk freestyle swimmer.'"

With his bowlegs, he looked like a smithy or a coal miner, but he became the best pure athlete in the game. In a photograph I have of him taken by the great Charles Conlon, you can see the muscles in his arms straining like iron cables, gripping the handle of what looks more like a club than a bat. On the field, his huge hands made it difficult to tell whether he was wearing a glove—which were big, puffy things in those days; he cut a hole in the palm and pulled out much of the stuffing to give him better feel. He had such a strong arm that, so confident was he of throwing a runner out at first, he enjoyed taking his sweet time, making his teammates nervous and pissing them off as they stood waiting for the throw.

He was the real deal. His final resumé included Major League records at the time for games at bat, extra base hits and total bases; in addition, he held National League records for doubles, triples and batting titles, and his 733 stolen bases rank third behind Billy Hamilton's 914. He could run like the wind, but if base stealing also has to do with fearlessness, he had that in excess as well. He was elected to the Baseball Hall of Fame in 1936, along with Ty Cobb, Babe Ruth, Christy Mathewson and Walter Johnson.

"Honus was neither angel nor saint," Finkel continues. "Some opponents thought him a fine fellow off a diamond but overly rough on it, and most umpires thought he kicked too much. Yet he also embodied the American dream as the son of immigrants who rose from humble roots to greatness. He was a gentle, hard-working man, a loyal friend and teammate who treated young players kindly, dealt with adversity, and inspired millions."

Pictured here is Honus Wagner's signature from the 1944 Pittsburgh Pirates team. (After retirement, Wagner served the Pirates as a coach for 39 years, most notably as a hitting instructor from 1933 to 1952.)

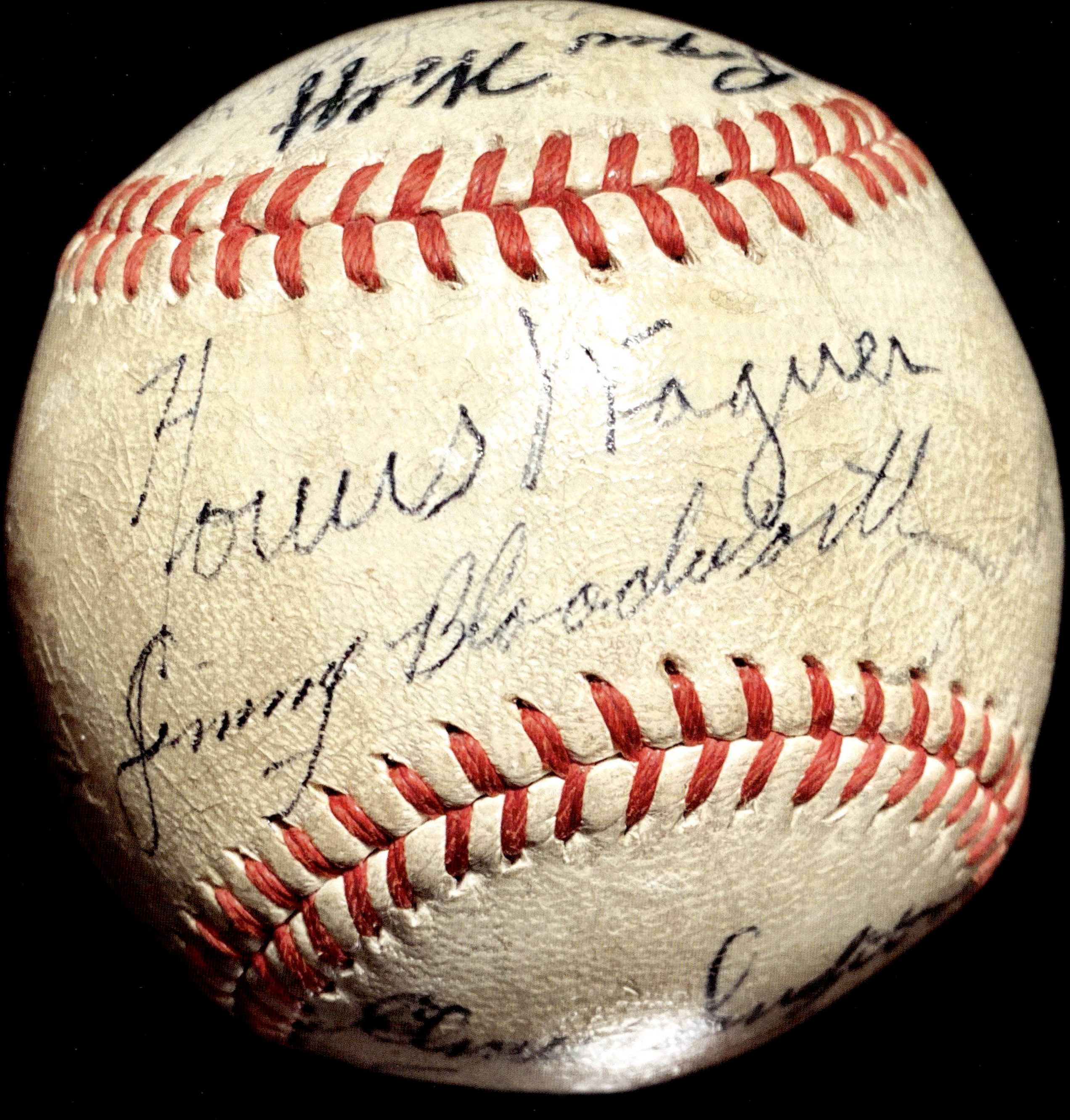
Honus Wagner
Jimmy Bloodworth

To Geddy
Good Luck
Ted Williams

TED WILLIAMS

OVER THE YEARS I've been fortunate enough to collect several baseballs signed by Ted Williams, one of the greatest sluggers ever to put on a uniform, including one that is personalized to me—though sadly, I never did meet the man; it was a thoughtful gift from a friend that I will never part with. I also have an oddity, a baseball signed by Ted Williams and George H. W. Bush, who first met in combat pilot training in 1942 (Williams had ended 1941 with the Red Sox and a .406 batting average but in the prime of his life enlisted to fight). Bush was an avid Astros fan, and the two hailed from vastly different worlds, but their friendship endured; they later became fishing buddies, and in 1988 Williams accompanied Bush on the New Hampshire campaign trail, both of them wearing bomber jackets. But by far the most interesting one in this group is the ball he hit for his seventh home run of 1953, (the year I was born) and career dinger number 331! (It was signed to "Biskie Belle," whoever that was. Do *you* have any idea?)

Bill Nowlin writes on SABR.org, "Any argument as to the greatest hitter of all time involves Ted Williams... One could probably count the legitimate contenders on the fingers of one hand. Most would narrow the field to just two players, Babe Ruth being the other one... If the name of the game is getting on base, no one ranks above Williams. His lifetime average was .482"... Think for a moment what that means: that he reached base safely almost *every other* time he went to bat.

Boston, meanwhile, was a highly competitive newspaper town that discovered trash-talking Williams was a good way to sell newspapers. (It didn't hurt that he was cocksure to the point of spitting in the direction of certain reporters or sniffing the air disdainfully when they walked past the clubhouse.) That resulted in a set of none-too-flattering nicknames that included "Terrible Ted" and "The Splendid Spitter." No wonder, then, that he took to fly-fishing—describing baseball his *second* favourite sport. He loved to fish on the Miramichi River, off the coast of New Brunswick, and when one spring I was invited to try my hand casting in the fresh, buggy waters of the nearby Sevogle, the locals had nothing but praise for the man. Fly-fishing for Atlantic salmon is a difficult, delicate art. Williams used to say he'd get one bite for every *thousand* casts—less than a .300 batting average, for sure, but reflective of the tremendous patience he also exhibited at the plate. He developed such a reputation for dismissing pitches as he waited for the perfect one to wallop, that more than one catcher complaining about a pitch being called a ball was told by the umpire, "If Mr. Williams didn't swing at it, it wasn't a strike."

After WWII, Williams returned to the game, received his first MVP award, helped Boston get to its first World Series since 1918, and led the league in OBP, total bases and runs; in 1947 he earned his second Triple Crown and led the A.L. with .342, 32 and 114; his accomplishments would surely have kept mounting, but for a series of injuries to his elbow (in spite of which he led the league in OBP and batting *again* in 1951) and, ultimately, returning to active duty in the Korean War, conducting perilous dive-bombing missions in an elite Marine Corps squadron—his wingman none other than future astronaut John Glenn. In 1953 towards the end of *that* war, he returned to baseball once more, batting .407, and kept on trucking despite ear infections, a broken collarbone and a bout of pneumonia: in 1957, at age 41, he hit .388 and led the league by twenty-three points over Mickey Mantle; his .526 OBP was the second highest of his career, as was his .731 slugging percentage and his 38 home runs. OMG, someone give this man a movie!

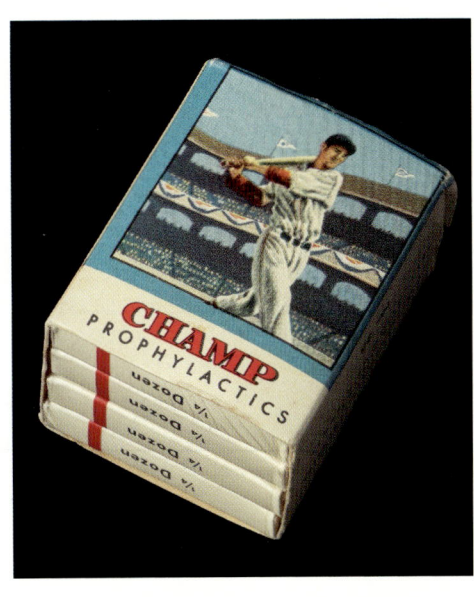

Yes, folks. Ball players do all kinds of endorsements!

1906 WORLD SERIES
(ED WALSH *and* MORDECAI BROWN)

ACCORDING TO THE certification paperwork of this marvellously ancient-looking ball, "The 1906 World Series pitted Chicago's cross town rivals against one another: the White Sox, led by the power pitching of right-hander Ed Walsh, versus the Cubs, led by southpaw Mordecai 'Three-Finger' Brown. It would mark the first National League pennant for the record-breaking 116-36 Cubs, while the White Sox won the AL pennant with a 93-58 record . . . This official Reach-brand, horsehide American League baseball is from that Series-deciding Game 6. Dark and discoloured by more than a century's worth of time, the game-used gem boasts discernible signatures from Both Walsh and Brown, the latter's just to the right of the sweet spot. An adjacent inscription reads, 'Final ball Sox win.'"

These two dudes were a *little* before my time, so I'm going to lean once again on the SABR site and an article written by R.A.R. Edwards: "Big Ed" Walsh was a Major League pitcher and manager from 1906 to 1912, for several seasons one of the best in the game until injuries shortened his career. "He was the last pitcher from any team to throw over 400 innings in a single season, a feat he accomplished in 1908, and was the last pitcher in baseball history to win forty games, hurling an incredible 464 innings, 73 $1/3$ more than any other pitcher in baseball. He tested the limits of endurance like no pitcher has since."

He was a respected spitball pitcher when spitballs were legal—when you could adulterate the ball, that is, any way you wanted.

"During the 1904 Spring Training with the White Sox and the Marlins in Springs, Texas, Walsh roomed with spitballer Elmer Stricklett, the same pitcher who had inspired Jack Chesbro to start experimenting with the pitch the year before. Stricklett taught Walsh the spitter, but the big right-hander did not start using the pitch for two years." Can you imagine all the goo that was coming off of that ball? It's surely got a *lot* of DNA on it.

Mordecai Peter Centennial Brown, meanwhile, was the ace right-hander of the great Chicago Cubs team of the first decade or so of the twentieth century, leading the greatest five-year record of any team in baseball history. He was given the middle name "Centennial" because he was born in 1876; and though you might think that "Mordecai" indicates a Jewish family, they appear to have been of Welsh, English and Cherokee heritage. He was nicknamed "Miner" Brown because he drove mule-drawn coal carts in the mines as a teenager, but his most familiar moniker was "Three Finger" (although in fact he had four and a half fingers on his pitching hand), having in his childhood lost most of his right index finger in a piece of farming equipment, and then broke his other fingers in a fall while chasing a rabbit. Result: a bent middle finger, a paralyzed little finger, and a stump where the index finger used to be, which enabled him to throw a bewildering pitch with lots of movement. He was, in short, the Django Reinhardt of baseball!

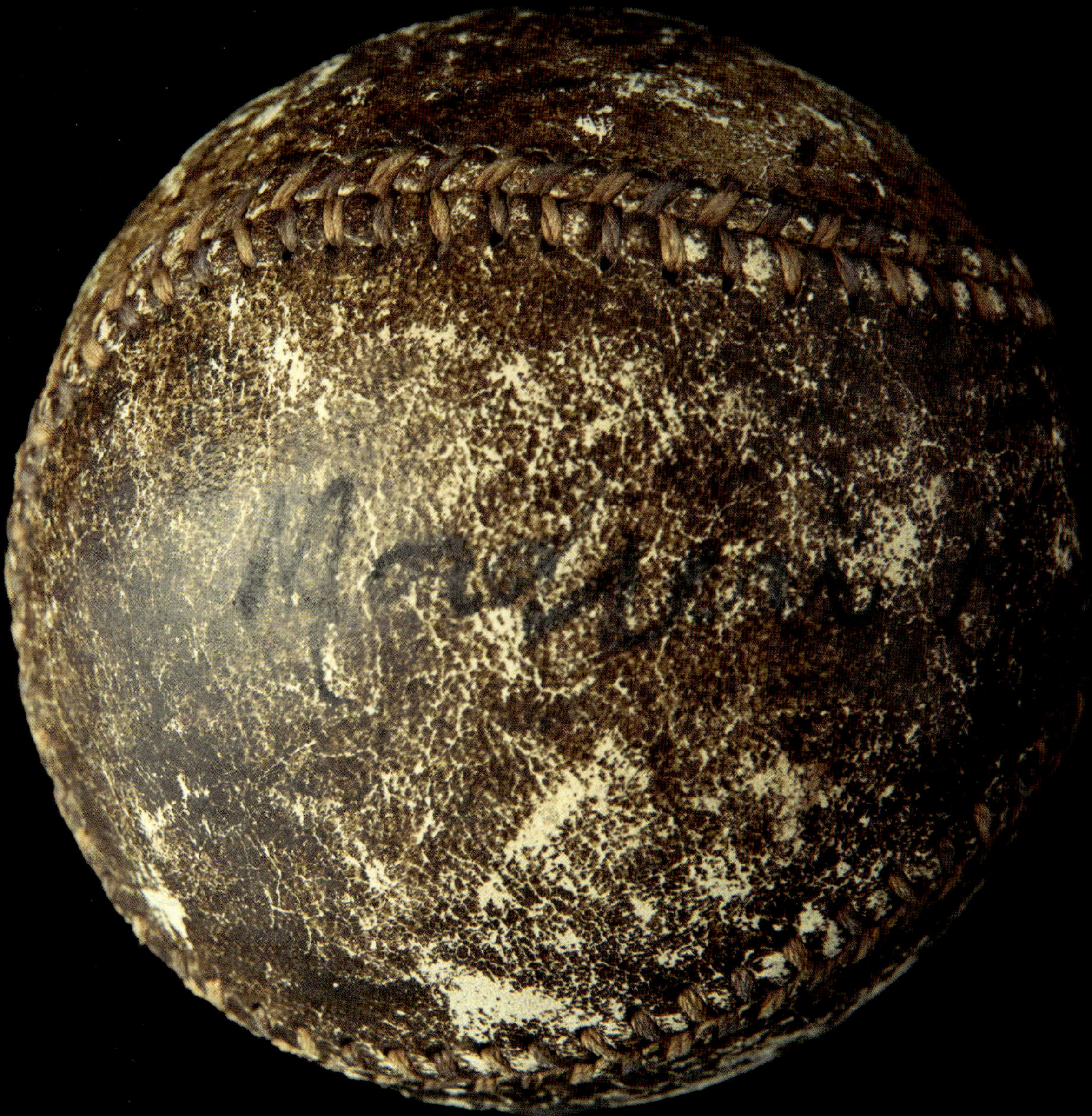

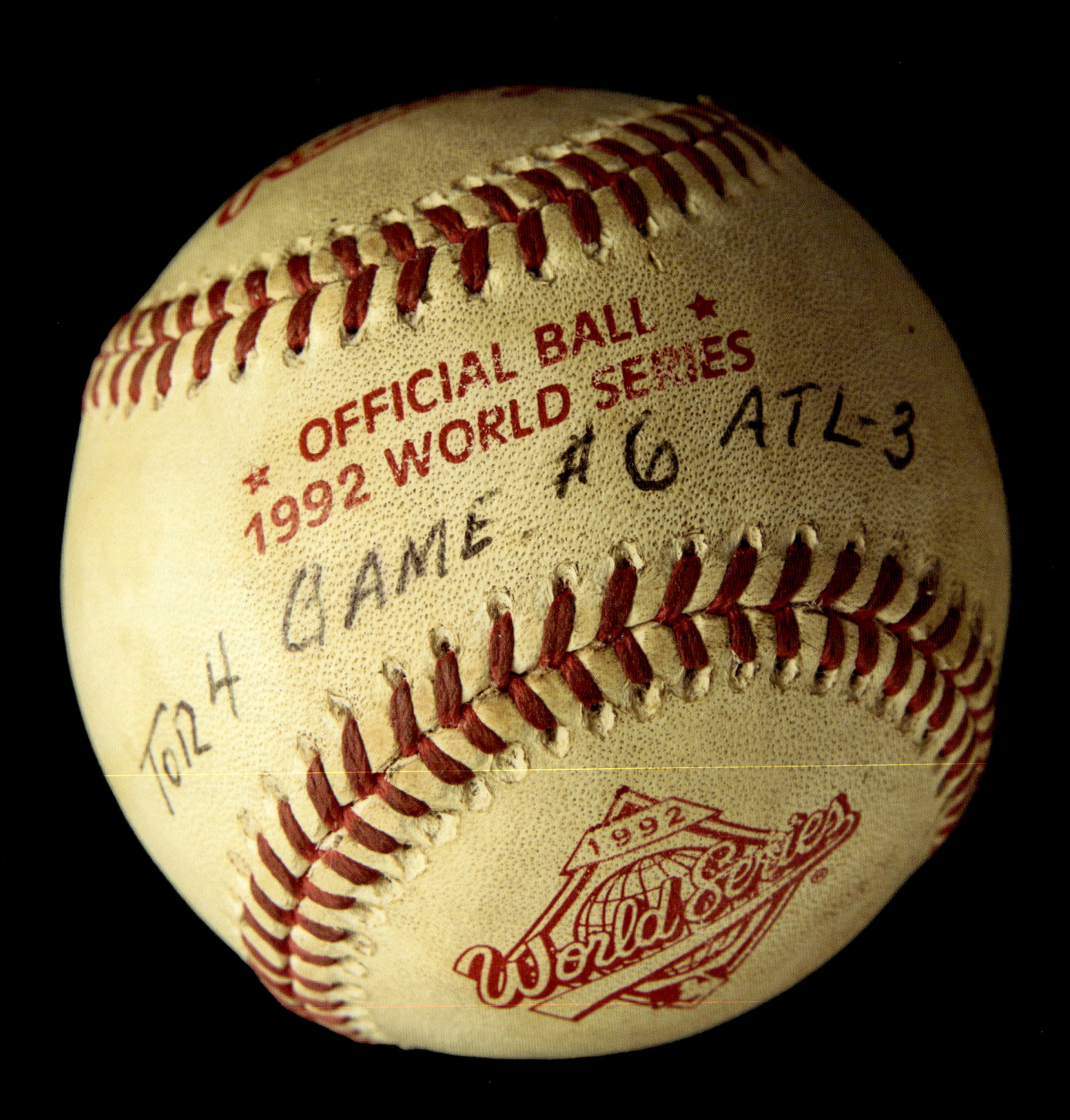

OFFICIAL BALL
1992 WORLD SERIES
GAME #6 ATL-3
TOR 4

1992 WORLD SERIES

THIS SIMPLE BALL represents the most glorious moment in my life as a Blue Jay fan, the game that won Toronto its first world championship. In 1992, I went with my brother to the Fulton County Stadium in Atlanta, where we sat in the section reserved for friends and family members of the players and coaches, and we were this little group of Blue Jays fans in a sea of foam tomahawks.

(Those were the bad old politically incorrect days, when Braves fans did the "Tomahawk chop" to the melody that used to signal Indians in old Hollywood westerns. I can see why that sort of thing offends a lot of people! I guess the argument some fans would make is that a brave is a noble person, a fierce warrior, but if a thing is offensive to a large group of people—and especially the first peoples of your country—I think you should give them a little credence and stop offending them. Cleveland changed its name from the Indians to the Guardians, but the Braves are still the Braves . . . while over in the world of football even the Washington team finally relented and dropped that offensive "Redskins" moniker.)

So anyway, we were very warmly treated—not like in Britain where if you're wearing the wrong colours at a football match you're taking your life into your own hands. We were welcomed and warmly taunted, told in no uncertain terms that we were going to lose. Yet we did *not* lose. It was an incredible game, its hero the great Dave Winfield, who laced the double that drove in the winning run. My brother and I were *ecstatic*. I remember counting out the outs towards the end of the game . . . *Only two more outs* . . . Only *one* more out to a *World Championship* . . . It was the most exciting moment of my life as a sports fan. It's *the* ultimate reward for being a fan: you're floating on air with the knowledge that this win can never be taken away from you.

After the game, we had the great privilege of partying with the Jays at their hotel. At the party I went up to Winfield and said, "I'm so happy to meet you. Congratulations! I think I was the happiest person in the stadium when you hit that double."

To which he replied, "No, *I* was the happiest person in the stadium."

All I could do was chuckle with embarrassment and say, "Oh, yeah . . . *Right*."

Years later—not until 2013, in fact—I came across a ball from that very game. It's not signed by any of the players, just by the umpire crew chief, John Schulock. But it's one that I will keep alongside the rest of my Blue Jays memorabilia for my grandson (and, hopefully, future generations of my family's Jays fans) to revel in.

THE 1927 NEW YORK YANKEES

ACCORDING TO THE Society for American Baseball Research (and this is about as succinct as you're going to get), "The 1927 New York Yankees are generally considered the greatest team ever to play the game."

The Yankees' owner Jacob Rupert is most often credited with building that team, though General Manager Ed Barrow probably had as much to do with it. The starting lineup was affectionately known as "Murderers' Row," mimicking the name of a section of New York City's Tombs prison, which had been applied to several different baseball teams before them—the 1904 Cleveland Naps and 1905 Yale teams, the Philadelphia Phillies and Athletics, amongst others, and the Yankees themselves two years before Babe Ruth joined—but really it's owned by the Ruth-Gehrig-era Yankees. Why, you may ask? Because they were a bunch of *killers*; they tried to effin' kill that baseball *every* time it was pitched.

It was a different game back then in that they didn't mix and match players the way they do today. With Ruth and Gehrig being lefties hitting in the heart of the order, you'd think that this Yankee team would be vulnerable to left-handed pitching, except that they were not your *ordinary* southpaws. In 1927, each of them had an OPS (the modern gauge of a great hitter: your on-base percentage added to your slugging percentage) of *over 1000* against lefties. Nobody was taking them out of the line-up, *ever*.

1927 was early in the "lively ball" period, but there's still plenty of evidence to back up the claim that these guys were the greatest ever. In 1927, the team batted .307, slugged .489, scored 975 runs and outscored their opponents by a record 376 runs. Centre fielder Earle Combs had a career-best year, batting .356 with 231 hits; left fielder Bob Meusel batted .337 with 103 RBIs; second baseman Tony Lazzeri drove in 102 runs; Lou Gehrig batted .373 with 218 hits, 52 doubles, 18 triples and 47 home runs, and a then-record of 175 RBIs (he slugged at .765 and was voted the AL MVP); Ruth amassed a *mere* .356 batting average, *only* 164 RBIs, a *scant* 158 runs scored and 137 times while slugging .772. In one game in July against the Washington Senators, the Yankees beat them 21-1, prompting the Senators' first baseman Joe Judge to say, "Those fellows not only beat you, but they tear your heart out. I wish the season was over."

It's a beautiful ball, in great condition. I don't think it's rubbed up, so it might not be an actual game ball, but it's an OAL (American League Baseball of the period) and pretty much the whole team is on it. All the biggies I just mentioned are there, plus bench players Benny Bengough, Cedric Durst, Mike Gazella, Johnny Grabowski, Ray Morehart, Ben Paschal, and pitchers Joe Giard, Waite Hoyt, Dutch Ruether and Bob Shawkey.

Can you imagine being a poor rookie pitcher trying to get through the Yankees' usual 1927 starting line-up of Combs, shortstop Mark Koenig, Ruth, Gehrig, Meusel, Lazzeri, third baseman Joe Dugan and catcher Pat Collins before, mercifully, getting a chance to face the pitcher in the ninth spot?

My god....

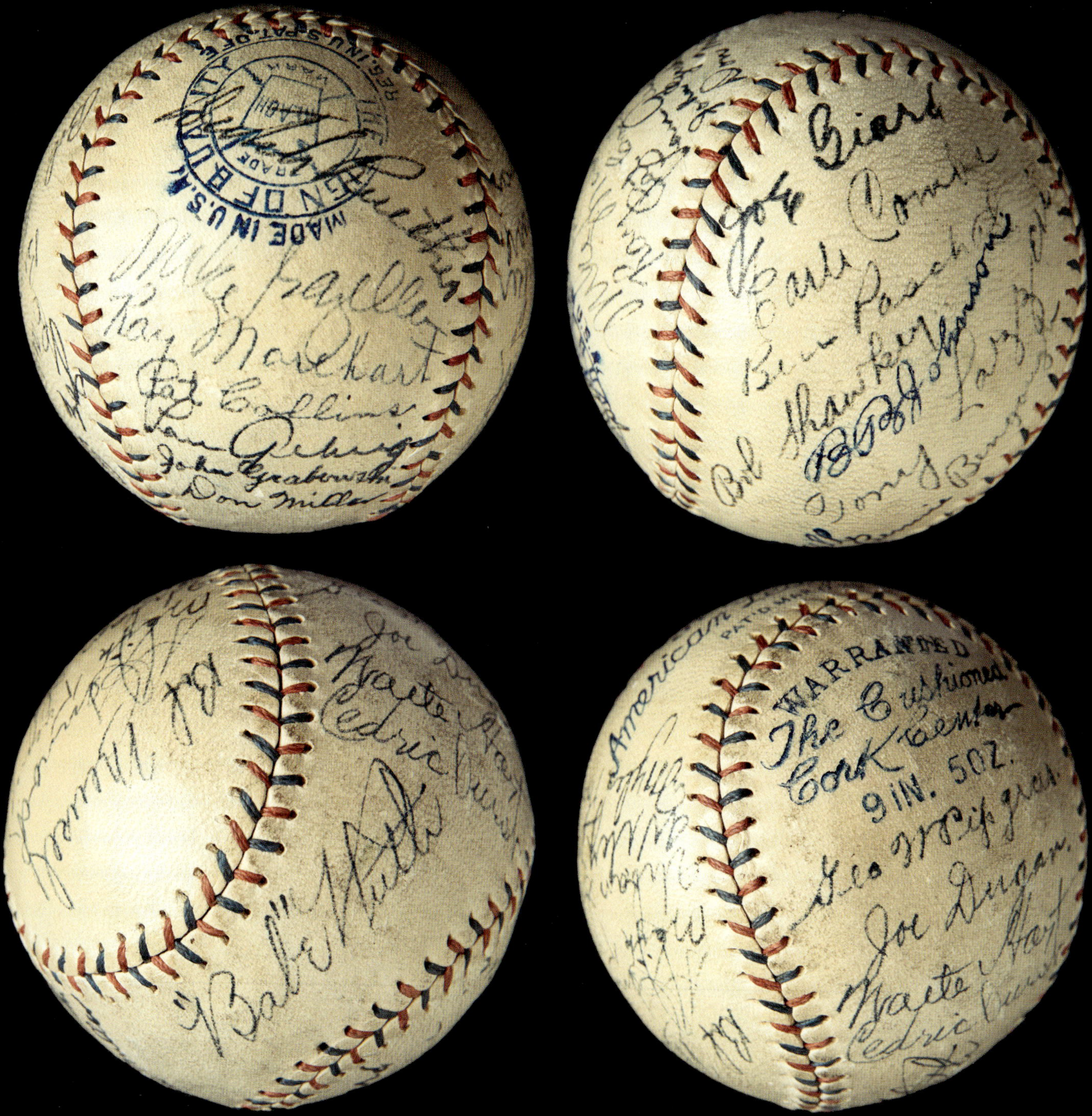
MADE IN U.S.A.
WARRANTED
The Cushioned Cork Center
9 IN. 5 OZ.
American
Joe Dugan
Waite Hoyt
Earle Combs
"Babe" Ruth
Ray Morehart

GIANTS
OFFICIAL BATTING ORDER
ST. LOUIS
DATE
ALSO ELIGIBLE
ORIGINAL
CHANGE
To Geddy
Good Luck &
Best Wishes!
WORLD SERIES
DAY PASS
DIVISION SERIES
LEAGUE CHAMPIONSHIP SERIES
Good for all Post Season Games
CLUBHOUSE
WORLD SERIES
ADMIT TO STADIUM AND FIELD ONLY
GAME THREE ONLY
(BADGE REQUIRED FOR CLUBHOUSE ADMITTANCE)
Name
Affiliation
GAME 3

MISCELLANEOUS MEMORABILIA

PICTURED HERE ARE some items that represent wonderful personal moments for me. First and foremost, see the set of cards on the left? Those are scoring cards used by Tony La Russa, former manager of the Cardinals, Athletics and White Sox. At every game he managed, he'd pull a couple of scorecards with both teams' batting order from his back pocket and scribble out notes in his personalised hieroglyphic shorthand, calculating how best to get an edge on the opposition. I watched him doing it for years, and eventually had the good fortune of meeting him and actually making friends. His family were Rush fans who came to many of our shows in California, and I'd always make sure that they had good tickets, and one day he asked if there was anything he could give me in return. I said, "Well, to be honest, I would love one of your scorecards." He was shocked that I even knew about them, but luckily for me, he'd never parted with any. He gave me several over the years, but the one that's pictured was the first: "Means everything to me that you would want these!" he wrote. I mean, how are you going to beat that? (How? He invited me to St. Louis to watch the Cards play the Red Sox in Game 3 of the 2014 World Series, facing the great Hall of Famer Pedro Martinez! Not only that, but before the game he told me to grab a bat and join the hitters in his office as they strategized the best way to approach Pedro. There I was, a total fish out of water but welcomed by all, into this inner sanctum! *That's* how.)

In another fine gesture the Cardinals' Ozzie Smith, who I'd only ever really met once or twice at spring training, gave one of his game gloves to the team's longtime equipment manager Rip Rowan to give to me. (Smith was one of the greatest shortstops to ever play the game. I used to love how he'd walk on to the field and do a somersault as part of his warmup routine every time.)

The first lineup cards Tony La Russa gave to me.

Then at top are some balls signed by people I became close with—my dear friends Mark Langston and Dave Stieb, for example—and some I met only briefly such as Bret Saberhagen, the Cubs' Bill Buckner, Robin Yount (one of the greatest *hitting* shortstops), my lifetime hero Sandy Koufax (pictured elsewhere in this book, I know, but it bears repeating!) and the great George Brett. I have many, many more that would not fit into one photograph, but which are a testament to what a lucky mutha I am.

Making friendships that have lasted a lifetime is something that as a mere fan you never really expect, and it's great when you connect thanks to a genuine commonality, not just because you're both well known in your respective professions. But perhaps my most cherished memory is from the time I attended Baseball's World Series of Golf, an annual tournament they hold in Pebble Beach, California, where after the season players from all the teams get to golf and drink and jaw wag, and where I found myself seated at a table with six or seven Major League pitchers—Bert Blyleven, the late Tom Browning, my host Bryn Smith, and Bob McLure among them. They were all left-handed except Blyleven and Smitty, and were debating the Standard Operating Procedure, if you like, of pitching to a left-handed batter. (That was as good as sitting down for a chinwag with Jimmy Page, Steve Howe and Jeff Beck!) The nugget I gleaned from being a fly on the wall that evening was something they all agreed on: that the first pitch a lefty throws to a left-handed batter should be a breaking ball, because they will always *take* it for a strike, even though they *know* it's coming. I've tested this theory whilst watching games, and I can say that more often than not, it's true! There you have it: a crumb from the table of the gods of baseball.

To Geddy,
The best to
you.
Enjoy the show
To Geddy
Thanks for the
music!
All my best
Geddy
my best

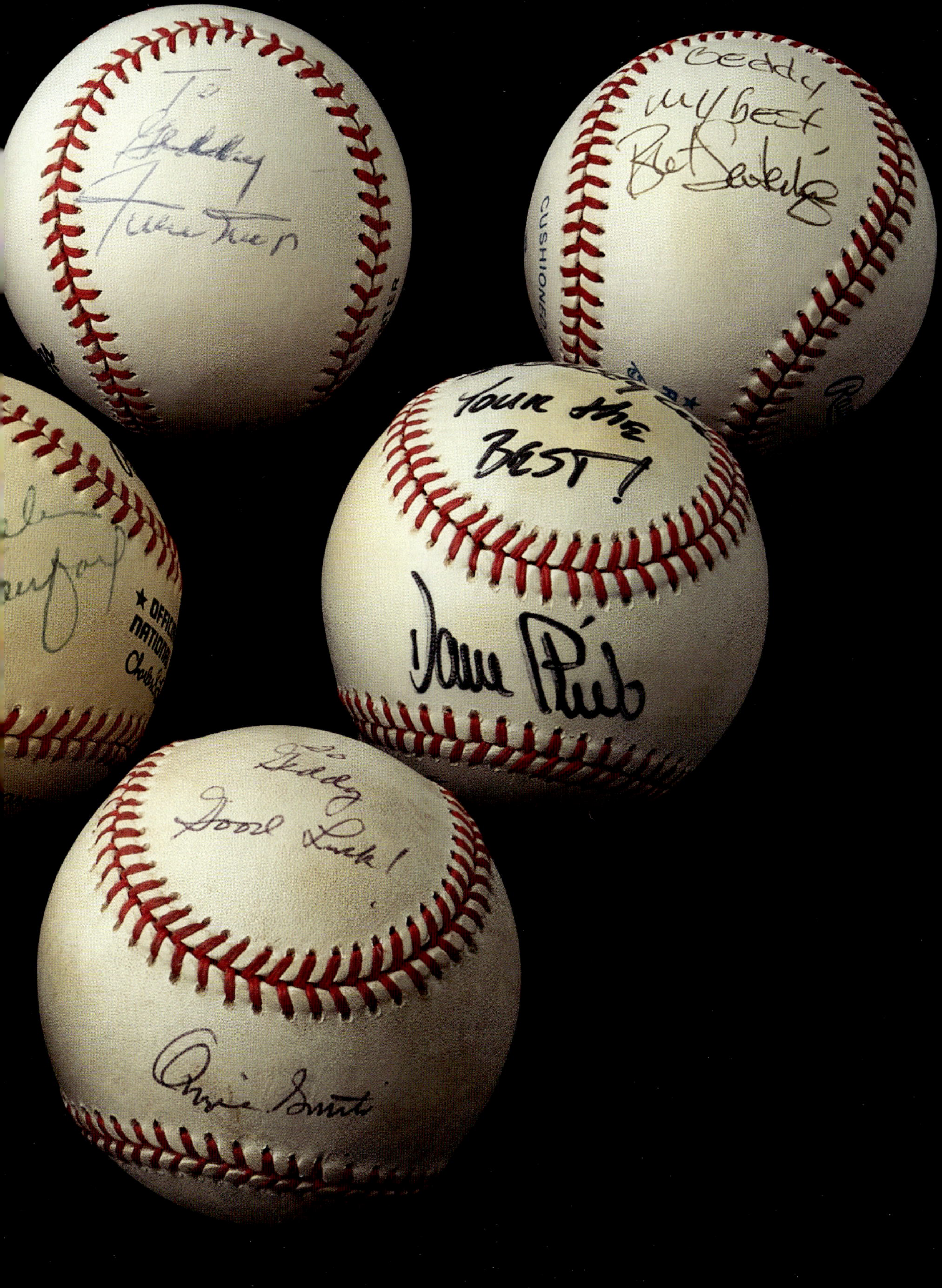
To Geddy
Geddy
my best
CUSHIONED
YOUR THE BEST!
OFFICIAL
NATIONAL
To Geddy
Good Luck!

RUSH

HERE'S A PICTURE of Alex, Neil and me, taken during soundcheck on our last tour—maybe even our last gig.

We didn't want to admit that it might be the last. Well, as far as Neil was concerned, it *was*; he badly wanted to retire, to spend more time at home with his wife and young daughter, but Alex and I were hoping against hope that that wouldn't be the case.

As part of our daily backstage ritual, our road manager Donovan Lundstrom would lay out on a table a selection of the numerous letters that venues had received from fans and arena personnel asking for autographs. After he'd eliminated the ones he considered most likely to have come from scalpers eager to put them on eBay (he had a great nose for smelling out the touts!), I'd slip in some baseballs to give to my really close pals as a little farewell memento.

I'd always liked the way certain players would append their signatures on balls with "Hall of Fame 1956" or "HoF 2001," so I decided to sign mine "Rock and Roll Hall of Fame 2013," and asked Alex and Neil if they'd sign them too. They did, but just for a short while, until finally Neil looked up at Donovan and said, "I think Deke has *plenty* now." Fair enough, Peke!

So that's how this ball came to be. And unfortunately, 2015 did end up being our very last tour.

ACKNOWLEDGEMENTS

I'd like to thank the following good folks for helping with this super fun endeavor. I could have danced all night!

- First, the SABR Baseball Biography Project (SABR.org), to whom I'm deeply grateful for permission to plunder their rich resource of historical knowledge. A huge thanks to all their fine writers.
- My good pals in the hobby and throughout the world of MLB.
- My dear friend Allan Stitt for his innumerable favours that go beyond friendship, and for encouraging me to create this memory book.
- Richard Sibbald for the stunning photographs featured throughout this book and his constant willingness to go beyond the call of duty.
- Daniel Richler, my tireless and perspicacious co-writer who always lends an air of poetry to the words I plop down on the page.
- Paul Kepple at Headcase Design for his wonderful eye and unerring good taste.
- Patrick McLoughlin for being so incredibly helpful in getting this book printed.
- My long-suffering partner Nancy Young for being so enthusiastic about me writing this book. (Really, she *was*!)
- And lastly, to my wonderful children for not complaining while watching Dad spend their inheritance on baseballs.

---

72 STORIES. Copyright © 2023 by Geddy Lee. All rights reserved.

Printed in Malaysia. No part of this book may be used or reproduced in any manner whatsoever without written permission except in the case of brief quotations embodied in critical articles and reviews. For information, address HarperCollins Publishers, 195 Broadway, New York, NY 10007.

HarperCollins books may be purchased for educational, business, or sales promotional use. For information, please email the Special Markets Department at SPsales@harpercollins.com.

Previously published in 2023 by Geddy Lee.

Photographs by Richard Sibbald on pages 2, 4, 6, 7, 10 (upper left), 11, 12, 15, 16, 18, 19, 20, 22, 23, 24, 27, 28, 30 (top), 31, 32, 35, 36, 37, 38, 39, 40, 43, 44, 47, 48, 51, 52, 55, 56, 59, 60, 62, 63, 64, 65, 66, 67, 68, 71, 72, 75, 76, 79, 80, 83, 84, 86, 87, 88, 90, 91, 92, 95, 96, 98, 99, 100, 103, 104, 107, 108, 110, 111, 112, 115, 116, 119, 120, 123, 124, 127, 128, 131, 132, 133, 134, 137, 138, 141, 142, 145, 146, 147, 149, 150, 151, 153, 154, 155, 156, 157, 158, and 159 © 2023 by Geddy Lee.

Photographs on pages 9 (middle right), 73, and 118 by Geddy Lee © 2023 by Geddy Lee.

Photographs on pages 9 (upper left, lower right), 11 (upper left), and 30 (bottom) by Andrew MacNaughtan.

Photograph on page 46: Bettmann Archive.

Photograph on page 130 courtesy of David Angelo.

Photograph on page 10 courtesy of the Negro Leagues Museum.

Photographs on pages 9, 10 (bottom right), 14, 62 (bottom), 81, and 155 courtesy of the Geddy Lee Archive.

Photographs on pages 13 and 53 by Marc Hamou.

Poem on page 136 copyright © 1949 by Ogden Nash, renewed. Reprinted by permission of Curtis Brown, Ltd.

FIRST HARPER EDITION 2025

Designed by Paul Kepple and Alex Bruce at Headcase Design. www.headcasedesign.com

Library of Congress Cataloging-in-Publication Data has been applied for.

ISBN 978-0-06-345019-6

25 26 27 28 29 IM 5 4 3 2 1